D1045262

The California Deserts...

The Westerners Brand Book
Number 11

THE CALIFORNIA DESERTS...

their people, their history and their legends

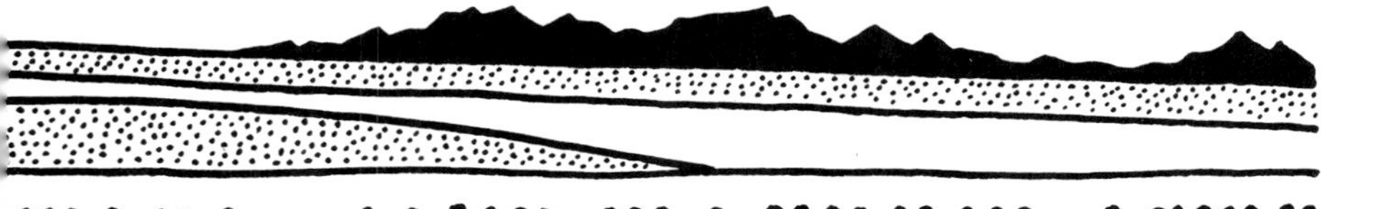

The Westerners

BRAND BOOK

Number 11

RUSS LEADABRAND . . . EDITOR

DON PERCEVAL . . . DECORATIONS

DR. HARVEY JOHNSON . . . SHERIFF

LOS ANGELES CORRAL . . . 1964

This is a limited
edition of 525 copies.
This is Number
84

Library of Congress Catalog Card Number 48-2575

PRINTED BY THE WARD RITCHIE PRESS

In memoriam
Alan LeMay . . . *Westerner*

The Westerners—Los Angeles Corral

Active Members

Edward P. Ainsworth
James N. Algar
Paul D. Bailey
Ray Billington
Homer H. Boelter
Loring Campbell
Arthur H. Clark, Jr.
Dwight L. Clarke
Henry H. Clifford
Iron Eyes Cody
Robert Cowan
Glen Dawson
Carl S. Dentzel
John Sky Dunlap
E. I. Edwards
James S. Fassero
Earle R. Forrest
Carroll Friswold
George E. Fullerton
P. W. Galleher
John B. Goodman III
Dudley C. Gordon
Everett Hager
A. Stevens Halstead, Jr.
Donald W. Hamblin
Col. C. W. Hoffmann
Holling C. Holling
Ernest M. Hovard
Lonnie Hull
Harvey S. Johnson, M. D.
Webster A. Jones
Dr. John H. Kemble
William Kimes
George Koenig
Russ Leadabrand
Don C. Meadows
Ben Hilliard O'Connor
Bert H. Olson
Don Louis Perceval
Sid Platford
W. W. Robinson
Charles N. Rudkin
August W. Schatra
Harvey Starr, M. D.
Ervin Strong
John Upton Terrell
Harlan H. Thompson
William B. Upton
Dwight Vance
Robert J. Woods

Honorary Members

Edgar N. Carter
Dr. M. R. Harrington
Lee Shippey
Arthur Woodward

CONTENTS

ILLUSTRATIONS

Preface

The winters in California are too short. They do not allow enough time to explore the desert country, to swim in the sea of history and legend and outrageous scenery that is Death Valley; to wander in the deeps of Anza-Borrego Desert State Park; to measure the tall rocks and the towering skies in Joshua Tree National Monument.

For much of the year the California desert is a fascinating land. It glows with the bright stains of a hundred humbled minerals, blushes under the press of tiny wildflowers. The palo verde, the smoke tree, the greasewood, the sages and the cactus add subtle colors. Even the desert sky is a different assortment of blues, depending on the mood of the day and the slant of the sun.

There is much following of footprints in the desert country. In Copper Canyon in Death Valley there are the imprints of prehistoric animals, preserved in a stone matrix. By following prospect holes, headframes, rubble and ruin it is possible to chart the course of the miner across the desert—from boom to bust. The railroads marched here too, and often only the skilled observer can follow the old roadbeds after the rails have been pulled up and the ties hauled away.

Towns stood in some of these lonely reaches of desert country; Army forts and way-stations for freighters and similar minor outposts. Mining brought most of the blossoming camps and the end of mining brought their demise. You can find their debris and fallen buildings in a hundred places: Copper City and Coolgardie and Denning Spring and Furnace and Lila C. and Old Dale.

There are reasons to explore the desert for days on end: lost mines and forgotten roads and lodes of turquoise and agate and bloodstone. Some come with camera, some come with sketch pad, some come only with the aches and ills of city living and are made well again.

For all its fearsome facade, the desert is a welcoming place. By early morning, when the light is a long and golden wash and the shadows reaching, there is the familiar and restoring sense of rebirth. Evenings, again decorated with long shadows, are soothing with purples and deep reds and lavenders tinting the sere hills.

Almost by color alone, the desert is a pleasant place. But more than that, the desert has the charm of length and the delight of room enough. Straight line roads travel unending until the horizon gobbles them up in a brief frantic tussle against the edge of the sky. The desert mountains are there for two reasons alone: for prospectors to prowl, and to cast shadows. The animals—squirrels and rats and rabbits and lizards—have an antic air about them: the living may be hard, but the living is good.

This is the California desert I had in mind when I started putting together my ideas for a Brand Book devoted to the subject. The desert is not the enemy that is painted by some. True, accidents happen here, and they are unfortunate. But there are simple rules one must abide.

I personally avoid the desert in the deep summer—not because I am afraid of it, but because I respect it. The rules then are inflexible. I can wait until October when the evening wind begins to have a bite in it again. I savor the Januarys when I bundle against the wind and cold in coat and gloves and hood, and walk, face down, prowling a remote playa looking for arrowheads. In March the exploring of lost mining camps is high adventure. Even in May, with strange bright little belly flowers carpeting the waterless wasteland, the desert is a pleasure. In the meantime there are books on the desert to savor.

It was people who feel as I do that I asked to contribute significant articles about the desert. All responded with enthusiasm.

E. I. Edwards, a normally peaceful man who will battle in defense of the desert's reputation, has supplied a detailed new chapter on the Death Valley story. Miss Nell Murbarger who loves the desert with a passion, has added to her explorations in the sandy past with an article on Inyo County's ghost towns.

A correspondence with Randall Henderson ended with his thoroughly delightful recollection of the early days on *Desert Magazine*.

I had long talked with Remi Nadeau about his great, great grandfather with the same name—old Remi Nadeau, the freighter. Nadeau cooperated with what is probably one of the finest studies of a desert pioneer yet put into hard covers.

My admiration for the archaeological work that Dr. Gerald Smith is doing in Bloomington, California, led me to ask him for a study of early man in the California desert. It was an exacting chore for him, requiring much research, but his finished manuscript is exciting.

L. Burr Belden retraced the Old Government Road in the Mojave country then found time in a crowded schedule to give us an article on that page of desert history.

Richard Bailey in Bakersfield loves the desert fiercely, particularly that in Kern County. He dug in depth at Red Rock Canyon and has come up with nuggets.

Paul Bailey, perhaps our most prolific author, closed the doors on a dozen other assignments to assemble an article with new material on a desert character without equal—Walkara, the horse stealer and slaver.

John Terrell has uncovered an incredible page of history in the fight for water along the Colorado River. And Horace Parker, looking for another source of water, has found Sackett's Wells for us—a worthwhile quest.

The idea for an article on Burton Frasher was warmly received by his son, Burton Frasher Jr. of Pomona. Frasher spent many hours with me, answering questions about his father and his family. And, beyond that, he went to great trouble making available to the Brand Book a collection of the fine historic Frasher photographs for reproduction.

On behalf of Nell Murbarger, I must thank Dorothy Cragen of the Eastern California Museum. To Floyd B. Evans and Jim Stevens, my thanks for photographic assistance.

Don Perceval, that most deliberate of desert artists, has captured the mood, too, of what we are trying to do here. He is a good friend; it is especially gratifying to have his work in this particular book.

For helping with the nerve-grinding chore of preparing the index, effusive thanks to Arthur H. Clark Jr. and Paul Galleher; the team that made up the publication committee supplied support and helpful ideas: Clark, Galleher, E. I. Edwards, Don Meadows and George Fullerton.

I thank the gentlemen of the Los Angeles Corral of the Westerners and especially the Sheriff, Dr. Harvey Johnson, for giving me such free rein with such an important venture. And for providing a sympathetic ear, a shoulder to cry upon when all seemed lost, a keen sense of rightness about the desert, savvy, knowhow, patience, common sense, I thank my good friend E. I. Edwards.

This is not a definitive volume on the desert by any means. But it pokes into a few desert camps where the historian has not been before. If you find it beautiful, thank Don Perceval and the gentlemen at the Ward Ritchie Press; if it is interesting, thank the authors; if you find it stimulating, praise the helpful editorial committee; if it disappoints you, blame me.

May you enjoy this corner of the California deserts. With time and effort, a gigantic monument could have been raised here to the lonesome country. But we have had a single short year, a year crammed with personal conflicts and crises.

It was only because I could go to the blessed desert once in a while and become restored that this book is here, now.

May you enjoy it.

—R.L.

THE GHOST TOWNS
of INYO *by* Nell Murbarger

STRETCHING FROM the Nevada border westerly 180 miles across Death Valley and on to the everlasting snowfields of the Sierra Nevada, California's second largest county embraces an amazing variety of topography and climate. Crystal trout streams, saline sinks, mountain lakes, desert flats, plunging waterfalls, mirages, glaciers, and sand dunes, plus an elevation of close to 15,000 feet, and a maximum-minimum temperature range of nearly 200 degrees, make up this incredible Land of Inyo.

Inyo is big and rugged country. It is cattle country; timber, hunting, fishing, camping, hiking, and pack train country.

It is also mining country.

For more than a hundred years these lands have poured forth a treasure of precious metals, base metals, and non-metallics—gold and silver, copper and lead and tungsten, borax and soda and salt. Besides contributing to the progress of the world and the welfare of mankind, these earth-given riches of Inyo have bolstered the economy of state and nation with multiple millions of dollars in new wealth. They have provided to thousands of men honest labor at good wages. Through property taxes they have built roads and schools. Homes have come into being because of them, and busy modern settlements have come to bloom in the wilderness.

Even the fringe benefits conferred by Inyo's mining industry have been great. To the amateur historian none of these residual rewards is more fascinating or thought-provoking than the many near-vanished ghost towns and picturesque ruins hidden away in Inyo's remote hills and canyons—the old camps that stand as inevitable sentinels in every land where mining long has been king. To the dreamer-of-dreams and dedicated prowler-into-the-past, to every soul who lends a sympathetic ear, each crumbling wall in these old towns whispers of the life and promise in the halcyon days gone; each silent ghost-site stands symbolic of peace and acquiescence, the priceless legacy bequeathed by a century of bonanza and *borrasca.*

Inyo's mining history, insofar as white men are concerned, dates from 1849 when members of the Jayhawker emigrant party, bound for the great goldrush in California's Mother Lode farther to the north, camped briefly near the rim of Death Val-

The mining camp of Lookout in the Argus Mountains of Inyo County. Picture's date is sometime between 1877 to 1879. Store belonged to Joseph S. Birchett.

The great mill at Panamint City, up Surprise Canyon in the Panamint Mountains. Most of the brick work of the structure is gone now.

ley—possibly on White Sage Flat, west of Wildrose Canyon. While hunting wild game in the vicinity, according to legend, one member of that party repaired his weapon with a makeshift gunsight whittled from a piece of soft metal collected on the spot. Later, he and a companion collected the bits of silver float that were destined to spark the imperishable legend of the Lost Gunsight Lode, even today a classic among lost mine tales of the Western United States.

Though the Lost Gunsight remains unfound, its lure was the magic magnet that drew other men to this then unfriendly and infrequented land. Within the first dozen years following the Jayhawkers' discovery, numerous mining claims were located, graves began sprouting on the hillsides, and the first outposts of civilization were established in the wilderness that was then Tulare County but soon would be Inyo. San Carlos, Bend City, Owensville, Chrysopolis, Kearsarge City—each came hopefully into being; each lived its brief span and died.

First mining district in the Inyo region was organized in April 1860 by the party of Dr. S. G. George, seekers of the Lost Gunsight. Situated in the Inyo range of desert mountains due east of the present town of Independence, the district was named after Colonel H. P. Russ, a member of that party, who staked the claim known as the Eclipse. Elsewhere in the county, at this same time, many other men were seeking—and a few were finding. M. H. Farley, a member of the Darwin French party, came to the Coso Mountains in 1860 and there made the first rich gold discovery on Silver Mountain. By midsummer of that year Farley had staked 90 claims and had named his mine the Olancha. Ore from this mine was packed six miles and hauled an additonal 12 miles to a point on the mesa west of the present small town of Olancha and about three-quarters of a mile west of U.S. Highway 395. The ore crushing mill built by Farley at this site is still identifiable by crumbling foundations.

First trading post in Owens Valley was established in August 1861 by Charles Putnam, whose stone cabin on Little Pine Creek evolved from a private dwelling into a general store, hospital, unofficial fort, and nucleus of the present county seat of Independence. Less than a year later, on July 4, 1862, Camp Independence was instituted by the United States War Department on Oak Creek, a couple of miles north of Putnam's. With this development, prospecting activities in the region took a sudden upward trend, since many of the soldiers stationed at the new fort were from California's Mother Lode district, therefore were thoroughly familiar with ores and the mechanics of mining.

Ranging out of the fort during the first month after its founding, one of the soldiers at Camp Independence made a discovery of free milling gold that resulted in the organizing of the San Carlos Mining and Exploration company. Before the autumn of 1862 the town of San Carlos had been founded between the Owens River and the toe of the mountains, four miles east of the fort.

San Carlos was everything a small mining camp should be. It had its saloons, its stores, its gun fights and funerals. Its steam-powered ore crushing mill, situated at the corner of Romelia and Silver Streets, went into operation July 4, 1864, heralding the event with resounding blasts of its steam whistle. Horse racing and a "grand ball" that evening helped to celebrate the joint birthday of mill and nation. For many years after San Carlos was only a ghost town, the tall masonry stack of this mill still marked its one-time site.

Meanwhile, three miles south of San Carlos, on a bend in the Owens River, the town of Bend City was settled in 1863. Although both San Carlos and Bend City attained peak populations between 2000 and 3000, it is likely that Bend City was a bit larger and more important than its sister town up-river. At one time in its brief history—the entire life of the town spanned less than four years—it was served by two hotels, the Marrow House being the "swell" place; a circulating library provided cultural refinement, and a stock exchange was listed among its institutions.

Chrysopolis, also on the east side of the river, was a "going" town by the autumn of 1863, as was Owensville, situated close to the present town of Laws. Although founded originally as a milling town and supply point for mines in the vicinity, Owensville soon developed into an agricultural town and, as such, was the most enduring of these four urban centers. An anonymous contributor, writing from Owensville to the *Alta California*, at San Francisco, in December 1863, reported: "I have just arrived with a party of fifty-six men, one family, eighty-two yoke of oxen, and saddle horses innumerable. The valley contains fifty-two claims of 160 acres each. . . ."

But even Owensville lost its last inhabitants in 1871, and its traces have virtually vanished from the earth. Even the graves in the old cemetery are lost to man's knowledge.

Another small ghost of the 1863 era is Ida, situated a few miles southeast of Independence. Original discovery of gold ore at this place was made by one Curtis Bellows who erected a ten-stamp waterpowered mill, at an asserted cost of $10,000, and on March 6, 1863, was shot and killed by Indians. So far as known to this writer there are no remains of either the little camp of Ida, or the mill it served.

During the period when the Confederate States raider *Alabama*, was inflicting devastating losses on Northern shipping, Southern sympathizers, prospecting in the rocky hills west of the present town of Lone Pine, discovered a mine which they named for the rebel cruiser—this mine, in turn, giving name to the highly-scenic Alabama Hills in which it was located. As the Southern miners were somewhat boastful concerning the prowess of the *Alabama*, fistic encounters between them and the local Unionists were not infrequent until June 10, 1864, when the Confederate raider was sunk off the coast of France by the *U.S.S. Kearsarge*. Soon after this event, Thomas May and C. McCormack, prospecting on the mountainside west of Putnam's, made a discovery of rich gold and silver ore and named their mine for the Union ship *Kearsarge*—thus striking back at the Alabama mine and its proprietors a few miles to the south.

The town of Kearsarge City soon began taking form and by 1866, when Inyo County was officially organized, had attained such size that its residents petitioned, unsuccessfully, for the county seat. Meanwhile, in 1865, the Benway and Company mill, waterpowered, had been built at a cost of $10,000; and in 1866 the Kearsarge Company erected a 20-stamp mill, steam-powered, at a cost of $50,000. Two other mines, the Silver Sprout and Virginia Consolidated, were placed in production, and everything was going beautifully in Kearsarge City, two miles above sea level, until the Day of the Avalanche—March 1, 1867.

But for the fact that most of her men were at work in the mines and mills, the loss of life might have been much greater. As it was, eleven cabins were swept away and others buried beneath the onrushing snow and rocks, one woman was killed, and two men suffered serious injuries. That night the entire population of the camp moved down the canyon to Gray's Meadows, and when the town was rebuilt it was in a safer location lower on the mountain.

Virtually nothing remains at the original site of Kearsarge City. The camp's three major mines—the Kearsarge, Silver Sprout, and Virginia Con—are filled with snow and ice. Some ruins mark the second site of the town; and a long, vertical scar on the mountainside traces the course of the tramway down which ore moved from mine to mill.

Of all the mining and milling camps that came into being during the first half-decade of Inyo's mining history, scarcely one survived until the present century. Nearest contender for that honor probably would be Cerro Gordo.

Mexican prospectors, working high on the west slope of Buena Vista Peak in 1865, made the discovery that was to launch the county's first major mining boom and the founding of Cerro Gordo City, greatest producer of silver and lead in the history of California.

One of the first arrivals on the Fat Hill was Mortimer W. Belshaw, mining engineer of San Francisco and Virginia City, who visualized in Cerro Gordo the nucleus of a second Comstock. Setting himself to the pleasurable task of controlling all the riches and potential riches in sight, Belshaw came close to realizing that goal. Acquiring ownership of the Union Mine, Belshaw, in 1868, erected Cerro Gordo's first modern steam-powered smelter, at a cost of $20,000, and built a toll road down the near-precipitous mountainside to the northeast shore of Owens Lake, dropping nearly 5000 feet in only eight miles.

Before many suns had set behind the Sierra summits to the west, the Belshaw smelter was pouring forth a steady stream of silver-lead ingots to be hauled away in massive freight wagons, their wheels chain-blocked and a dozen mules hitched to each to slow its descent. Reaching the bottom of the so-called "Yellow Grade," the bullion freighters began a grueling three-weeks' journey around the north end of Owens Lake, south toward the pres-

Last building standing in Greenwater, California; taken in May, 1950.

Remaining buildings at old Skidoo in the Panamint Mountains. Larger building is gone now.

ent town of Olancha, thence south and southwesterly across the Mojave Desert to San Pedro and tidewater.

About a year after the erection of Belshaw's smelter, the Owens Lake Silver-Lead Company built a $25,000 steam-powered smelter on the northeast shore of Owens Lake, near the lower terminus of the toll road. At this smelter was handled ore from the Santa Maria and San Felipe mines, of Cerro Gordo, and here came into being the rock-and-adobe town of Swansea, its name derived from the famous smelting center of Swansea, in Wales.

Even with 32 of Remi Nadeau's largest freight teams and wagons in constant service, silver ingots poured from the two smelters with such abundancy that the teams could not haul them away. In an effort to eliminate this bottleneck, James Brady, superintendent of Owens Lake Silver-Lead Company, built the *Bessie Brady*, a ferry-type paddlewheeler, 85 feet in length with 16-foot beam.

Christening of the *Bessie Brady* in midsummer 1872 was a gala occasion that drew to Ferguson's Landing more than 20 wagon-loads of spectators, plus many horsemen, assembled from the length and breadth of Owens Valley. After little Bessie Brady, daughter of the superintendent, had broken over her namesake's prow a bottle of wine, the *Bessie Brady* steamed out on the lake carrying aboard some 130 jubilant excursionists. As the lake was then 23 miles in length, with a maximum width of 14 miles—approximately the present size of Lake Tahoe—it afforded ample room for cruising, and the balance of that festive day was devoted to dining, wining, dancing, and sightseeing, all at company expense.

Later, the *Bessie Brady* buckled down to the thankless life of a cargo boat, making one round trip daily from Swansea at the foot of the lake and return, about 18 miles each way. On outbound trips she carried around 70 tons of silver ingots and, returning, bore mountainous loads of freight, as well as passengers en route to the busy lake port and the mountaintop mining camp. So far as the transportation bottleneck was concerned, however, it only shifted across the lake from Swansea to Cartago, as the new landing on the south shore had been named by its principal merchant, John Baptiste Daneri.

The efficient *Bessie Brady* was simply delivering silver ingots faster than the freight teams could haul them away. By January 1873 there had accumulated on the wharf and in the streets of Cartago some 18,000 silver bars, representing a total worth of more than $600,000. Several persons, it is said, ingeniously employed these silver ingots in the construction of winter shelters for themselves, stacking the bars in brick fashion to form small cabins which they roofed with poles and canvas. In an effort to reduce this silver hoard there were eventually in service between Owens Valley and San Pedro some 80 teams, each comprised of 16 powerful mules and three wagons.

Unfortunately, the inexhaustible mine has yet to be discovered, and the great Cerro Gordo sleighride eventually came to an end. In 1879 the last load of bullion from the Belshaw smelter went down the tortuous grade to Swansea, and after the production of some $17,000,000 in silver and lead, citizens of the Fat Hill began looking for new locations where the future seemed to hold more promise.

During the past 85 years, Cerro Gordo has experienced several brief revivals. In 1911 Louis D. Gordon visualized potential profit to be gained by working the old tailings dumps for their zinc content. To that end he expended a quarter of a million dollars to build a six-mile tramway from the mountaintop camp to Keeler (which had come into existence with the building of the Carson and Colorado in the 1880s). This operation kept the old mining camp eating with some regularity until the Depression years of the 1930s. Again, during World War II, the mining of tungsten brought about another brief flurry of activity.

At the time of my visit to Cerro Gordo, in 1957, enough ruins remained there to delight the heart of any ghost town buff. Still standing, in good condition, was the two-story American Hotel (for which the water bill, in this dry camp, is said to have averaged $300 per month). There were also the mine buildings, the old smelter chimney, several cabins, plus numerous foundations and broken walls. Leading away from the skeleton of the camp toward the white expanse of Owens Lake, long before robbed of its water and left to die in the desert sun, was Louie Gordon's old tramway. Leaping from ridge to ridge, its black cables still held aloft their burden of ore buckets, swaying and creaking in the wind hundreds of feet above the bony face of the mountain.

Fortunes of Swansea and Cartago necessarily paralleled those of their fountainhead. A flash flood filled the big Swansea mill with debris and it was never reactivated. The *Bessie Brady* burned at her dock in 1882. (A second ship, the tug-type *Mollie Stevens*, built to draw barges laden with timber and charcoal from Cottonwood Landing to the Swansea dock, had sunk in midlake in 1877.) Both of the lake ports gradually wasted away until little remains to mark their one-time sites. At Cartago Landing, about midway between the present settlements of Cartago and Olancha, are still some signs of the old wharf, built in 1872; at Swansea still may be seen a part of the old furnace, as well as scattered fire bricks, silver slag from the smelter, and a handsome historical monument to mark the site.

Cerro Gordo's most active decade (1868-78) also saw the birth and death of Panamint City, another Inyo County silver camp situated in the Panamint Range about 50 airline miles to the southeast of Cerro Gordo.

Even though Panamint City never distinguished herself as a producer of fortunes, her fame will never die. Like Bodie, Virginia City, and Tombstone, her name will go down in history—or what passes for history—as one of the greatest, the richest, the roughest, the rowdiest; truly a superlative among mining camps.

After finding silver float near the mouth of Surprise Canyon in 1872, three prospectors—Richard Jacobs, W. L. Kennedy, and Bob Stewart—made their way up the near-precipitous chasm, climbing some 5000 feet in only five miles, and were amply rewarded when they found silver-copper ore assaying $2500 per ton! News of the rich discovery soon reached the ears of John Percival Jones and William Morris Stewart, both of whom were then reaping fortunes from Nevada's Comstock. Jones and Stewart bought a group of claims, organized a company, and almost before it was possible to say "silver strike!" the big rush was under way.

First to open a saloon in the new camp was Dave Naegle, who would later gain lasting fame by shooting and killing Judge David S. Terry. Naegle's saloon, the Oriental, with $10,000 worth of fixtures and furnishings, including a solid walnut bar, was advertised in the press of that day as "finest on the Coast, outside of San Francisco."

In addition to the posh Oriental and 18 other grog shops, Panamint's single, mile-long Main Street was bordered by six general stores, a bank, brewery, meat market, sundry other shops and services, and a newspaper, the *Panamint News*, which published its first edition November 26, 1874. Along this same street were situated nearly 200 miners' cabins and tents, not a few of which were occupied by men wanted by the sheriffs of Nevada and neighboring states. At its head, Main Street debouched into the district known as Maiden Lane where Martha Camp and her girls offered their charms.

About all Panamint City lacked, (besides law and order and sundry other cultural refinements), was wheeled access. During the first several months of its boom the camp was served only by pack mules and burros that toiled up the steep, dusty canyon in long, heavily-burdened queues. (Small wonder that eggs sold at $2 a dozen, hay at $200 a ton, and other commodities accordingly.) Eventually a toll road of sorts was built through the canyon to the new silver camp, and the pack trains were replaced by stages and ox-drawn freight wagons.

Panamint boomed, reaching its peak population in the winter of 1874-75 when, it is said, some 5000 persons jammed the basin at the head of Surprise Canyon. Two thousand is likely nearer correct. In either case, business lots sold for as much as $2500 each, a Masonic lodge was organized, and the big store of the Surprise Valley Mill and Water Company began stocking such dandified items as canned asparagus and French bonnets. Meanwhile, an unusual number of characters were being hauled off to Boot Hill in the two-wheeled butcher's cart that did double duty as a hearse, and the first baby born in camp was presented with a case of champagne.

Panamint, unfortunately, was no second Comstock. It was not even a good, honest, second Cerro Gordo. Though considerable development was done in the Panamint mines, and there was erected in camp a magnificent smelter with a 250-foot brick stack, the money that flowed into camp from the pockets of investors invariably was of greater volume than the emolument that poured forth in the form of dividends.

In August 1875—even as rumor was being circulated that Panamint's veins were pinching out—the big smelter went into its initial production on ore of the Wyoming and Hemlock mines. The yield was fair—around $100 to the ton—but not good enough to withstand the demoralizing shock of Black Friday, that same month, when the Bank of California closed its doors and its cashier, William Ralston, was found dead in San Francisco Bay.

Less than two months later, T. S. Harris passed through his Washington hand press the last issue of *Panamint News*, and the boomcamp boys began filtering down the canyon. Fortunately, much of the town's population had taken its departure before the day of the cloudburst, July 24, 1876.

When rain-swollen clouds crashed against the Panamint peaks on that torrid summer day, there was barely time for the mill whistle to blast a single shrill warning before the town was engulfed in a roaring deluge of flood water. Thundering the length of sharply-tilted Main Street in a wave six feet in depth, the flood carried away virtually everything in its path. Stone buildings collapsed like eggshells, wooden structures were borne aloft like canoes. Billard tables, chicken houses, beds—complete with their straw ticks and blankets, barrels, every conceivable item of furniture and furnishings, went swirling down Surprise Canyon, pounding against the rocks, breaking to splinters on the jutting walls of the narrow gorge.

Minutes later found the flood subsiding, but the City of Panamint was gone forever. Fifteen of her people were drowned, most of her buildings had been demolished, and the laboriously-built toll road through Surprise Canyon had been swept away so completely it might never have existed.

When I visited Panamint, about ten years ago, there was then still standing a major portion of the smelter, dominated by the great, square stack built of bricks locally made and fired by Chinese labor. Stone walls of the big company store were standing, roofless, and a brooding chimney marked the site of Louie Munsinger's brewery. Otherwise, the townsite was a melange of caved cellars, crumbled foundations, and fragments of stone walls. Whether those walls originally had sheltered bawdy houses or Miss Della Donoghue's Wyoming Restaurant, was impossible for this chance visitor to know. One thing seemed fairly certain—they had not harbored churches.

Panamint simply wasn't that sort of camp.

So far as that goes, neither was Ballarat, where a population of 1700 souls was more or less adequately served by 23 saloons.

Though situated less than 13 road miles from the camp in Surprise Canyon, Ballarat did not come into existence until almost two decades after Panamint City had gone down the drain. Named for Australia's great old mining center, the Inyo County town owed its existence to mineral discoveries made on the west slope of the Panamint Range in the early 1890s, particularly to the Ratcliffe mine, which is credited with an ultimate production of around half a million dollars. Other Ballarat mines that may have hit the $100,000-plus category were the World Beater, the Gem, and the O Be Joyful.

Like Panamint, Ballarat was a "fun" town, a horseplay town, a town beset by laughs and tall tales, and peopled by near-legendary characters such as Copperstain Joe, John Lemoigne, Pete the Frenchman, Wild Bill Corcoran, Judge Joe Goose, Sparkplug Sherlock, Shorty Harris, Johnny-Behind-the-Gun, and others. Chris Wicht, who continued to operate his saloon long after the town, otherwise, had died, often recalled that in Ballarat's heyday there had passed over his bar as much as $65,000 in a single month.

The wasted bones of the town still huddle on a desert flat at the foot of the Panamints, four miles east of the Trona-Death Valley road. Two or three old pensioners still make it their home, and the desert wanderer, Seldom Seen Slim, sometimes may be seen there. Scattered over the flat are half a dozen old cabins fabricated of adobe, tin, boards, and any castoff that may come to hand; but the men that made Ballarat one of the great camps of the desert all have taken their way down the Long Trail that has no turning.

Of Inyo's ghost-haunts there is almost no end.

The old Eclipse mine, discovered in 1860, eventually became the Reward. A mill was built, and a prosperous little gold camp grew up around it. The Reward mine and mill continued to operate until shortly before World War II, and the site of the town, about eight miles southeast of Independence, still contains a few interesting ruins.

In 1877 gold was discovered in the next canyon north of Hunter Canyon, on the Saline Valley side of the Inyos, and the mining camp of Beveridge came into being. Due to its rough, isolated location, it is said there was never a wagon road into the camp; that all supplies, including a piano, were packed in on mule back from Lone Pine, and all ore was carried out in the same manner. Over the years there have been several attempted revivals at Beveridge, the last about 1916; but location of the old site is all but lost to man's knowledge.

During its brief span of years the camp of Belmont, near Cerro Gordo, chalked up a production record of some $500,000 in high-grade silver. Water purchased at Cerro Gordo at three to five cents a gallon, it is said, was carried by burro back to the even dryer camp of Belmont were it was resold at 50 cents a gallon.

In the Argus Range, southeast of Darwin, the town of Lookout burgeoned in 1877, a pack trail over the mountains connecting the camp with its major source of support, the silver mines of Minnietta and Modoc, (the latter owned by Senator George A. Hearst, father of the late publisher William Randolph Hearst). Due to the fact that the arid Argus Range provided little wood that could be converted into the charcoal necessary to smelt the Modoc-Minietta ore, Senator Hearst had constructed in Wildrose Canyon in the Panamint Mountains, about a dozen miles to the east, a group of beehive-type kilns. After being burned in these stone ovens, the charcoal was hauled by muleteams across Panamint Valley to the smelters. In addition to the old kilns, still standing in excellent preservation, today's ghost seeker may visit the old Modoc mine via a marked dirt road leading westerly from the Panamint Springs-Trona highway.

Other one-time villages and camps, of which there remains almost no known record, include Lake City, laid out at the south end of Owens Lake in 1862 and virtually deserted by 1868. Millspaugh is another of the places that existed, but of which there seems no present history; nor does anything seem to be known of the town of Reiley—except that it is listed in the 1883 *Report of the Director of the Mint* as "one of the 17 most important settlements and towns in Inyo County."

Opening years of the 20th century found thousands of prospectors combing the hills in search of a second Goldfield or Tonopah, two great camps then going their delirious way in the Southern Nevada hills. Out of this renewed flurry of activity sprang an entire new crop of Inyo County mining camps. Though colorful and lively, virtually none of these camps of the 1906-10 era was founded on the strength of good, sound ore deposits, and all eventually were destined to find a place in the lengthening roster of ghost haunts.

Lee, a gold camp in the Funeral Mountains, had a Board of Trade organized in 1907 with 25 charter members. . . . Zabriskie's adobe ruins stand alongside Highway 127, not far from Tecopa Hot Springs. Ryan and "Old" Ryan—at the site of the Lila C. mine—were borax towns. Kruger was a gold camp four miles south of Keeler City. There was Chloride City, and Harrisburg, and Keane Wonder. Latimer, a town in Butte Valley east of Ubehebe Mountain, was named for J. E. Latimer, Cleveland traction tycoon. The townsite was surveyed and platted, streets named, and building lots sold; but he who goes looking for it today should have a sense of humor and plenty of time to devote to the search.

There were the copper towns. Copper-crazy towns, complete with crisp stock certificates, page advertisements in mining journals, gentlemen in frock coats, and White Steamers bouncing over rough desert roads. Of all the copper camps in Inyo County, none attained more notoriety than Greenwater, an outgrowth of the earlier camps of Kunze and Ramsey. Within a month after the main claims were sold to Charles M. Schwab, president of Bethlehem Steel, there were more than 1000 boomers assembled at the townsite on the eastern slope of the Black Mountains. Within a year, Greenwater had a population of more than 2000, served by two local newspapers and a lively magazine, a $100,000 bank, an array of shops and saloons, several illegal gambling halls featuring faro, roulette, and poker; and building lots on Main Street were tagged at $2000 each. Water, freighted in from an outside source, sold at $7.50 a barrel, and when fire broke out in the office of the *Greenwater Times*, it is said, the owners had to stand by and watch the building burn to the ground because the water to save it would have cost more than the plant was worth.

The Charles M. Schwab Merger Company, capitalized at $25,000,000, for some time spent $30,000 a month on development of their mines . . . but the mines never developed. The town, already tottering on the ropes, went down for the count with the Panic of 1907. George Graham Rice, one of the greatest shyster promoters of all time, later called Greenwater "the monumental mining stock swindle of the century," and stated that the public, in only four months' time, invested and lost at Greenwater more than $30,000,000.

Another monumental swindle was Leadfield, in Titus Canyon. It was here that C. C. Julian, of petroleum fame (or infamy?) sired a fantastic stock promotion in 1926. Hundreds of Southern Californians, hauled royally to the nearest railroad station aboard the 15-coach "Julian Special" of the Tonopah and Tidewater Railroad, left behind their money and took away with them memories of a gala occasion and sheafs of beautifully-engraved and thoroughly worthless stock certificates. In August 1926, the Leadfield post office opened with mail for 200 persons. Six months later it closed with mail for one last straggler.

Another ghost of the 20th century is Skidoo, a camp whose life spanned the decade 1906-16. Soon after the discovery of gold ore by Harry Ramsey and One-Eye Thompson, the new camp on Tucki Mountain boasted five saloons, two general stores, two barber shops, three restaurants, three lodging houses, two dance halls, an assay office, poolhall, a clubhouse, branch bank, and a newspaper, the *Skidoo News*. There was even talk of building a branch railroad westward across Death Valley to the burgeoning boomcamp, which was taking on an air of permanence; its boothill cemetery, at least, was beginning to fill. Several of its graves were of persons who had succumbed to the elements, and two others dated from the day that Joe Simpson, saloonkeeper, shot and killed storekeeper Jim Arnold and was summarily lynched by Skidoo's irate burghers who didn't approve such goings-on.

When I last visited Skidoo, in 1953, there remained at the site several old buildings, including one large boarding house and sundry cabins, but I am told that none of these structures remains today.

Not so thoroughly obliterated is the townsite of Tramway whose ruins are visible from the highway about five miles northwest of Keeler. Here was the lower terminus of a 13-mile electric tramline built in 1913 to transport salt over the Inyo Mountains to the north shore of Owens Lake. During the total of nine years that the tram operated, approximately 30,000 tons of salt were processed and shipped. Costs of operation, unfortunately, were too often greater than the gross profit and the salt project fell by the wayside in 1930. The mill was torn down years ago, but several old cabins and a boarding house still mark the site of this rather unusual mining venture.

Last, and by far the most pathetic in this woefully incomplete roster of Inyo County's ghost haunts, is Manzanar in the Owens Valley between Lone Pine and Independence.

Originally settled by homesteaders in 1860, these lands, about 1910, were subdivided into small orchards by George Chaffey and Associates, of Los Angeles, and in one year 20,000 apple trees were planted in the tract. A large general store was opened in 1911 by a man named Hatfield, who also operated the post office. A school was established, a commercial club organized, and community life flourished. Came then the era of the Big Water Grab, the flowing irrigation canals went dry, the young orchards died for lack of water, and the heartbroken farmers moved away.

The town of Manzanar had been a sorry little ghost many years before World War II broke on the scene and Uncle Sam found himself in need of a War Relocation Center for Japanese residents of the California Coastal area. Manzanar, strangely enough, was chosen for that dubious honor. Many large buildings were erected—dormitories, dining rooms, commissaries, administration buildings; trees and gardens were planted, and the little ghost town bloomed anew as the temporary home of 10,000 displaced Japanese.

With the war's end, Manzanar's erstwhile citizens were permitted to return to their homes, the buildings were razed, and the little ghost town went back to sleep.

Today's motorist, traveling U.S. Highway 395 between Lone Pine and Independence, may notice to the west of his road two strange little buildings whose stone walls slope upward to shingled roofs; whose empty windows, like sightless eyes, look out over a jumble of broken foundations and cement platforms and weeds and ruin, and on across the dead townsite to the long, snowy backdrop of the High Sierra Peaks.

These buildings were the gatehouses.

This was Manzanar.

One of the ghosts.

RED ROCK CANYON
by Richard C. Bailey

RED ROCK CANYON, located a hundred and twenty-five miles north of Los Angeles and twenty-five miles north of Mojave, is a spectacular gash at the western extremity of the El Paso Range where it joins the higher Sierra Nevada. It is now well-known by reason of the magnificent sweep of freeway that serpentines between the red cliffs from which its name is derived. Travelers along U.S. 6 have often described the area as a sort of California Bryce. Others are reminded of portions of the Grand Canyon. Comparisons like these are warranted, although in extent Red Rock is considerably smaller than these more famous natural attractions.

Size apart, it also differs from these in another important respect. It will come as a surprise to thousands of visitors who have camped in its gulches and picnicked at the foot of its colored cliffs to learn that Red Rock is privately owned. A number of unsuccessful attempts have been launched to acquire the area as a state or national park but to date all such proposals have made little progress.

Although its genesis is in the distant past, Red Rock became known to history little more than a century ago. The accidental discovery of gold at Sutter's Mill in 1848 set off a tide of emigration from the East that was soon to alter completely the course of California history.

In their eagerness to reach this land of promise a number of emigrant divisions chose to follow the questionable routes in traversing the unknown mountains and desert expanses that barred their way West. Among these were several groups popularly known as the Death Valley parties. After blundering into the great basin with the macabre name these units made their painful escapes south and west over wastelands considered among the most awesome in North America.

In January, 1850, a number of these footsore survivors camped in Red Rock on their way south to safety. They were the Bennett and Arcane families plus a division of the Illinois Jayhawkers. The former had recently been rescued from Death Valley by Lewis Manly and John Rogers who had returned from Southern California with food barely in time to save their lives.

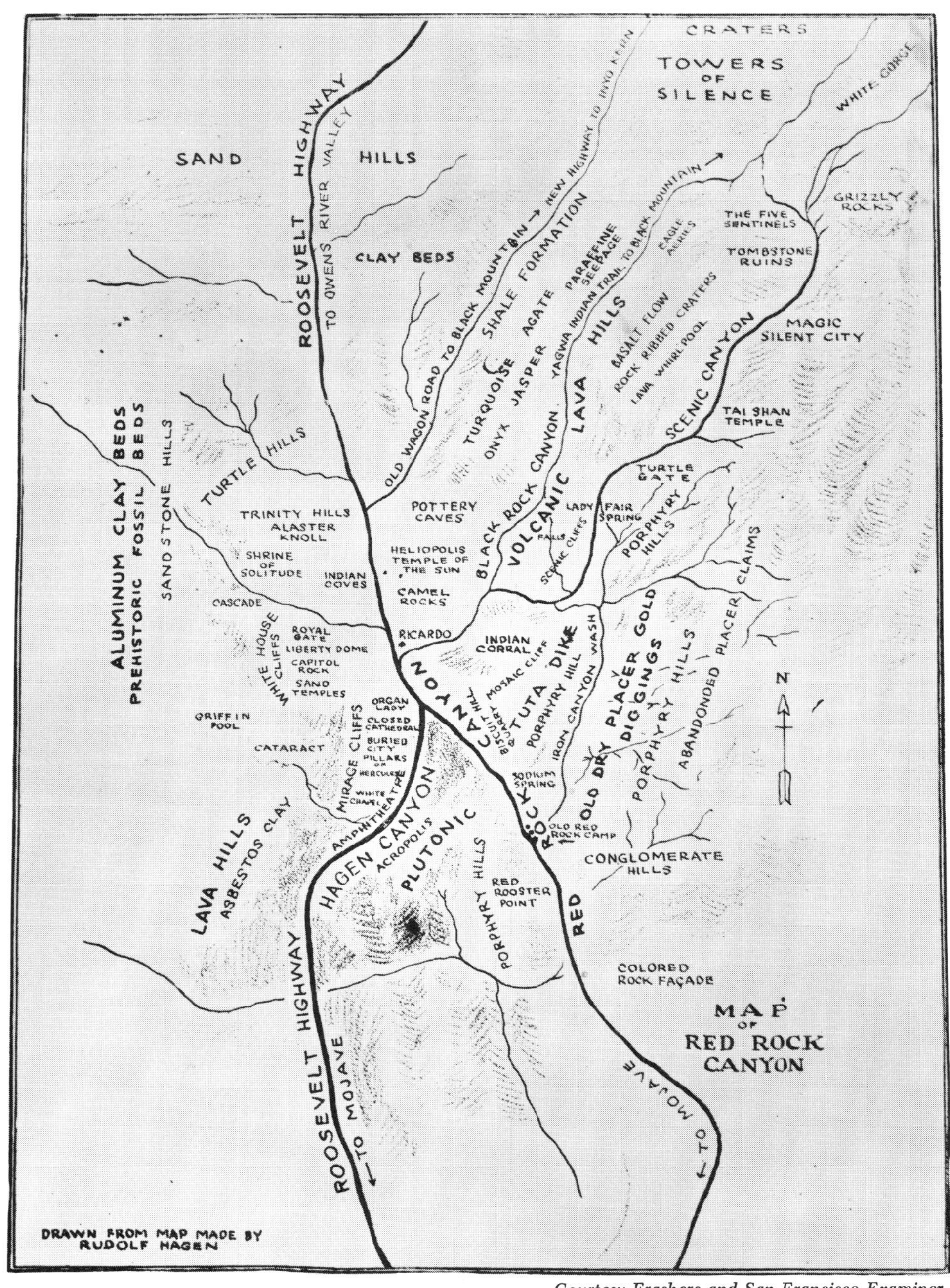

Courtesy Frashers and San Francisco Examiner

Old newspaper map shows some of the main points of interest in Red Rock Canyon area.

Neither they nor the Jayhawkers were apparently impressed by the wonders of the canyon through whose depths they passed. In later years, if they thought of it at all, it was most likely to recall how hungry, cold, and weary they had been at this time. Four decades later Lewis Manly in his famous book, *Death Valley in '49*, was content to state simply that the pass was now known as Red Canyon. His descriptions of other points on their route are often vivid and detailed, and his failure to enlarge on what he undoubtedly saw here is inexplicable.

There were two Germans with the Jayhawkers, although not of their party. Somewhere on their route out of Death Valley one of them is credited with having discovered a number of rich placer nuggets. The other, a John Galler (or Goller), was not in the least interested at the time. However, after his companion's death, Galler tried unsuccessfully to relocate the spot where his friend had found the nuggets. It has been suggested that the actual site was Red Rock Canyon, later the scene of a considerable placer rush.

Because of its geographical location Red Rock was not seen by great numbers of early western travelers. Those heading north from Southern California en route to the San Joaquin Valley and the distant Mother Lode usually turned off at Oak Creek and other passes through the Tehachapis. Others, trekking southward from Owens Valley, invariably swung west at Walker's Pass and made their way into the San Joaquin via the Kern River area. Had it lain a few miles either north or south, Red Rock would undoubtedly have been hailed as an outstanding landmark in the annals of pioneer desert wayfaring.

The formations of Red Rock date back to late Tertiary times. Judged to be at least 2,500 feet thick, they are composed mainly of bedded volcanic tuffs, sandy and shaly beds, and two lava flows. Their strikingly tilted facades have been eroded and weathered into fantastic and weird forms.

An imaginative observer has described a two-story bastion of red rock carved in relief from the gray hillside as the "citadel." Another outstanding sight is the "white house cliffs," composed of numerous towers and domes. Sand-laden winds and the rains of centuries have carved out myriads of strange shapes along the lava-capped parapets that flank the main highway and line the adjacent gulches branching off to the east and west. As in looking at cumulus clouds one can see anything he chooses—a camel's head, praying nuns, organ pipes, toadstools, even ferocious-appearing gargoyles. For those with an archeological bent, there is a particularly splendid "buried city."

During the Pliocene period, perhaps two million years ago before the uplift of the present Sierra Nevada Mountains, the appearance of this area was decidedly different. A study of fossil plant material indicates a less arid climate than at present, and considerably more herbage. Among the animal fossils found in the canyon's Ricardo strata were several species of horses, camels, antelope, a ruminant hog, mastodons, and two kinds of rhinoceroses. With them were the bones of flesh eaters, represented by dogs, wolves, and cats, including a primitive saber-tooth. Coeval human remains, however, have not yet been detected.

At least five species of trees have been discovered in the fossil beds. The locust is the most abundant tree, and with it are found fragmented sections of oak, pine, and cedar.

It is generally agreed that 1893 was the year that placer gold activity at Red Rock began on an extensive scale. However, even then there were rumors that some prospecting had been conducted here during the 1860's. In 1894, a W. J. Langdon is reported to have found a location notice posted by a Hiram Johnson bearing the date of 1853. On a nearby rock Langdon observed a pair of rusty gold scales, and not far distant, by the remains of an old fireplace, he found a black whiskey bottle containing about six dollars worth of gold dust.

During the 1890's hundreds of miners sifted the sands for gold among the basal conglomerates and tuffs that lined the beds of the various gulches. That their efforts were richly rewarded is evidenced by the report that around sixteen million dollars in gold was taken from the canyons within a few years. The largest nugget known to have been found here was unearthed by Dave Bowman in Santa Monica Canyon. Having no scale large enough to determine its weight Bowman, with the help of Clinton Todhunter, another miner, estimated its worth by balancing the nugget against a four-pound single jack and four cans of condensed milk. They were not far off its actual value which approximated $2,000.

A view of the "buried city" in the Red Rock Canyon area of Kern County.

One of the animal forms to be found in Red Rock Canyon —this one looks like a camel.

Another fortunate prospector was Rudolf Hagen, who has been credited as the rediscoverer of Red Rock Canyon gold in the 1890's. Coming here in the spring of 1893, he and his associates are said to have washed more than two and a half million dollars worth from surface workings. They are then reported to have spent a considerable amount of this in litigation to protect their claims. One of his partners was Charles Canfield, a well known pioneer producer in Kern County's Midway oilfield. Hagen subsequently acquired quite a few thousand acres in the Red Rock area, and a considerable part of this property is now held by his heirs.

But all of the gold in the El Paso Range was not found in Red Rock alone. Four miles to the east in Last Chance, there were numerous claims, while some miles farther east toward the end of the range lies Goler Gulch and Summit Diggings where still more millions in gold were taken from the dry stream beds and hillsides. As happened in many districts a comparative few hit it rich while the rest were not so fortunate and scarcely scratched enough on which to get by. In Reed Canyon near Goler Gulch another large nugget was found in 1893 which is said to have brought $1,900. Others in the same area ranged in value from $10 to $50 apiece.

Although white miners have been chiefly responsible for our current knowledge of Red Rock and its neighboring terrain, the presence of their ancient and immediate predecessors should not be overlooked. Throughout the numerous gulches, and over the ridges and hillsides of this volcanic territory, there exist considerable reminders that man was here long ago. Primitive rock shelters and once-occupied caves abound, particularly several miles east of Red Rock at Black Mountain, tallest peak in the El Pasos. Hundreds of rock circles and many pictographs are scattered over a wide area. Meager information received from old miners, who likely secured their "facts" at second or third hand, points to the likelihood that Black Mountain was long ago a sacred place and the site of annual religious ceremonies. The position of some of the stone rings, especially those perched on the very top of the boulder "pyramid" at the western end of the highest ridge, are strongly suggestive of ceremonial usage.

Investigators have referred to these unknown builders as the

"Old People" and have made educated estimates that portions of their handiwork may date back 15,000 to 20,000 years. Possibly they were the same artists, or their relatives, who carved the older petroglyphs that appear in such proliferation in the canyons on the eastern rim of Indian Wells Valley north of China Lake. Within a few years the mystery of these ancient folk may be resolved. An archeological group from Southern California is presently engaged in a long-range survey that should eventually clarify many details respecting origin and daily life that are now obscure.

The more recent Indians are better known. Anthropologists term them the Shoshone-Comanche, but to nearly everyone else they are popularly known as Mojave Indians because of their residence in the Mojave Desert. The word "Mojave" is supposed to be a corruption of Chemehuevi. Obviously, name-calling here is no simple matter. To add to the confusion there were also numerous tribal groups, each with its individual name.

These desert Indians were nomadic through necessity, and permanent year-round campsites were the exception. Mesquite beans formed their staple food, but in season they ate many kinds of seeds, berries, and roots. In the desert their diet included lizards, snakes, grubs, and insects, as well as any small mammals they could catch.

For houses they prepared circular wickiups of brush and willow. Their basketry was excellent and their tightly-woven water bottles were highly prized by other Indian nations in California. Many of these are found in basket collections hundreds of miles from the spot where they were fashioned.

The early sheep industry contributed an interesting episode to Red Rock history. In 1879, following a long spell of drought in the San Joaquin Valley, sheepmen sought to avoid bankruptcy by seeking markets far removed from their home ranges. In May of that year flockmaster J. J. Lopez of the famous Rancho El Tejon began his drive of 16,000 sheep from Cow Wells south of Mojave via Red Rock Canyon to Green River, Wyoming. Despite the strenuous efforts of Lopez and his herders during the succeeding six months, nearly half of his charges were lost due to storms and arid conditions along the trail. This amazing trek by Lopez, who afterwards served as general superintendent of the Tejon for many years, is ranked among the greatest sheep drives ever attempted in Western America.

Cattle are also no strangers to the area, for long before the placers of Red Rock and Goler were discovered, the brothers John and William Cuddeback had large herds ranging over Fremont Valley south of the El Pasos. Although much of this acreage is now under irrigated cultivation, cattle in limited numbers are still found here.

The early trail through Red Rock was always difficult due to the sandy soil. It was subject to frequent washouts by torrential cloudbursts which even now rage through the gulches during winter months. Freighters and stageline drivers, however, for many years cursed their way through the gorge over this unimproved road on the passage between Los Angeles and Owens Valley. Their alternative was the detour around the east end of the El Pasos which was difficult and too long to be practicable.

Ricardo, a canyon stopover, was established during the 1890's by the early miner Rudolf Hagen, and named by him in memory of his son Richard. The original building fell victim to a flood some years ago and was rebuilt a short distance to the west. This later structure is now abandoned and near obliteration.

During the 1920's the road through the canyon was first blacktopped with oilsand. Then in 1931 a modern paved highway section was dedicated, which in 1958 was succeeded by today's four-lane expressway. A short distance within the southern entrance, where the concrete bridge spans the main streambed, the present roadway passes almost over the original site of Ricardo. Early accounts mention the nearby location of Sullivan's Spring where miners and travelers secured drinking water. This spring still exists a few hundred yards northeast of the road, protected by weathered timbers placed here long ago. Two miners, named Sullivan and Black, ran a placer claim in the vicinity in 1899; the spring is presumably named for the former.

In 1908 the City of Los Angeles contracted with the Southern Pacific Company to construct a nine mile branch rail line from Cantil Siding up Red Rock Canyon to the site of the aqueduct. This standard-gauge line was completed in January, 1909, and operated almost continuously for twenty-two months. It was then dismantled and its material sold to the railroad and the U.S. Reclamation Service.

Once a cloudburst ripped out a section below the canyon's south entrance, and a number of the twisted rails lie rusting in the wash, not far off the present highway. Nearby stand the remains of a stone and earthen dam built by Hagen; most of this was also carried off by a canyon flood.

The entire aqueduct was completed in October, 1913; and since that date has transported water over 225 miles of desert and mountains to the expanding metropolis in the Los Angeles Basin. The principal section through the Sierra, west of Red Rock, required the drilling of a two mile tunnel through a soft sandstone formation, an operation that was completed in seven months. The tunnel was then completely lined with concrete during the next eight months. During the month of August, 1909, this job saw the establishment of a new world's mark for rock drilling when crews of the Jawbone Division cut a record 1,000 feet, eclipsing all former standards.

Red Rock has been a popular mecca for "rockhounds" since the hobby's birth several decades ago. Although the area has yielded considerable material, diligent searchers can still find a variety of excellent specimens. Among these are agate, quartz crystals, and small opals. Chalcedony in various mixtures and colors is also present, as well as brown, green, and red moss jasper. As has already been mentioned, petrified wood is still available, but the once noted "petrified forest" in Last Chance Canyon no longer exists. The fossil remains, formerly so plentiful on the surface, have been entirely carried off by voracious collectors.

Gone also are the bighorn sheep that ranged the high ridges surrounding Red Rock in former days. Nor are there any survivors of the great herds of prong-horn antelope that grazed in the gulches and over the broad expanse of Fremont Valley. Their final extermination occurred well within the memory span of persons yet living.

However, man and his guns have not succeeded in divesting Red Rock of all wildlife. Small mammals and birds are well represented though understandably wary. Desert jack rabbits and cottontails can be glimpsed scooting from bush to bush, and lucky observers may spot an occasional coyote or kit fox trotting down one of the sandy washes. There are also gophers, as well as rats and mice of various species.

During summer months a host of lizards constantly dart over the rocks and blistering sand. Rattlesnakes are also present in moderate numbers. A surprising variety of birds pass through the canyon. They include finches, warblers, wrens, linnets, and thrashers. Hawks, mourning doves, and mocking birds are also fairly common. Ravens, buzzards, owls, and the fast-moving road runner apparently make this their home on a year-round basis. With patience, bird watchers could undoubtedly run up an impressive list of feathered visitors.

Red Rock abounds in most of the plants common to the Mojave Desert. Some of the more familiar are the Joshua tree, mesquite, creosote bush, and desert holly. Wet winters usually bring out brilliant patches of wildflowers the following spring, which invariably entice thousands of sightseers to the area. Other attractions during this season are the impressive Easter sunrise services held annually in the canyon. These observances, which began in 1928, have continued to the present with few interruptions.

The desert seems to have a strange fascination for unusual individuals, and the El Pasos certainly never had a stranger resident than William Henry Schmidt. This man, better known as "Burro" Schmidt, spent thirty-eight years alone digging and blasting a half-mile tunnel completely through a granite mountain. So far as can be determined he carried out his prodigious task, using the simplest of tools, merely for his own satisfaction; only a fraction of the rock removed contained ore of any value. At the tunnel's completion in 1938 Schmidt became a celebrity when Bob Ripley featured him in one of his "Believe It or Not" cartoons. Schmidt died in 1954 at the age of 82; and his tunnel, located on an upper ridge of Last Chance Canyon, is still regularly visited by the curious.

Charley Koehn, who homesteaded Kane Springs between present day Cantil and Saltdale in 1892, was another early personality. Often referred to as the "Bismark of the Desert" and the "Wild Dutchman," Koehn built up a small settlement near his spring. During the boom of the local placers he became their chief supplier of garden vegetables and hard liquor.

Koehn was around for quite a spell, and during his last years he was the fellow movie companies contacted when they required wagons and mules for their filmmaking in Red Rock. Even prior to the 1920's, before the talkies, the canyon was a favorite Hollywood locale for outdoor scenes. More recently its cliffs have formed the background of numerous sound extravaganzas. Its terrain has also become familiar to television viewers since western episodes are frequently filmed here.

Quite a few "oldtimers" spent their last years in Goler Wash on the southern flank of the El Pasos, but their modest shacks are now possessed by late arrivals. The possibility of earthquakes is evidently of small concern to them for their dwellings in this shallow trench stand directly atop the Garlock Fault.

Red Rock Canyon is one of the geologic and scenic wonderlands of California. Perhaps through the concerted efforts of those most concerned it will soon achieve park or monument status, thus insuring its preservation for all time as a recreational area. Such a possibility will be heartening to those who have enjoyed its pristine attractions and thrilled to the tales of its varied and colorful past.

EARLY MAN *in the* CALIFORNIA DESERT

by Gerald A. Smith

TODAY VERY FEW descendants of the historic Indians remain on the desert. The greatest number are members of the Mojave and of the Yuma tribes of the Colorado River. A few Indians of Shoshone, Chemehuevi and Paiute ancestry are found on the Mojave Desert. Certain locations on the Colorado Desert remain the home of the Desert Cahuilla.

Sociological changes have resulted in a new migration of Indian peoples from Arizona and New Mexico. These have come to our Southern California deserts, not to hunt or to gather turquoise, but to work for the Santa Fe Railroad. Greatest in number among these are the Navajo. Thus we see today the beginning of a new Indian industry on our Southern California desert. The Navajo women have brought their knowledge, their skill and their materials, and are even weaving the traditional Navajo rugs.

The record of man's coming to the Americas, his occupation of the Western Hemisphere, and the development of his multifaceted culture is but one chapter in the fascinating continuing drama of man's world-wide physical and cultural evolution.

At present, the oldest known evidence in the world indicating the existence of true man is an occupation site in Olduvai Gorge, Africa. There the British prehistorian, Dr. L. S. B. Leakey, has found assemblages of rocks suggesting crude shelters, crude simple tools made to a set and regular pattern, fragmentary animal bones and human bones all on the same living floor. By the potassium-argon technique, the University of California has given the site an age of about 1,750,000 years.

Actually, the study of ancient man is still very much in a state of flux. Dating, physical evolution, and migration routes are but a few of the problem areas being studied by anthropologists all over the world. Geologists have never been completely in accord regarding a beginning date for the Ice Age or the Pleistocene, but the majority have agreed that it was about a million years ago and coincided with the appearance of Man. Olduvai Gorge, with a date of nearly two million years, has thus made the age of Man and of the Pleistocene a geological problem of the first magnitude.

It is currently believed by most anthropologists that Man developed his stone-age culture in Africa and ultimately spread into Europe and Asia. The number of people living in Africa at the time of expansion into Europe and Asia was perhaps small at first. Improvements and innovations in tool types, as in all new basic inventions, were exceedingly slow. This was also true of the spread of Man and his culture.

Hundreds of thousands of years apparently passed before Man reached northeastern Asia, and ultimately crossed the Bering Strait and spread throughout the Americas and occupied our California desert.

The Pleistocene period of geological time is generally divided into four major periods of glaciation separated by interglacial periods with climates suggestive of modern times. Regional names have been applied to the periods. In Europe, the Fourth Glacial Period is called the Wurm; in America, it is called the Wisconsin. Within the Wisconsin Glacial Period there were advances and retreats of the ice. These intervals have regional names. In Western America, the two major advances are called Tahoe and Tioga. Scientists believe that Man reached America before or during the early part of the Wisconsin. Much work needs to be done by geologists and archaeologists before we will have even a reasonably reliable approximation of the age of the Wisconsin Period or of the coming of Man to the Americas.

All current evidence indicates that even the first migrants to America were people physically very similar to Man today and are therefore referred to as "wise men" or homo sapiens. One cannot be sure that these first people were Indians or even that they were of the Mongoloid race. Scientists do know that the American Indians, when first discovered by the Europeans, represented a composite of that segment of humanity closely related to the Mongoloid Race. The term "Indian" is used to refer to any aboriginal inhabitant of the new world. The ancestors of the Indians of Southern California may have belonged to a culture which existed thousands of years ago in an era as far away as the Gobi Desert of Asia. They came to America across the Bering Strait region, band after band, as they expanded their hunting and food gathering over a period of a great number of years.

Certainly the increasing population pressure in Asia and the movement of herds of camels, horses, elephants and other animals over the arm of land connecting Asia and America induced Man to move with the herds at least as early as the Tahoe Advance. Man's first journey into the new world may have occurred at least 45,000 years ago. At that time, much of Canada and the northeastern United States were covered with ice while Alaska, and probably the Bering Strait, the coast of Southeast Asia, as well as a large strip of North America southeastward to Mexico were open grassland. This area at such a time would have been rich in game and inviting to Man, the hunter. Perhaps the first Americans followed large herds of mammoth south through this open grassland area. The early people would have moved with the herds—perhaps returning to their homes when the herds moved back, perhaps actually migrating a few miles in a year's wanderings. It must have taken many generations to reach the area known in historic times as the great American Grasslands. Other groups continued to cross from Asia to America and with the growth of population, in time the Indians covered all the land of North and South America.

While Man is called a hunter when he came to America, it must be remembered that as yet no stone spear points have been found that are older than 20,000 years. Actually, none older than 14,000 years have been firmly dated. Perhaps Man had wooden spears in America much earlier, but none has been found and dated. Probably it would be more accurate to speak of the early migrants to America as hunter-scavengers who habitually caught small animals, but who, to kill larger animals, were in large measure forced to rely on the assistance of natural predators equipped with claws and fangs.

During the fourth glacial period of the Pleistocene, the Great Basin, of which the California desert is a part, was dotted with many pluvial lakes, connected by a network of streams. Everlasting snow capped the higher mountains. The present deserts, now so barren, were green and well-watered. The vegetation of the area provided food for herds of mammoths, camels, horses, and other mammals which in turn provided food for man. Perhaps Indians first discovered the California desert over 30,000 years ago.

During recent years, exciting new evidence has been discovered at Tule Springs, Nevada, by Ruth D. Simpson and M. R.

Harrington,[1] of the Southwest Museum; on Santa Rosa Island by Phil Orr,[2] of the Santa Barbara Museum; and at Lewisville, Texas, reported by W. W. Crook and R. K. Harris.[3] Such evidence suggests that men were eating mammoth, camel and other large animals in the West 30,000 years ago. Mammoth bones found with projectile points have so far been dated at only about 14,000 years. Perhaps this may indicate that mammoth continued to roam over much of North America and may have been hunted by man for a period that lasted more than 20,000 years. At this time the evidence for early Man on the California desert is not conclusive for an age of 30,000 years because of various reasons. There is lack of agreement as to the validity of radiocarbon dating; there is danger of contamination of samples; there are problems of interpretation of deposits containing carbon and artifacts. There are conditions of deposition and even of soil content, which all combine to make absolute dating difficult.

Archaeological investigations now being conducted by Ruth D. Simpson above the Pleistocene gravel bars at Manix Lake have resulted in the discovery of tools suggestive of ones found in Europe, Africa, India, Asia, and Java which were made before the Wurm or Wisconsin Glacial Period began. It will take much more research and study to determine the age of the almond-shaped hand-axes and associated tools found on the terraces of Pleistocene lakes of the California desert and elsewhere in the West. Ruth Simpson has initiated such a study with her analysis of the early lithic artifacts from Coyote Gulch and Manix Lake situated in San Bernardino County. The diagnostic specimens from these assemblages are bifacially flaked "coup to poing-like" implements similar to those of the Old World Lower Paleolithic period. These well defined implements are too numerous and too well made to be considered "quarry debris," as some writers have claimed. We do not anticipate an age comparable

[1]Harrington, Mark Raymond, and Simpson, Ruth DeEtte, "Tule Springs, Nevada, with other evidences of Pleistocene Man in North America." *Southwest Museum Papers*, No. 18, Los Angeles, 1961.

[2]Orr, Phil C. "Radiocarbon Dates from Santa Rosa Island," I. Santa Barbara Museum, *Bulletin* No. 2, Department of Anthropology, Santa Barbara, 1956.

[3]Crook, Wilson W. and Harris, R. K. "Hearths and Artifacts of Early Man Near Lewisville, Texas, and Associated Faunal Material," Texas Archaeological Society *Bulletin*, Vol. 28, pp. 7-97 Austin, 1957.

to that of the Old World, but indications are that Man on all continents at some time passed through the same cultural evolutionary stages.

The oldest recognized man-made artifact assemblages apparently fall into three groups: collections of small stones characterized by planned recurring edge-flaking; collections of large "coup de poing-like" tools with large scrapers, choppers and prepared cores; and scarce inventories of specimens of bone. This latter assemblage occurs both in the western United States and Mexico where there has been abundant Pleistocene fauna. The hand axes and associated tools have been found at sites in Wyoming, Utah, Arizona, California, Nevada and Baja California. The edge-flaked assemblage has been reported thus far only in the Death Valley-Mojave Desert region.

Between the scattered oldest known sites in the western United States and the formidable mass of evidence from radiocarbon-dated sites 9,000-14,000 years old, there exists a gap in our knowledge. Until that gap is filled or otherwise explained, many questions pertaining to the age and evolution of American prehistoric culture complexes will remain unanswered.

Probably for a clearer picture of American archaeology our greatest need is for more dateable sites and artifacts from this interval.

Ten thousand years ago, the mountain glaciers that characterized the southern expression of the Pleistocene were retreating and the Pluvial climate of the country we now know as the California desert was ending. The region during this period was occupied by men, now skillful hunters who were equipped with the atlatl and with spears and lances tipped with a variety of stone projectile points. This is the stage of American archaeology known across the Americas as the Paleo-Indian Period.

Numerous sites on our Southern California deserts are being exposed today because of the vast amount of construction, flood control, and military activities. At more than ten such sites, fossil bones of the mammoth, sloth, camel, and horse of the Pleistocene mammalian assemblage have been discovered in association with charcoal or with stone tools which indicate the presence of Man.

From the implements left, it is evident that early primitive bands of people varied at least in skill and technique of chipping

Some of the early man stone implements found in the California desert area.

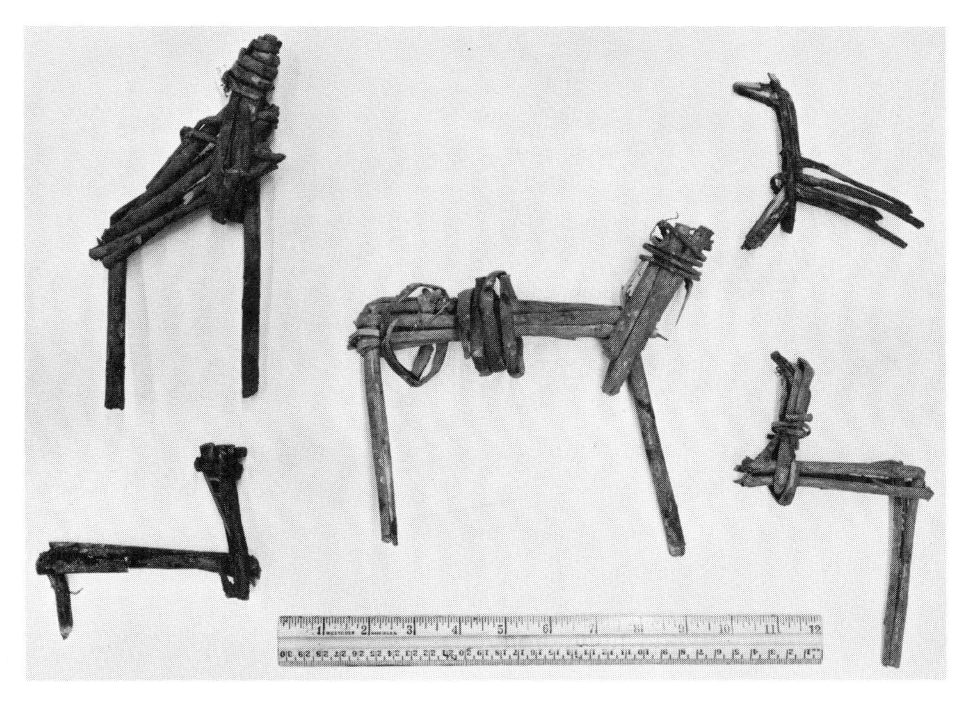

Curious split twig figurines found in a California desert cave.

stone tools. Archaeologists have named these different early bands with place names from the geographical location where such new style of tool or new technique of manufacture was first found. Consequently, even though it is not known what the physical appearances of these people were, they may be referred to as Pinto Basin people, Lake Mojave people, Gypsum Cave people, and Amargosa River people, etc.

One of the earliest of these different culture complexes found wide spread throughout the California desert has been well described by Elizabeth and William Campbell,[4] as a result of their archaeological research of Pleistocene Lake Mojave. Evidence of Man's occupation around the Pleistocene lake on an ancient beach at a specific elevation was discovered in the nature of a wide variety of refined percussion flaked implements. Tufa from this beach has been dated at 9600±250 years. The tools indicate that these ancient people were hunters who may have fashioned shafts of wood with stone scrapers, tipped them with large stone projectile points, and thrown them at game with the aid of the atlatl approximately ten thousand years ago. It is possible that the game these ancient ones hunted consisted of the now long extinct camel and horse, as well as bighorn sheep and pronghorn antelope. A considerable amount of archaeological investigation has supported the Campbells' conclusions. Malcom Rogers[5] once referred to the artifact assemblage of this kind as belonging to the early Playa industry. William Wallace[6] believes this projectile assemblage to be the oldest certain remains attesting to human occupation found in the California Desert.

As time passed and as the land became warmer and drier, people changed to meet the requirements of new climatic conditions. Archaeological evidence indicates that in various locations widespread throughout the California deserts an early Indian population added seed grinding tools to their culture for the

[4]Campbell, Elizabeth W. Crozer, and William K., "The Lake Mohave Site" in "The Archaeology of Pleistocene Lake Mojave; A Symposium." *Southwest Museum Papers*, No. 11, Los Angeles, 1937.

[5]Rogers, Malcolm J., "Early Lithic Industries of the Lower Basin of the Colorado River and Adjacent Desert Areas." *San Diego Museum Papers*, No. 3, San Diego, 1939.

[6]Wallace, William J., "Prehistoric Cultural Development in the Southern California Deserts." *American Antiquity*, Vol. 28, No. 2, p. 172, 1962.

preparation of a new food to add to their former apparently preponderantly meat diet. This phase of early Indian occupation of the desert is best known by the term Pinto Complex and is described by Elizabeth and William Campbell[7] in their report of the Pinto Basin. Hunting was still of great importance to Man, but the appearance of the slab milling stone and mano for grinding seeds into a flour perhaps indicated the beginning of a change in diet which may have been stimulated by a change in climate and vegetation. Perhaps the people of the Pinto Culture Complex created some of the petroglyphs we find scattered throughout the desert today.

At about the time of the Lake Mojave or Pinto Complex, there appears to have been an influx of people onto the California Desert from Southern Nevada. These Indians possessed a somewhat different lithic material assemblage. This culture complex is best described by referring to the classical work of M. R. Harrington[8] in his written account of the excavations of Gypsum Cave, Nevada. The makers of these stone tools were hunters. They fashioned excellent stone projectile points of a distinctive shape to fasten to their short spears which were thrown effectively with the atlatl. Evidently the Gypsum Cave people hunted the ground sloth and bighorn sheep. Several years after the publication of Dr. Harrington's report, C-14 dates of 8,500-10,000 years were obtained.

At the Newberry Cave in the Mojave Desert of San Bernardino County, archaeologists have discovered artifacts associated with bones and a tooth of the ground sloth and with the bones of the bighorn sheep. Some of the projectile points resemble those found at Gypsum Cave by Dr. Harrington and may indicate some relationship to a late aspect of the Gypsum Cave complex. Consideration of the entire artifact assemblage from Newberry Cave evidences a greater similarity to the early Amargosa or Basketmaker implements. Split-twig figurines constituted one of the most interesting groups of artifacts found at Newberry Cave. It is believed that the figurines were made and used as a

[7]Campbell, Elizabeth, W. Crozer, and William H. "The Pinto Basin Site." *Southwest Museum Papers*, No. 9, Los Angeles, 1949.

[8]Harrington, Mark Raymond. "Gypsum Cave, Nevada." *Southwest Museum Papers*. No. 8, Los Angeles, 1933.

part of some hunting ritual which may have had some magic for insuring success for the hunter. These split-twig figurines are similar to those found and reported by Douglas W. Schwartz,[9] from caves in the vicinity of the Grand Canyon and dated by the radiocarbon method as being approximately 3,500 years old.

Lithic material similar to that found at Newberry Cave has now been reported from numerous sites scattered throughout the deserts.

The climate and animal life had become much like that found by the earliest historians of the California deserts. The campsites of the Amargosa or Basketmaker people are usually found near still existing water. These people had not yet learned of the bow and arrow, but still clung to the ancient spears and atlatls. During their early stages, they relied on baskets and fibres for vessels and bags. As these people experimented and traded, they gradually learned to make pottery, fashion jewelry of green slate and shell, and in time may even have practiced some primitive agriculture in certain favored locations. The entire period of time covered by the Amargosa-Basketmaker occupation is marked by an increase in the use of grinding slabs, personal adornment evidenced by shell, stone, and paint pigments, and indications of clothing such as fragments of woven matting and fibre sandals.

The stage in the archaeological culture sequence of early Man of the California desert following that of the Pinto Basin complex, would undoubtedly fall into the Amargosa-Basketmaker lithic assemblage which has been described by Malcolm Rogers and somewhat later by William Wallace. This culture complex is represented by many sites extending over the greater portion of the Mojave desert. The entire period covered by Amargosa-Basketmaker occupation is marked by an increase in the use of milling stones. Perhaps this indicates a growing scarcity of large game and man's greater dependency upon seeds for food.

Evidence for the Amargosa-Basketmaker Complex appears in artifact assemblages from many sites extending beyond the Mojave Desert to include a great portion of the southern Great Basin and the Sonoran Desert. Although described more than twenty-

[9]Schwartz, Douglas W., Lange, Arthur L., and DeSaussure, Raymond. "Split-Twig Figurines in the Grand Canyon." *American Antiquity*, Vol. 23, No. 3, January, 1958.

five years ago, and although it apparently had wide distribution temporally and geographically, recognition and designation of the Amargosa-Basketmaker Complex as such has occurred only sporadically. This is an illustration of the weakness of the development of uniform typology and communication between prehistorians even in a single region. These two problems will continue to plague archaeologists throughout the Americas for many years.

Numerous Amargosa-Basketmaker sites in the southern Great Basin, which really includes our Southern California deserts, have yielded a rich assortment of lithic implements, both grinding tools and projectile points. The projectile points and related chipped stone tools dominated the apparently earlier Amargosa-Basketmaker occupation. Grinding stones became more numerous and true arrowpoints appeared in the last stages of this occupation.

Much of the material described by Alice Hunt[10] (1960) as late Death Valley II and Death Valley III reflects Amargosa-Basketmaker influence if not actual Amargosa-Basketmaker occupation. Much of the occupation around Troy Lake in Manix Basin was distinctly of the Amargosa-Basketmaker Phase.

The definite rock alignments and petroglyphs which constitute an enigmatic aspect of southern desert archaeology may well date from Amargosa-Basketmaker times. Prehistoric Indians may have placed the rocks in the various formations for trail signs, for some religious purpose, or, more likely, for some purpose associated with hunting activities. Some of the rock formations may have been hunting blinds or used to hold down brush fences so that large game such as bighorn sheep or antelope could be driven in certain directions past waiting marksmen. The rock alignments occur at many places in San Bernardino County, occasionally in Inyo County, and of late are frequently reported in Riverside County. Many of our desert petroglyphs (designs pecked or cut into rock) and pictographs (designs painted on rocks) may have been made by people of the Amargosa-Basketmaker Culture Complex.

[10]Hunt, Alice "Archeology of the Death Valley Salt Pan California" *Anthropological* Papers Number 47, University of Utah, 1960.

Perhaps future study will more precisely delimit and define the Amargosa-Basketmaker occupation of our deserts and perhaps then we shall know whether Amargosa and Basketmaker people had a common origin or if one was derived from the other.

While milling stones remained a secondary trait until late Amargosa-Basketmaker times in the desert, they are dominant on sites in the lower mountains and southern interior valleys of Southern California at an apparently much earlier period of Indian occupation. As yet there are no Carbon-14 dates for these sites, but the lithic material does suggest strong similarities to La Jollan and Topanga Culture Complexes nearer the coast which are at least 7,000 years old.

We know, of course, that even the most successful hunting peoples would augment a meat diet with berries, bulbs, and other plant products. The question of whether any of the early people of the deserts were essentially gatherers rather than hunters remains unanswered.

Evidence appears to be growing that would support the belief that very early bands were essentially both hunters and gatherers, with only the emphasis changing as climate and ecology changed. Certainly in Southern California's valleys and along its western slopes of the San Bernardino Mountains, the earliest people known were seed gatherers.

David Banks Rogers[11] of the Santa Barbara Museum, first described the stone culture of such people in the Santa Barbara region in 1929 when he referred to them as "The Oak Grove People." Later writers have recorded discoveries of similar lithic material.

Studies from San Diego County, conducted by Malcolm J. Rogers (1939) of the San Diego Museum, and from Los Angeles County, studies by Robert F. Heizer and Ada Treganza[12] of the

[11]Rogers, David Banks, *Prehistoric Man of the Santa Barbara Coast.* Santa Barbara Museum, 1929.

[12]Heiser, Robert F., and Lemert, Edwin M. "Observations on Archaeological Sites in Topanga Canyon, California." University of California, *American Archaeology and Ethnology,* Vol. 44, No. 2, pp. 237-258, University of California Press. Berkeley, California, 1947.

Treganza, A. E. and Beerman, A. "The Topanga Culture, Final Report of Excavations, 1948." University of California *Anthropological Records,* Vol. 20, No. 2, Berkeley.

University of California and those of Edwin F. Walker[13] of the Southwest Museum have supported the report of David Banks Rogers. In San Bernardino and Riverside Counties, these basically grinding-complex sites are located on crests of high rounded hills overlooking the valleys. The stone artifact assemblages secured from such sites correspond to those found elsewhere dated at approximately 7,000 years.

Evidence from southeastern Arizona now dates "ancient seed grinders" as living about the same time as the makers of projectile points which were used by the hunters of prehistoric animals. Further research is needed to determine whether the different cultures of Southern California represent different contemporary peoples, the same people at different times, or the same people living under different ecological conditions, following a variety of food gathering operations.

As early as Amargosa-Basketmaker times, there is evidence of considerable trade between the Indian peoples of Southern California and the Southwest. Trade routes linked the Great Basin with coasts of the Pacific Ocean and the Gulf of California. With increased population the refinement and diversity of culture complexes, trade increased and well-defined trade routes were established across the desert. Some extended through the high passes of the White, Inyo, Argus, Panamint, Sierra and Coast Ranges; others crossed the lower passes of the desert ranges and followed the open ways between the transverse ranges. Many of these trade routes continued to be used into historic times. One of the most important of these followed the Mojave River across the desert.

Our California Desert has long attracted "rockhounds." Some of the people who long ago liked pretty stones may have made periodic visits to our deserts to collect turquoise and paint stones as well as agate, jasper, and chert for manufacturing various tools.

Malcolm J. Rogers,[14] in 1928, found unmistakable evidence of

[13]Walker, Edwin Francis. "Five Prehistoric Archaeological Sites in Los Angeles County, California." *Frederick Webb Hodge publication Fund VI.* Southwest Museum, 1951.

[14]Rogers, "Malcolm J. Report of an Archaeological Reconnaissance in the Mojave Sink Region." *San Diego Papers.* Vol. I, No. 1, San Diego, 1929.

very early Pueblo turquoise mining activity near the town of Baker, in San Bernardino County. He located other sites between Granite Wells and Crucero. At more than fifty locations, Rogers found stone hammers, picks, and pottery shards relating the turquoise miners to the ancient Pueblo people of Southern Nevada or Arizona. In all probability, this Pueblo element came from southern Nevada, apparently also the source of the earlier movement of Amargosa-Basketmaker people who reached various parts of the Southern California desert at an earlier period. In the Turquoise Mountains, extensive digging had been done by these prehistoric Pueblo miners. Some of their pits were thirty feet long, twelve feet wide and twelve feet deep. Many tunnels branched out from the mining pits as the Indians endeavored to follow the turquoise seams. Numerous mining tools of stone have been found which were used to break up the rock and dig out the precious blue stone.

Probably Pueblo agriculture did not spread west of the Colorado River Valley and the evidence of Pueblo occupation reflects expeditionary and trade contacts, not permanent village sites. Rogers did discover what appeared to be a small Pueblo colonial settlement on East Cronise Lake, where rock outlines and a quantity of Pueblo pottery and other artifacts indicated an occupation of longer duration.

No one knows just what happened to the early hunters and gatherers who at various times occupied the Southern California deserts. Perhaps some settled along the Colorado River to become the prehistoric Mohave and Yuma. Some archaeologists believe the ancestors of the modern Hopi combined with some of the earlier inhabitants and later still moved on into northern Arizona. Perhaps this movement marked the entrance of the Paiute and Chemehuevi bands onto the southern desert. It is even possible that the Cahuilla, Serrano, and other bands of so-called Mission Indians were the ones left on the deserts and interior valleys when the ancestors of the Hopi moved northeastward.

It is evident that the material culture of the immediate prehistoric Yuman and Shoshonean Indians as found in Southern California was somewhat different from that of the "Ancient Ones."

The deserts during the immediate prehistoric period were

essentially as we know them today. Grasslands were gone and so were the lakes and most of the rivers. Water holes were few and far between. Gone were most of the large animals. Deer, bear and mountain sheep remained in the mountains and antelope roamed on the desert periphery.

Again there was population pressure as more and more people were forced into areas of dependable water. There was movement into the valleys and coastal area and the deserts were left to small hardy roving bands who moved from spring to spring as they gathered sufficient food for bare existence. These bands served as traders to peoples both east and west. They hunted small game with bows and arrows, using unique methods of snaring game with hand-wrought cordage, and constantly gathered and ground seeds for a basic diet. To secure sufficient food for survival was always a major challenge on the desert. No edible plant or animal was spared in the desert Indians' search for food.

It would seem that Man changed very slowly over the many years of the prehistoric periods. We know from historic records that he changed little while living in the California deserts during the two hundred years between 1540 and 1776. We know, too, that Man is capable of changing quickly when the necessity arises. We are witnessing the change today in the material culture of very primitive groups in other parts of the world as they change from the use of the primitive drum to television in just one generation. We know that change can and did come quickly to the Indians of Southern California as they moved from war clubs to machine guns during the period between1850 and 1918.

The future of the remaining descendants of the original pioneers of the Southern California deserts is now linked with the future of all mankind.

PHOTOGRAPHER *of the* DESERT *by* Russ Leadabrand

BURTON FRASHER may not have been the first man there, but in many cases he was the first man there with a view camera. . . .

Frasher and his camera went everywhere in the California desert wasteland and that was long before pavement and four-wheel drive vehicles.

The sandy washes of Death Valley knew Frasher in 1920 when the best way to get there was up the washboard roads out of Barstow, over flinty Jubilee Pass and through the sugary sand into Furnace Creek Ranch and its little date palm grove. On his many trips into the desert country Frasher's cars broke down, became stuck in the sand, were slowed by weather and stopped by wind. But he kept going back into the desert with camera and film "on any excuse."

In the beginning it was as much just an itch, call it a hobby, as it was anything else. There was not much market in those early days for large and arty scenes of Death Valley and the surrounding desert country. Later, when Frasher began funneling his energies into the creation of picture postcards, views of the strange California desert country went all over the world. Frasher became a kind of postcard king of the Southwest. His tripod-footed cameras might be found sitting on any rise between Washington and New Mexico. And since part of the fun for Frasher was in the going, he drove his cars into the desert until he could drive no farther and then he walked, camera and tripod over his shoulder, to get the view from the farthest hill.

Frasher postcards are seldom seen these days, but their passing does not mean that the work of this inquisitive explorer has gone for naught. His earliest views—some 1500 glass plates—have already been turned over to the Pomona Valley Historical Society in Southern California for safekeeping and for use by historians in the future. The enormous bulk of his later work, some 60,000 celluloid negatives, guarded in fireproof vaults in Frasher's photo studio in Pomona, will soon be transferred to the Historical Society's archives.

Some of those early Frasher glass plate negatives might surprise some collectors of Southwest scenes: group pictures of fruit packing house workers. This was the beginning of Frasher as a traveling photographer. . . .

Burton Frasher was born in the Denver, Colorado area on July 25, 1888. His father died (or disappeared) early forcing Burton, the eldest child, to go to work. Even then there was interest in photography by the Colorado boy; photography, exploring the mountains of Colorado, fishing. But for a living Frasher took to making boxes, first for a department store in Denver, a meat packing firm, a milk company, finally at fruit packing houses. Making fruit boxes for packing houses then became his first trade.

In time, around 1910, Frasher and Harry Wilson, his partner, came to California where the big interest in raising fresh fruit had started. Frasher became a box maker boomer, traveling to areas of the West where fresh fruit was being harvested and packed.

Even then Frasher carried a camera—it was a large formal 5 x 7 inch view camera, possibly made by Crown. The camera and tripod and portable darkroom all went into the sidecar of Frasher's motorcycle. In 1912, when he married Josephine Angel from Yakima and took his bride with him on his box making chores, Josephine went in the sidecar, too.

With the big, old camera Frasher took some scenics, but the collection of earliest plates show mostly an assortment of groups at packing houses from Southern California to Northern Washington.

Then, in 1914, just before Burton Frasher, Jr. was born, the Frashers settled down in Lordsburg, California, and opened a portrait studio with a sideline of photo supplies and stationery. Lordsburg would, in time, become LaVerne.

Frasher found himself doing more and more commercial photography and portraiture. By 1921 Frasher moved to Pomona, bought out Ayers Stationery and enjoyed a growing business.

While he had hung up the hatchet and the apron of the box maker the itch to travel stayed with him. In a Model T Ford Frasher sought out the sandy lonesome of the Mojave Desert country, pushing all the time closer and closer to Death Valley.

His first trip into Death Valley, made with a group of friends, was in the winter of 1920, according to Burton Frasher, Jr. who has no journal or diaries of his father to guide him, only a collection of sometimes dated negatives and an uncommon memory.

Frasher recalls that the route in those days was something like this: out of San Bernardino over the Cajon Pass to Barstow, and beyond. This far in those days on those roads was itself a day's drive. From there the route was north through the Silver Lake area to Jubilee Pass, through that passage into the lower end of Death Valley proper and up through that gritty wasteland to Furnace Creek. It was on this trip, Frasher recalls, that his father's party started running low on gasoline. They drove the touring car from Furnace Creek to Ryan and from there a call was placed to Death Valley Junction. Frasher waited at Ryan until the little train brought the tins of gasoline over from the Junction. Frasher and his group returned to Furnace Creek, drove north up through the Valley, crossing over the mountains finally to ruined Rhyolite. And such a Rhyolite it was. Burton Frasher, Jr. recalls it from a later trip. . . .

"All the wooden buildings were still standing. We spent the night in one of the town's best preserved buildings, an old church. We had to sweep the whisky bottles off the church pulpit to put down our bed rolls. In the old newspaper office the files of the paper were still in place. There were hundreds of Rhyolite and Bullfrog stock certificates scattered across the floor of the bank. I was a great collector, or wanted to be in those days. I wanted to take it all with me. But my Dad was opposed to it. 'Leave some for the next man', was his motto. I took a few things. The next time we were there it was all gone. From the first visit the wooden buildings started to vanish at Rhyolite and the collector's items had vanished."

If Burton Frasher was bearish on collecting curios, he did like to put everything worth seeing on film. There are pictures in the Frasher collection of Rhyolite of that day.

Subsequently Frasher's excursions—almost always with his wife and child—took them and the cars of the day into the lonesome desert region. There are some wonderful pictures in the Frasher collection of old Pierce Arrows and Hupmobiles. As a rule Frasher drove new cars or nearly new cars into the desert on his trips. He knew the dangers of a breakdown in remote places, and Frasher sought out the remote places. Titus Canyon—and this was before C. C. Julian built his road from Rhyolite into the swindle town of Leadfield—was a place that Frasher sought out. He drove to the north end of the Valley and got to know that strange Death Valley character, Death Valley Scotty, and the recluse, Albert Johnson. It is said that while Johnson and Scotty lived Frasher was the only commercial photographer allowed to take pictures inside the castle. There was an earlier castle, but it was partially built and then torn down. Frasher took no pictures of it and none may exist.

At the north end of the Valley, north still from Scotty's Castle, at Sand Spring, Frasher took pictures of a scattering of dead cattle and their bones—they had nothing to do with emigrants or their disasters. It was an unsuccessful experiment to run cattle in the mineral saturated wasteland.

Even in those days the sound of the words "ghost town" intrigued young Frasher and he remembers Scotty and his father talking about a place that cannot be pinpointed today—the vanishing mining camp of Ubehebe, which was located somewhere on the eastern side of Tin Mountain. Frasher photographed the Keane Wonder Mine and Chloride City.

Many made their first trips into Death Valley as a result of seeing Frasher's pictures. Burton Frasher, Jr. recalls:

"H. W. Eichbaum, who was driving a bus on Catalina Island for Wrigley at the time, saw some of Dad's pictures of Death Valley and talked with one of Dad's desert friends. I think it was the pictures of the sand dunes that impressed him. He went up to Death Valley, founded Stovepipe Wells resort, and by 1926 or 1927 had built the Eichbaum Toll Road—the Mt. Whitney Toll Road—from Darwin Wash up over Towne's Pass down into Death Valley. In the beginning Stovepipe Wells was just a collection of small huts and some tents."

The Frasher picture file records the site.

All historians credit Eichbaum with opening Death Valley to the motoring public. Frasher introduced Death Valley to Eichbaum.

How did Frasher navigate in this lonesome desert land in those days? Burton Frasher, Jr. recalls that on his earliest trips his father used a National Geographic map of some sort. Research reveals only a 1906 or 1907 map in the National Geographic magazine. There were U. S. G. S. Maps in the day which showed the major tracks through the desert, and the Automobile Club of

Burton Frasher, Death Valley Scotty and Josephine Frasher, with cameras and camera car in Death Valley.

Southern California had a map printed just before 1920 which Frasher might have used that would have been helpful.

It was not in the desert, where the Frashers ran into few people, but at Carson Camp at Silver Lake in the Sierra Nevada where the idea of going into the postcard business was born. The proprietor there asked Frasher to provide him with "some of his pictorial views" in postcard form which he could sell at the resort. Frasher agreed and found himself in the postcard business, an enterprise that would continue to a degree even after his death.

On subsequent trips to the Death Valley area Frasher tried to follow the old twenty mule team borax wagon route out of the Valley via Wingate Pass. His car of the trip could not make the rough crossing and he had to turn back.

Once coming back from Death Valley across the mid Mojave Desert with Copper City as their destination the Frashers ran into a fast-approaching night. There was a well at Copper City, an abandoned camp in the desert south of Death Valley. It was near dark when they reached the town, tired and thirsty. They found the well at abandoned Copper City without trouble, but the well had a dead horse in it. It was a dry camp that night.

Burton Frasher, Jr. recalls getting stuck in the sand near Stovepipe Wells at one time. He recalls breaking springs on their car at Salt Creek and having to wait for a week for repairs or replacements.

The Frashers were in Bodie before the last big fire and have photographs to prove it. Tioga, Mammoth, Aurora, on the edge of the desert country, were visited by the Frashers. On many of the trips Mrs. Frasher took motion pictures of their adventures. Frasher liked the mountains and fishing and they made numerous pack trips into the High Sierra region after fish and after pictures.

Among the desert personalities that Frasher counted as friends were Eichbaum, Scotty, Johnson, W. A. Chalfant (the publisher of the Owens Valley newspaper and a respected author and historian), and Harry Gower (the man who opened the Furnace Creek Inn).

Chalfant took Frasher with him through Death Valley when he was putting together his book, "Death Valley, the Facts," and some of Frasher's photographs illustrate the book.

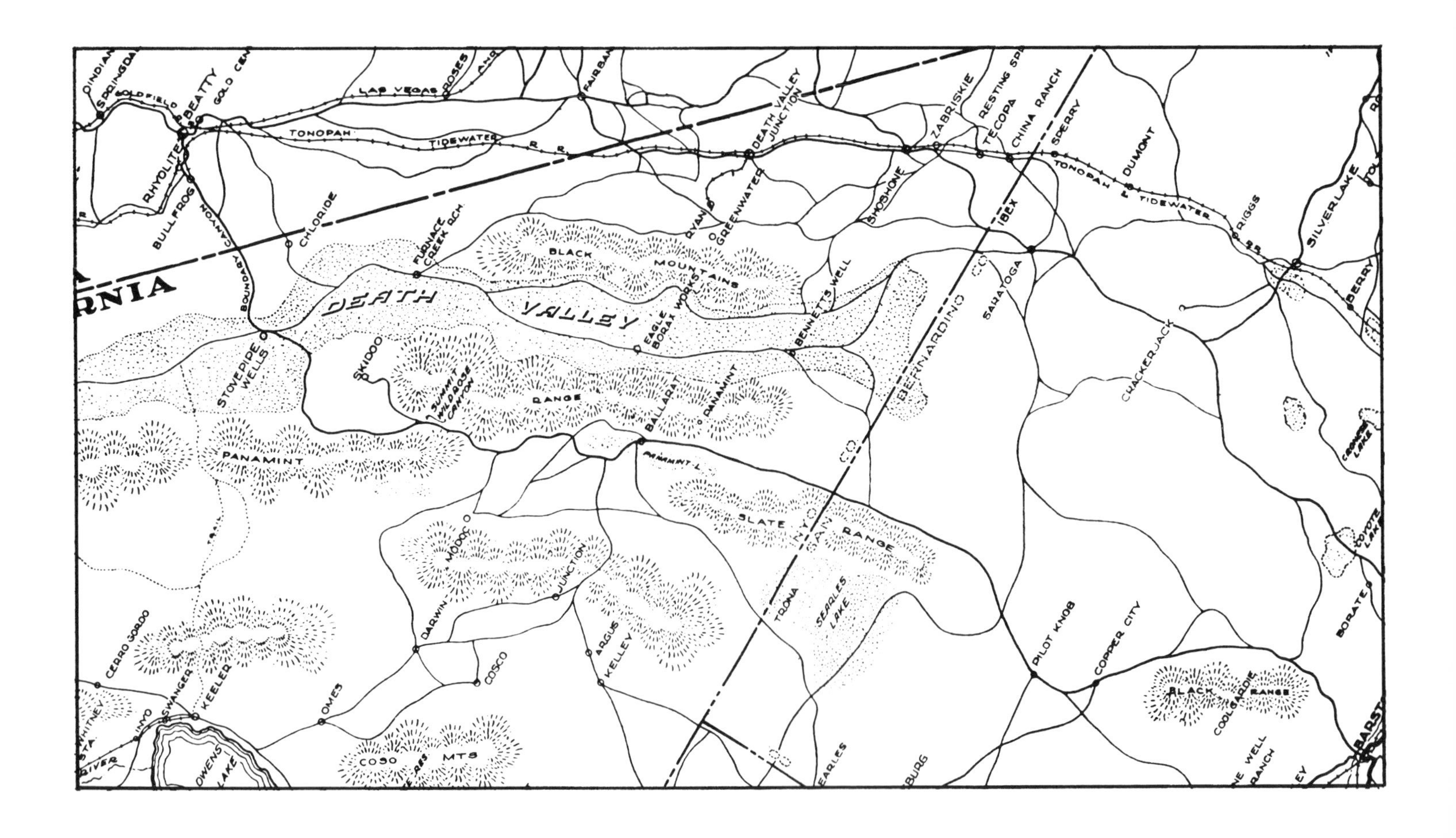

RNIA
DEATH VALLEY
BLACK MOUNTAINS
PANAMINT RANGE
PANAMINT
SLATE RANGE
SEARLES LAKE
COSO MTS
BLACK RANGE
OWENS LAKE
BERNARDINO CO
INYO
TONOPAH & TIDEWATER R. R.
BEATTY
RHYOLITE
BULLFROG
GOLDFIELD
SPRINGDALE
INDIAN
GOLD CEN
BOUNDARY CANYON
CHLORIDE
FURNACE CREEK RCH
STOVEPIPE WELLS
SKIDOO
SUMMIT WILDROSE CANYON
EAGLE BORAX WORKS
BALLARAT
PANAMINT
BENNETT'S WELL
RYAN
GREENWATER
DEATH VALLEY JUNCTION
SHOSHONE
ZABRISKIE
TECOPA
CHINA RANCH
RESTING SP
SPERRY
DUMONT
RIGGS
SILVERLAKE
BERRY
IBEX
SARATOGA
CRACKERJACK
LAS VEGAS
ROSES
FAIRBAN
TONOPAH
TIDEWATER
MODOC
JUNCTION
DARWIN
COSCO
OMES
ARGUS
KELLEY
TRONA
PILOT KNOB
COPPER CITY
COOLGARDIE
BORATE
COYOTE LAKE
CRONESE LAKE
CERRO GORDO
KEELER
SWANGER
WHITNEY
EARLES
BURG
NE WELL
RANCH
BARST

Frasher's photographs illustrated other books of the area. The WPA guide, "Death Valley, A Guide," published in 1939, carries a number of fine Frasher photographs. So do books by C. B. Glasscock, William Caruthers and others. But, strangely, none of the Death Valley authors of the day mention the doughty photographer in their chronicles.

Once, in a Buick, the Frasher family was snowed in for three days at Keyes Point in Death Valley, but such events seldom disturbed Frasher. He frequently camped atop Dante's View for days waiting until the weather was just right for some of his sweeping pictures of the Valley and the Panamints to the west.

Frasher's most unusual piece of equipment was a 7 x 17 inch banquet camera made by Crown. The extremely wide angle device was preferred by the desert photographer because it did not present the problems of distortion found in some of the cranked panoramic cameras of the day. The 7 x 17 inch negatives did provide problems of filing, but Frasher took hundreds of pictures with the oversized camera. The pictures are pinpoint clear.

Frasher preferred a 5 x 7 inch Crown view camera for much of his work. He disliked telescopic lenses, experimented with some of the faster films when they first appeared but each time went back to the slower films which he knew and trusted.

A tripod addict, Frasher haunted junk shops and pawn shops always on the lookout for old Crown Primo cameras which he cherished. He employed different filters, liked them primarily because they gave the sky grades of value which were missing in most desert photographs of the day.

Frasher learned quickly that the best pictures in the desert were taken early in the morning and late in the afternoon. Photographers still agree wholeheartedly with this philosophy.

By 1929-1930 Frasher wandered farther and farther afield seeking new subjects for his burgeoning postcard business. He employed photographers and salesmen. He drifted into Arizona and New Mexico and discovered the Indians there and found them fascinating. He made friends with them in his own manner and was given access to their secret rooms and their private dances.

In 1941 Josephine died. Frasher remarried later that same year. His widow, Margaret, is still living.

Frasher died of a heart attack in 1955. He was 67 at the time. The operation of the photo studio was assumed by Burton Frasher, Jr., himself a prize-winning photographer. Young Frasher sold the postcard business—by then consisting mostly of colored photographs—in 1959 but he still gets requests for postcard prints of some of the older black and white pictures. These he supplies—the orders are small but there is a strong link of *auld lang syne* between Frasher's and the resorts and small firms that order.

Frasher's collection of old glass plates and celluloid negatives is one of the largest still intact in the state.

Of all the country that was focused in the groundglass of Frasher's cameras, it is obvious that Death Valley was his favorite. It was here that Frasher returned again and again, year after year. It is hard to measure what he contributed to the desert country, but the fact that in return it gave the pioneer photographer much pleasure and an assortment of moods and faces, cannot be doubted.

* * *

In the portfolio of Frasher photographs that follows, an assortment of Frasher camera views is reproduced. It was difficult to make a selection, to keep it as small as it had to be for such a publication as this. It would have been easier to have run a section of hundreds of Frasher photographs, for there are hundreds to choose from. In most instances selection was based on items in the photograph that indicated a date, although precise dates are not always available. From the condition of the old mining camps, from the model of the new cars that Frasher drove, from these things we can approximately date these delightful photographs from Burton Frasher who drove the sandy washes into Death Valley first in 1920 and continued his visits for 30 years.

—R. L.

A Portfolio of
Desert Area Photographs
from 1920 to 1939 by
Burton Frasher

It was by means of impressive photographs such as this view of Grotto Canyon that Burton Frasher drew attention to Death Valley in the 1920s and 1930s.

The automobile is a Hupmobile, the road is in an unnamed wash in the Death Valley area, and the date is 1926.

A photograph taken in the early 1920s shows one of Death Valley Scotty's rustic outposts north of the Castle site. Identified in the picture are the photographer, Frasher, on the left end; and author W. A. Chalfant, wearing the hat and seated, at the far right.

Pictures like this one taken in the 1920s added macabre interest in the Death Valley area. This view shows dead cattle—starved or poisoned by bad water—somewhere in the Sand Springs region.

Possibly taken on Frasher's very first trip into Death Valley,
is this photograph of the old railroad station at Rhyolite, Nevada.

A tiny hotel and a great big sign: this is Leadfield, C. C. Julian's swindle town in Death Valley. Leadfield was born in 1926—died the following year.

Another view of Leadfield in the Grapevine Mountains of Death Valley. Street name on signboard is Julian Avenue, after town's founder C. C. Julian.

The ruins of the old Keane Wonder Mine in Death Valley with Frasher's photo car in the foreground.

The original bottle dugout at Stovepipe Wells—the spot is considerably east of the site of the present resort.

When Stovepipe Wells first came up it looked like this —tents and small wooden huts.

The new sign in front of the Rhyolite bottle house says: "Restored, January 1925 by the Famous Players —Lasky Corp." Sign has long since vanished.

There were no paved roads in Death Valley in 1926 when this picture was taken by Burton Frasher.

On this 1926 trip to Death Valley Frasher drove the Hupmobile out into the Devil's Golf Course, the salt flats area.

Wooden buildings still stand in Rhyolite in this picture taken early in the 1920s. Wood cannibals quickly made off with lumber in the old ghost camps.

This is the sign that stood over the road from Death Valley west out of the Valley via the toll road built by H. W. Eichbaum. The location is near Stovepipe Wells resort.

An excellent study of Death Valley Scotty —Walter Scott— taken at the doorway of the then new Scotty's Castle.

A Frasher masterpiece—Mr. and Mrs. Albert Johnson and Death Valley Scotty at ease within the comfortable Castle.

Albert Johnson and some of the Shoshonean Indians who once lived near the Castle.

Millionaire builder of the Castle, Albert Johnson, in the structure's power room. Time exposure photograph taken with available light.

When it was occupied Scotty's Castle was ruled off limits to Death Valley visitors. Frasher was one of the few commercial photographers allowed inside the sprawling structure.

Considered a most rare photograph is this Frasher view of the old Hopi Chief Tewaquaptewa within a kiva at Old Oraibi fashioning kachinas. Photographers, let alone white photographers, are rarely allowed within the kivas.

A view of the main street—Pine Street—in Aurora, Nevada, before most of the old buildings were torn down for the bricks.

The old Esmeralda Hotel in Aurora with three of the town's last residents: Andy Anderson, Gus Peterson and Ferd Walker.

Almost nothing remains at Aurora today. Frasher and one or two other photographers preserved the only evidence we have of how the boom town looked.

The brick salvagers were already at work in Aurora when this picture was taken. The four photographs in this series were probably taken in the mid-1930s.

This is Little Lake, California, in the old days —probably around 1930.

The gasoline-electric train that made the Tonopah and Tidewater run between Death Valley Junction and Ludlow in 1929.

There is no clue to the exact date of this fine photograph of Darwin, California. Many of the structures appear to be occupied.

Easter sunrise services in the sand dunes in Death Valley. It was photographs like this beautiful camera view that brought curious tourists to desert sites that Frasher had photographed in the 1920s and 1930s.

AN HISTORIAN'S SEARCH *for* SACKETT'S LOST WELLS *by* Horace Parker

FOR MANY YEARS I had been interested in relocating the site of historic old Sackett's Wells.

Oddly enough, their location was a subject of common knowledge during the exciting days of the Butterfield Overland Mail. The well-known Sackett's Wells station was one of the farthest south and east of all the Butterfield stations in California. During 1861 and 1862, in their marches across the desert to protect Arizona and New Mexico from Confederate invasion, the California Volunteers were ordered by Colonel James H. Carleton to make camp at Sackett's Wells. Earlier, during the 1850s, the site was used by the several Boundary Commissions and by Railroad Survey Parties. In 1856 the Government Surveyor, R. C. Matthewson, referred to them as "the celebrated Sackett's Wells."

Despite the voluminous notes I had accumulated, it wasn't until 1962 that I was able to make an on-the-ground search for the lost station and wells. For several years prior to 1962 the area had been closed to public entry because of the U. S. Navy bombing and strafing operations.

Throughout the years I consulted many so-called old-timers asking them if they knew of the whereabouts of Sackett's Wells. Most of them had a ready answer and some of these were quite interesting. Like the time at Ocotillo Wells when I sat on a lunch counter stool next to a tanned and wrinkled old desert character. I asked him if he knew anything about Sackett's Wells. He said he did. Said he had actually been there. On this particular occasion he had been prospecting around Carrizo Mountain and had located an old trail leading to the top. Once on top he explored around a bit, when suddenly he noticed the outlines of a cross cut into the flat face of a boulder adjacent to a large crack in the rocks. The crack was too narrow for the burros to enter, so he tethered them to some nearby mesquite and slithered his way into the opening. Within a short distance he stepped out into a small, bowl-like valley surrounded by steep, circling boulder walls. Cottonwoods and palms were growing in a little water-soaked cienega. Farther up, along one side of the valley, he noted a small stream of water. He walked over and tasted it. It was cold and sweet and flowed from a spring hidden beneath the rocks.

Under one of the huge cottonwoods he saw a small, single-room, windowless sod house still roofed and well preserved. It was constructed of cienega-cut sod bricks, similar to those used in the construction of the original Butterfield Stage station at Vallecito. He opened the door and found the cabin to be completely furnished, as though the owner expected to return within a short time. There were old iron kettles, heavy crockery dishes, battered knives and forks; and the bed frame was covered with woven strips of rawhide. In a corner stood a full keg of black powder. Near the door were two large Indian ollas and a smaller cooking olla. In the course of our conversation, the Old Timer mentioned having seen enough furnishings in the little sod cabin to crowd a spacious warehouse. He even included some old Spanish armor and swords and vessels, as well as numerous Indian ceremonial artifacts.

When he finally stepped outside the house, he noted a number of caves among the surrounding boulders at the edge of the little valley. Most of these contained pictographs and, in their gloomy depths, he could discern Indian ollas. What really caught his eye, however, was a strange out-cropping of black quartz. Not obsidian. *Quartz.* He picked up a piece and was surprised to find it riddled with strings of wire gold. He broke a sample with his pick and the bits of quartz continued to be held together by the wire gold. It was rich stuff. He gathered fifteen or twenty pounds of the highgrade ore; and he figured its value in the thousands of dollars.

Near the sod house was a boulder with a huge mortar hole worked into it; and alongside were some long rock pestles. This was where the gold had been milled, because both the mortar and pestles still had thin sheets of gold adhering to them.

It was late in the afternoon when he slipped through the crack to check his burros. He decided to hurry back to camp at Carrizo and show his partner his find. Before he left, however, he determined to obliterate the cross on the rock marking the crack. He pecked and chipped away at it until no visible sign remained.

Back at camp he showed his partner the black quartz with its wire-gold, and he told him about the hidden valley. During the night his partner silently packed the burros with nearly everything they had, including the highgrade ore, and deserted. At daybreak a series of terrific cloudbursts hit the Carrizo area and there were flash floods flowing everywhere. The trail to the top of the mountain was entirely destroyed and the terrain so altered by floods he couldn't locate the spot where he had entered the crack. Worst of all, he had destroyed the incised cross so effectually he could not find it. He diligently continues his search for Sackett's Wells in the hidden valley whenever opportunity presents. He *knew* it was Sackett's Wells right enough, because there—carved in a wooden header over the door of the sod house—was the name "Sackit."

Quite sensibly, after being beguiled by all this Pegleg Smith type nonsense, I determined to rely upon more reliable sources of information.

The first, and most obvious, of these sources was Conkling's three-volume work on the Butterfield Overland Mail. According to Conkling, in October of 1858 the name Sackett's Wells was changed to Hall's Well Station in honor of Warren Hall, superintendent of this division of the Butterfield Mail. Conkling sets the locale of the station as two and a half miles northwest of Plaster City on the west side of Coyote Wash. The station was said to be comprised of an adobe building with corral attached and a well dug in a dry arroyo. Had there been an adobe building and corral, it should not be too difficult to locate the site, either from the low mounds of remaining adobe or from possible stone foundations.

However, in passenger Bailey's itinerary of the initial trip of Butterfield's first east-bound stage out of San Francisco (October 1858), no mention is made of a stop at either Hall's Well or Sackett's Wells.

The United States Census for 1860, of San Diego County, lists "Sacket sta.", valued at $1200, with 2400 pounds of barley, 5 horses, and George Taylor—keeper—at $40 per month. Significantly, no mention is made of Hall's Well Station.

In Lt. Sweeny's Journal of 1849-1853 (edited by Dr. Arthur Woodward), I found that Sweeny—of Fort Yuma fame—had "spent the day with Mr. Bartlett and other gentlemen of the Commission (Boundary Commission), at Sackett's Wells about 40 miles this side of Vallecito on the 5th of June (1852). . . ." In Dr. Woodward's annotations I found he had listed a location similar to Conkling's, but added—"They (the Wells) were named for Russell Sackett, a station keeper."

In John Russell Bartlett's personal narrative of the Boundary Commission we read: "June 5, 1852. Reached the water-holes called Sackett's Wells, 24 miles from Carrizo. . . . After digging about six feet the water began slowly to enter, and by dipping it up with a basin, we managed to supply our animals. The desert where we are now encamped is an open and remarkably level plain. . . . distance from Carrizo Creek twenty-five miles."

In the official records of the War of the Rebellion, we find this mention: "Sackett's Well when cleaned out affords a good supply of excellent water; it is a mere water-hole, without any marks to distinguish it at the distance of 200 yards; men must be kept away from the brink, as it is liable to cave." This was written October 28, 1861.

On April 26, 1862, Colonel James H. Carleton, in a letter to Capt. Shinn encamped at San Felipe, writes: "I shall cause all the water at Sackett's Wells to be saved for you; but these wells are drying up, so you must not count on even one gallon per animal. Have all your kegs filled at Carriso Creek. Have your barley soaked, so as to feed soaked barley at Sackett's Wells five quarts per animal. At Sackett's Wells you will find a feed of hay."

From the several Railroad Survey Parties (1853-1856) come the following: "The water supply at Sackett's Wells consists of three wells sunk in an arroyo bed, which itself lies four feet below the general level; the wells are about six feet deep, and the water oozes in about five feet down, flowing through a thin stratum of sand which overlies the clay bed constituting the bottom of the wells. Should this last be cut through the water sinks, and it would be necessary to go several feet down to meet another clay layer. A fourth well was dug at this time by a Mexican party traveling along. The water is good, not saline, and agreeable to the taste; it oozes out of the sand layer slowly but steadily, requiring six minutes to fill a two gallon pail. In one of the wells a barrel has been sunk, which should be done with all, and an adobe building should be raised around them. The clay at the bottom of the wells is a yellow, tenacious argil, and advantage might be made of it for brick manufacture, or using it merely puddled as a material for the sides of the wells." "Sackett's Wells does not owe its water to this source (the overflow of the Colorado River), deriving it from a small under current between clay strata, which may be the remains of small streams rolling from the sierra, and losing themselves in the porous sands. This supply is, however, so sparing, the original stream so trifling and so uncertain in its flow, and the annual fall of rain almost nothing, that to make deep sinkings, or artesian borings, on the desert, along the line of trail, would likely be a complete failure. . . ." "At Sackett's Wells the supply of water is abundant, and is derived from holes sunk in an arroyo or bed of stream leading into the channel of Cariso Creek. This point is fairly on the open plain of the desert. . . . From Sackett's to the Colorado River the desert appears to the unaided eye a perfect level. . . ."

R. C. Matthewson, Government Surveyor in 1856, records in his field notes: "In sec. 29 is located the celebrated 'Pozas Coyotes' or 'Sackett's Wells.' These wells are situated in the bed of a sandy, dry arroyo. On the surface there is no vegetation or any sign whatever that indicates a difference between this and other parts of the arroyo and yet upon sinking here to the depth of from three to five feet an abundant supply of pure clear water is obtained, while a few chains above or below not a drop can be found by sinking to a much greater depth. The water is apparently running but although I dug into a variety of places around it I could not ascertain its direction. By digging a few feet into the sand below the surface of the water there is found a layer or stratum of clay, and when this is perforated through the water sinks and is lost in the sand underneath."

With these rather detailed descriptions of Sackett's Wells during the 1850s and 1860s, I attempted to find the earliest mention of them and perhaps the time of their discovery and also something of their discoverer. In Bolton's work on the Anza expedition of 1774 we read that the party camped between present day Yuha Wells and Harper's Well in a dry arroyo which they named *Arroyo Seco*. The distances covered would appear substantially correct. The Anza party could have heard of water in an arroyo in the general vicinity of Sackett's Wells, yet failed to find it.

The earliest American report I could find was a handwritten notation on a crude manuscript map of the territory made by Lieutenant Cave Couts. On December 3, 1849, he notes that good water had been found by digging a few feet in an arroyo by one of the teamsters. He gives the location as about twelve miles northwest of Third Well, or Indian Wells, which is essentially correct for Sackett's Wells.

After the Civil War, travel along this portion of the old Butterfield Trail, or Southern Emigrant Trail, past Indian Wells, Carrizo Creek, and Vallecito all but ceased. There were new routes opened between San Diego and Yuma as well as from Los Angeles, San Bernardino and Yuma. Many of the old watering and camping spots were either by-passed or forgotten. Occasionally Indians, Mexicans and desert prospectors, or people living in the desert, used the old road. That was all.

Bailey, in his well-titled book, *Golden Mirages*, states in a footnote that Sackett's Wells were lost in a sandstorm in 1867. A few others expressing this same view, report the date as 1875. Yet the *San Diego Union*, in a September 22, 1895 item giving the report of a traveler on the condition of the desert trails, states: "Going north from Indian Wells, water is at the surface at Laguna, Sackett's Wells, and at Carrizo." In Mendenhall's Water Supply Paper of 1909 and in Brown's Water Supply Paper of 1918, no mention of Sackett's Wells is included.

And now we come to one of the *real* mysteries concerning the old wells. Who was Sackett, and when were the wells named? We do know that the christening occurred sometime during the period between December 3, 1849 and June 5, 1852.

It is easier to determine who Sackett was *not* than to discover who he actually *was*. I have referred to Dr. Woodward's notation that the wells were named for a "Russell Sackett, a station keeper." I have searched the more common Butterfield sources, the 1860 census for San Diego County which lists all the Butterfield Stations, personnel, and equipment between the Laguna Station (Elsinore) and Fort Yuma. Nowhere can I discover a listing for "Russell Sackett." I checked the entire census rolls for San Diego County and City for 1850 and 1860, with not a single Sackett listed. I could not find the name on the rolls of Kearny's Dragoons, Cooke's Mormon Battalion, nor among the soldiers stationed at San Diego and Fort Yuma from 1850 to 1860. He never attended West Point, was not listed among the Army officers before and throughout the Civil War, is not on any pioneer list I consulted including Bancroft's.

There was one exception. While checking random sources in the Huntington Library, I did find mention of a Sackett—of a *Russell* Sackett. In a list of postmasters for Los Angeles between 1850 and 1900, I found record of a "Russell Sackett appointed May 5, 1865." Apparently he was an attorney and a former Justice of the Peace, but "nothing is known of his antecedents." Newmark mentions a Sackett in Los Angeles engaged in the kerosene business. In another historical journal was a brief reference to a "Judge Sacket" during vigilante days in the northern part of the State. A check of the San Francisco Vigilante rolls, however, revealed no Sackett. So, for the present, Sacket—or Sackett—of Sackett's Wells' fame still remains a mystery.

Eventually, then, several of us started off one bright fall morning on our first on-the-ground search for Sackett's Wells. We were confident. With our knowledge we should be back by early afternoon to announce our discovery. We swung into the site of the Old Carrizo Stage Station and checked the speedometer mileage on the Jeep. If everything went well, seventeen or eighteen miles should bring us into the vicinity of Sackett's Wells. We followed Carrizo Creek for five miles to Blue Hill or the "steep pitch" out of Carrizo Creek over the mud hills mentioned in nearly all the early itineraries.

After topping Blue Hill we followed the plainly marked tracks, of what we assumed to be the old road, through a short stretch of barren mudhills. After emerging from the mudhills we found ourselves on a flat, alluvial plain extending from the eastern slopes of the mountains to the west into the depths of the Salton Sink. The vegetation was sparse, parched and stunted; and surely this must have been a dismal sight for the early travelers. This was my first trip over a territory which had been closed to travel for nearly seventeen years. I recognized the rusted pipe standards of the old Jasper water-markers first set across this arid waste in the 1890's. Carefully we checked our progress on the topographical map. At seventeen and a half miles we came to where the road dipped over the north bank of Coyote Wash. The mileage was right; perhaps Conkling was correct in his location of the wells after all.

Coyote Wash is between ten and fifteen feet below the surface of the flat-appearing plain. The banks of the wash are irregular with finger washes of varying sizes and depths extending from its sides back into the plain and forming shallow barrancas. We decided to begin our search along the northern bank, looking for green vegetation growing above the plain and for indications of a shallow arroyo. At the same time we would watch for signs of moisture, old roads, old foundations, man-made debris, wooden well copings and anything else that might serve as a clue. We agreed to cover an area within a radius of about a half mile on foot and in the Jeep.

As the search progressed the entire party seemed to drift instinctively eastward toward the railroad trestle over Coyote Wash of the narrow gauge railroad running between the gypsum quarry in Fish Creek and Plaster City. We could see Plaster City plainly about two miles south of us.

Suddenly with a shout of excitement one of our party held up a small muleshoe. It was handmade and obviously old. Was it of Spanish or Mexican origin, or was it from a later period? This question is still undetermined. Our enthusiasm was whetted for a time; but after some hours of fruitless search I was becoming discouraged.

This territory is so barren and relatively flat that it seemed impossible to conceal anything unusual from view. Unfortunately there were new and old wheel tracks running all over the place. Were we on the old Butterfield Trail or some later road bulldozed by the military? Distances from Carrizo could be misleading, depending on their route and direction. We could be miles off our course in one direction or another unless we were on the original road used in the itineraries. There are no conspicuous landmarks; therefore none is mentioned in the old accounts. Flat as this territory appears, it is cut up with numerous broad, shallow washes from a quarter to a half mile in breadth. Old roads and wheel tracks dipping into them are lost in the sand and are difficult to pick up on the opposite bank. We were at an impasse for the present and more work would have to be done to determine the exact route of the old road. I had a feeling the road we followed was too far west. So we abandoned the search.

A few days later, while I was out on the desert, one of the Bow

Willow rangers got word to me that a Southern Pacific brakeman in El Centro by the name of J. A. Kinkead claimed to know the exact site of Sackett's Wells. By telephone I made a date to meet him in a few days at his trailer near Dos Cabezas.

I returned to Bow Willow and that evening I met and visited with "Jade" Kinkead in his trailer in back of the old dolomite mine near Dos Cabezas Station. "Jade" was a typical desert wanderer; and by the light of kerosene lamps he showed me interesting objects he had picked up here and there on the desert. In his collection was part of a human skull; also half a muleshoe, the exact mate to ours, which he had picked up in approximately the same territory where we had been hunting near the railroad trestle over Coyote Wash. But according to Kinkead the site of Sackett's Wells was several miles west of the trestle.

The story he told was that, while camping with his wife and searching around on the desert, they had unearthed what appeared to be an old wooden well coping on the banks of a shallow wash. As he discussed and described the find, and the territory about it, I was sure that we would locate the lost wells the next morning.

A cold blustery wind had been blowing the night before and by morning it not only continued to blow but was gaining in velocity. It was one of those cold, overcast, windy desert days with gusts of swirling sand and gravel. The area into which we were going was noted for the severity of its sandstorms. But, irrespective of the weather, nothing was going to stop my search for Sackett's Wells. I picked up Kinkead and, well bundled up, we started on the long, cold Jeep ride to Plaster City and then onto the western end of the old *Jornado del Muerto* and the probable site of the lost wells.

I was heartened as "Jade" picked his way confidently along the Butterfield Trail to where his trailer had formerly been parked. We bore southwest off the old road across a broad, shallow wash and through a low growth of creosote bush interspersed with galleta grass. On the southern border of the wash "Jade" indicated where his wife had dug out a stump of petrified wood. Surely enough, the clay-soil had been disturbed and there were bits of partially petrified wood exposed. A few hundred feet west of this spot was where the old wooden coping had been found. Off-hand it appeared as though some digging and backfilling had been done in the area.

The wind was blowing a gale and sand was constantly getting into our eyes. Kinkead started to dig enthusiastically in this spot with the trenching tool from the Jeep. I watched for a few minutes and then decided to search the sloping, flat mesa for other man-made signs. The hard clay surface of the mesa was covered with the typical paving of waterworn, sandblasted and variegated pebbles, interspersed with pieces of drab-gray petrified wood so commonly found in this part of the Colorado Desert. Geologists tell us these pebbles and bits of wooden flotsam had been dumped into the Salton Sink millions of years ago by the Colorado River. A rusted, modern sardine can was all I found. A few hundred feet southwest of where "Jade" was digging was a surveyor's stake and cap with the notation T15S, R11E, S36 and S31. All this checked out with the 1902 State Mining Bureau Map of San Diego County, which had Sackett's Wells roughly indicated on it as being in the southwest corner of T15S, R11E.

"Jade" dug here and there but couldn't find the remains of the old coping again. We were both discouraged. Despite the corner stake the general territory didn't look too promising to me unless we could find the coping. Finally, with our eyes lined with sand from the wind, we decided to give up.

Kinkead, obviously disappointed, wanted to show me some curious things he had found within a radius of three or four miles of this spot. We ran across what appeared to be some exposed human bones in a shallow, blown-out grave in a wash. The skull, however, was missing. He showed me some old well casings, a curious pit well dug on the shores of a dry lake near where he had found an old prospector's cache of matches and canned goods, the remnants of a downed aircraft, and other miscellaneous sites and objects. Then we retraced our steps to the vicinity of the railroad trestle where he had found the skull and half muleshoe.

Most interesting of all, on the mesa north of the wash of the skull and muleshoe, Kinkead showed me the outlines on the mesa's surface of an old campsite. There were a series of square outlines littered with rusting tobacco cans where obviously the tents had been set up. Along what appeared to be a former picket line was desiccated horse manure covered with blowsand. One broad area was littered with skeins of twisted bailing wire in the typical manner teamsters used to dispose of it. In another spot was the coke and iron from the blacksmith's forge. At the time, all this seemed interesting but of little significance—it was just an old horse camp or cavalry bivouac. The bits of iron and rear cleats cut off the horseshoes indicated that the shoes had been manufactured and not handmade and the nails found in pieces of lumber were round. Accordingly, I estimated the era of the camp as being around 1910 or 1920. That was my last outing with Kinkead.

In the fall of 1963, I set up camp at Bow Willow to concentrate entirely on the search for Sackett's Wells. I had heard new rumors and reports in regard to the lost wells. It seems there had been some "fraudulent surveys in the early days" in this general area which resulted in errors on the maps of nearly a section (mile). The external boundaries of the townships had been determined by Lt. George H. Derby, of *San Diego Herald* fame, in 1854. Should the surveys vary, it is impossible to use a map to pinpoint a spot, particularly if one is not familiar with the survey used.

The story is briefly this. Between 1856 and 1912 the government extended contracts to private individuals to survey various parts of the country. On occasion, in the more remote and rugged parts the surveyors under contract cheated. Instead of making the actual survey they merely guessed and faked it. This is what occurred in some of the areas around Sackett's Wells. So Dean Jennings, Surveyor for the Division of Beaches and Parks, decided to go back to Matthewson's original survey of 1856 and ascertain if he located and included Sackett's Wells in his survey. He located Matthewson's original survey maps and notebook of *calls* in 1856, with Sackett's Wells boldly indicated in the files of the Bureau of Land Management in Riverside. Only a surveyor acquainted with the surveys in this area could unravel the mystery from the 1856 survey.

Time slipped by until April, 1964. One night, while at Bow Willow, one of the Rangers took me into Ocotillo where I met Dean Jennings. He showed me the corrected maps and work he had done on Sackett's Wells.

On our first meeting I mentioned and described Kinkead's horse camp which Dean had not found. On a subsequent trip in

April he located the horse camp. Strangely enough, the camp was on the mesa immediately north of the wash or arroyo in which Dean had pinpointed Sackett's Wells from Matthewson's original survey of 1856. It might well be a happy coincidence that the chance finding of the unknown horse camp, by Kinkead, could be the missing part of the puzzle in authenticating the actual site of lost Sackett's Wells.

What was the old horse camp doing in this particular part of the desert? It has every indication of having existed for weeks and perhaps months. Adjacent as it is to two railroads, the gypsum railroad and about two miles north of the former San Diego and Arizona Eastern, it could be an old railroad construction camp. I have seen similar sites in and around Dos Cabezas. If it was for the gypsum-railroad, with a relatively minor grading job, why didn't the camp move along with the construction crews? If it was a camp used during the building of the Arizona Eastern why was it located nearly two miles from the right-of-way at Plaster City? If this was a cavalry camp why pick this particular spot in the desert? How can the lack of kitchen midden and a can dump from the mess tents be explained? There seems to be one word to answer these questions logically—water.

Water is extremely scarce in this part of the desert, and particularly was this true during the early 1900's. Ordinarily it would have to be hauled to a stock camp. The grading crews were obviously ahead of the tracks so water for the stock would have to be tediously hauled in horse-drawn water wagons. This could hold true for both railroads. Now let us assume there was available a local water supply. It might be economical to establish a semi-permanent camp adjacent to this water even if it meant driving the stock a few miles to work. The lack of kitchen debris might be explained by the fact that the mess tents were along the right-of-way, closer to the bulk of the workers of which the teamsters were only a small part. They would eat at the mess and ride the stock to the horse camp where they would bunk overnight. I have not seen a camp in the desert, even if the can pile was washed away in a flash flood, that didn't have pieces of broken crockery lying around the site of the mess tent. Yet we failed to find evidence of such items here. Such an absence was not indication of neatness, else they would have picked up the discarded tobacco cans and baling wire.

Because of the time factor we had no opportunity to make a concerted attempt at digging for water. We did dig two or three feet in two places and found moist clay and sand. The water may not be near the surface in this location for a number of very obvious reasons. What was perhaps a four-foot arroyo a century or more ago may today be a ten or fifteen foot deep, dry wash. Flash floods and not sandstorms could have spelled finis to the wells. Where originally the water flowed over thin clay strata near the surface, these strata could have been destroyed in the flooding. And the present water, if any, would now be many feet below the surface of the wash. According to recent scientific reports involving weather and the deserts of Southern California, the last twenty years of drouth have been the most severe in four centuries. In the little desert community of Ocotillo the source of water is from wells at a higher elevation which may conceivably have tapped or depleted the source at Sackett's Wells. However, because of the condition of the mesquite in the wash, I think we'll find it.

We may identify the site in other ways. I want to query some of the reliable old-time informants in the area. I have been told one of the older members of the pioneer McCain family knows the site of Sackett's Wells. I want to check on the statement that water was on the surface in this general area during the 1920's. I am also curious to know if, in some dusty and forgotten ledger in San Diego, there may be a list of the construction camps and their sites during the building of the Arizona Eastern. Dean Jennings has access to some metal detecting equipment and we'd like to give this a try. Most of all, Sackett, bless his old elusive past, must have left his name somewhere—in between a scalawag and a saint.

* * *

AUTHOR'S NOTE: Surveyor Dean J. Jennings pinpoints the original location of Sackett's Wells as follows:

From the U.S. Gypsum Plant at Plaster City, Calif. go north along a dirt road on the east side of the mining railroad 1.5 miles to Coyote Wash. Continue North 0.2 mile to the Arroyo in which the wells are located. (From this point the wells were located upstream, northwest, 0.4 mile). To reach the site of the wells by Jeep, continue north along the dirt road 0.4 mile to a dirt road crossing the mining railroad. From the railroad crossing drive southwest 0.2 mile through the old horse camp found by "Jade" Kinkead to the bank of the arroyo in which the wells were located. The site is located at latitude 47° 21′ 40″ north and longitude 115° 51′ 10″ west and is further described as bearing east 3200 feet from an iron pipe and brass cap which was set by Wilkes in 1913 to mark the west ¼ corner of Section 32, T 15 S, R 11 E, S.B.M.

BIBLIOGRAPHY

ANZA, JUAN BAUTISTA DE, ET AL. *Anza's California Expeditions* (5 vol.) 1930. Berkeley. Univ. of California Press. Edited by Dr. Herbert E. Bolton.

BAILEY, PHILIP. *Golden Mirages*. 1940. New York. The Macmillan Co.

BARROW, H. D. *Los Angeles Postmasters 1850-1900*. Hist. Soc. of So. California and Pioneers of L.A. Co.; 1900-1901-1902; Vol. V.; pp. 49.

BARTLETT, JOHN RUSSELL. *Personal Narrative of Explorations*, etc. (2 vol.) 1854. N.Y. Appleton & Co.

BOWERS, STEPHEN. *Reconnaissance of the Colorado Desert Mining District*. 1901. Sacramento, Calif. State. Min. Bur.

CONKLING, ROSCOE AND MARGARET. *The Butterfield Overland Mail* (3 vol.) 1947. Glendale. Arthur H. Clark Co.

COUTS, LT. CAVE JOHNSON. *From San Diego to the Colorado in 1849*. 1933. Los Angeles. Zamorano Club. Edited by William McPherson. Also original Journal in Huntington Library.

DERBY, G. H. *Survey Notes and Calls for 1854, T 15 S, R 11 E, SBM*. Microfilm. Riverside. Bur. of Land Management.

EDWARDS, E. I. *Lost Oases Along the Carrizo*. 1961. Los Angeles Westernlore Press.
—— Personal correspondence.

EMORY, LT. COL. WM. H. *Notes of a Military Reconnaissance, Etc.* 1848. Washington. House Ex. Doc. 41; Senate Ex. Doc. 7.

HARRIS, BENJAMIN BUTLER. *The Gila Trail*. 1960. Norman. Univ. of Oklahoma Press. Edited by Richard H. Dillon.

HUNT, AURORA. *The Army of the Pacific, etc.* 1951. Glendale. Arthur H. Clark Co.

LANG, WALTER B. *First Overland Mail* (1 vol.) 1940.

MACDOUGAL, D. T. ET AL. *The Salton Sea*, etc. 1914. Washington. Carnegie Inst.

MAPS

San Diego County Map. Fox & Wiley. 1883.

General Map—U.S. & Mexican Boundary Commission in years 1850-1853.

Ms. Maps of Lt. Cave J. Couts. 1849-50.

Skeleton Map of Southern California. 1869. Photostat Bancroft Library—Map F, 867, 1, 1869, R8.

Johnson's California with Territories of Utah, Nevada, Colorado, New Mexico and Arizona—1864. Pub. Johnson & Ward.

State Mining Bur. Map of San Diego Co. 1902.

MATTHEWSON, R. C. *Survey Notes and Calls for October, 1856, T 15 S, R 11 E, SBM.* Microfilm. Riverside. Bureau of Land Management.

PARKER, HORACE. *Anza/Borrego Desert Guide Book* (2nd Ed.) 1963. Balboa Island. Paisano Press, Inc.

SAN DIEGO COUNTY AND CITY AND UNITED STATES CENSUS ENDING JUNE 1, 1860. Photostat. San Diego. Serra Museum.

SWEENY, LT. THOMAS W. *Journal.* 1956. Los Angeles. Westernlore Press. Edited by Arthur Woodward.

War of the Rebellion—Official Records of the Union and Confederate Armies. Series 1; Vol. L; Part 1; The Pacific Coast, January 1, 1861—June 30, 1856. Serial #105. Washington, D.C.

WELLS. Serra Museum, San Diego. Vertical File, #608.

WILLIAMSON, R. S., BLAKE, W. P., ET AL. *Pacific Railway Survey Reports.* 1853-1856. Washington. Beverly Tucker, Printer. Vol. V; VII.

WOODWARD, ARTHUR. *Lances at San Pascual.* 1948. Cal. Hist. Soc. Spec. Pub. No. 22.

FORGOTTEN ARMY FORTS *of the* MOJAVE

by L. Burr Belden

In the lengthening shadows of late afternoon a faint pair of wheel marks may be discerned leading in a general east-west direction across the center of the Mojave Desert* about midway in the huge triangle bounded by the diverging routes of U.S. Highways 66 and 91 and by the Colorado River.

This trace of all but obliterated wagon tracks, along with a few crumbling stone ruins mark the route of what was, some 110 years ago, Southern California's principal transcontinental link with the East. The route was called the Old Government Road, even when it had a mere decade of life—old because a newer and shorter road had been broken through to reach the then rich gold diggings in La Paz, Arizona Territory, and because Uncle Sam has switched from land to water transport for supply of its frontier garrison at Fort Mohave.

It was President Franklin Pierce's secretary of war, one Jefferson Davis, who directed the scouting of a road from Fort Defiance, A.T., west. This assignment was entrusted to Lt. Edward F. Beale in charge of the Army's famed camel corps. Beale's strange caravan was ferried across river on a steamboat which had arrived coincidentally at the Mohave villages. The camel caravan plodded west over the desert to Soda Lake, then ascended the Mojave River to about today's Helendale where Beale turned with the bulk of his animals to his ranch at Fort Tejon. Two camels were sent to Los Angeles via Cajon Pass. It is recorded that in the Mormon town of San Bernardino a school holiday was decreed to permit the children to see the two camels.

The old trail had been surveyed by L. A. W. Whipple in 1854. Survey, in reference to a pioneer road, meant a few key point observations and a scouting journey.

Long before Beale and Whipple, however, the route over the central Mojave had been a path of commerce. Its initial chapter was as a trade trail used in primitive commerce between desert and coastal Indian groups. It was over this route that the mis-

*In the interest of consistency we have followed the decision of Geographic Board (*Sixth Report*) which has decided on the spelling of Mojave for the California names, but approved the spelling of Mohave for names on the Colorado River, including the name of the Indians there. This is also in keeping with Erwin G. Gudde (*California Place Names*) and Will C. Barnes (*Arizona Place Names*).—Editor

sionary-explorer Fr. Francisco Garces traveled in the spring of 1776 nearly four months before representatives of 13 east coast colonies signed the Declaration of Independence in far off Philadelphia. Father Garces had detached from the second Anza expedition at Yuma, explored up the Colorado River to near the Grand Canyon, and, after returning to the Mohave villages headed west for San Gabriel Mission.

Fifty years after Garces, a bronzed Westerner, an Anglo-Saxon trapper and trader, one Jedediah Strong Smith, left the rendezvous of mountain men near the Great Salt Lake, pushed south through the Utah country to reach the Colorado River, followed that stream down to the same Mohave villages where he too turned west to follow the Garces route into San Gabriel. Smith, despite a suspicious California reception and warning in 1826, was back a year later. On his second trip his company had been mauled by the same Indians who had been his friends the year earlier.

The *entrada* of Garces and the overland arrival of Smith have been chronicled in historical works, the former notably in the two-volume *On the Trail of a Spanish Pioneer*, by Elliot Coues, and the latter in significant volumes by Harrison C. Dale, Maurice Sullivan and Dale Morgan.

After Smith the desert crossing slumbered for more than three decades. Then, in 1853 and 1854 came the surveyors, Lt. R. S. Williamson first, then Lieutenant Whipple with wagons and even a pause at Piute Springs where crops were irrigated.

The gold rush brought a world into movement and it is not surprising that some argonauts decided to break a trail west from Santa Fe. The popularity of the route was dimmed when Indians attacked a caravan on the banks of the Colorado. Punishment followed as troops were sent overland through Cajon Pass.

To assure continued peace, a fort, Fort Mohave, was established in 1859, in the midst of the Mohave villages. Supplies were initially sent overland through the Cajon and across the desert. The old Indian trail used by Garces and Smith, the route surveyed by Whipple, became a well-recognized thoroughfare.

Then there was unrest farther north among the Shoshonean groups in Owens Valley with attacks on settlers. Major Moses McLaughlin left Visalia, rounded up what Owens Valley Indians

Photo by J. G. Stevens

Ruins of redoubt at Marl Springs.

Outpost redoubt at Rock Springs.

he could find and moved them onto a reservation at Fort Tejon, a strongpoint on the ranch of the same Lieutenant Beale who served as Indian agent. The McLaughlin expedition and the establishment of Camp Independence in the Owens Valley may have quieted matters locally but these moves set loose numerous marauding bands who eluded the Army and preyed on the overland wagon trains.

Major James Carlton established a string of camps and fortified points along both the Salt Lake Trail and the Old Government Road. On the Salt Lake Trail redoubts, much like stone corrals, were built at Bitter Spring and Resting Spring. An adobe fort, or strongpoint, was built at The Vegas—today's Las Vegas. On the Mojave Desert route a base camp, Camp Cady, was built downstream from Daggett. A redoubt was built for Capt. Winfield Scott Hancock who had established Fort Mohave. This was the noted Civil War general and later presidential candidate. Camp Rock Springs was made a secondary supply point. It also boasted a post office briefly. In the Piute Mountains, where Whipple had found irrigated crops, Carlton built a fort. He named it Fort Beale in honor of the camel caravan's leader.

Travel on the Old Government Road grew until the *San Bernardino Guardian* claimed 2,000 wagons a year were using the route. John Brown, Sr., an ex-mountain man, had moved to San Bernardino. He built a toll road through Cajon Pass and, in 1860 established a ferry across the Colorado River. To operate the ferry Brown hired a Mohave chief, Sic-a-hoot, but the Indian had trouble keeping Brown's money separate from his own.

In the 1927 annual publication of the Historical Society of Southern California a portion of Brown's diary is printed telling of some of that pioneer's troubles with the ferry which he retained for but a year or two. The time was an eventful one. On one inspection trip Brown lost a wagon on the desert.

Brown was forced to abandon his wagon in the Devil's Playground, a 30-mile stretch of shifting sand dunes between Soda Lake and Marl Spring. He made it to the spring, filled a water cask, and returned in time to save the lives of others in his party. Marl Spring, a few miles north of today's Kelso, had been noted by Lieutenant Whipple. Later, in the years immediately after the Civil War, Marl Spring was made a Government strongpoint

Remains of the crude barracks at old Camp Cady.

Ruins of the main building at old Fort Piute.

with a diamond shaped log stockade protected by blockhouses. The refuge was large enough to accommodate several wagons. The camp at Rock Springs was moved to Marl Spring.

The string of little forts across the Mojave Desert gave a feeling of security to travelers, possibly unjustified, for early Southern California newspaper columns contain references to attacks both on civilian travelers and on the military. The monthly returns from Camp Cady which the writer obtained in microfilm from National Archives are replete with notations of desertions and of garrisons weakened by a full guardhouse.

Typical of the public complacency the *Los Angeles News*, in its July 14, 1860 issue, reported:

"Major Carleton has built these strong redoubts on the line of emigration, which will be of essential service in the future. Each redoubt is capable of accommodating a large company with their animals and wagons, thus affording protection to those traveling the road. They are all, of course, in the immediate vicinity of springs which were opened up, and of reservoirs constructed and capable of containing a large supply of water. At Camp Cady a redoubt was built and at Soda Springs, 36 miles distant, another which is named Hancock Redoubt. Both are on the main road down the Mojave; another at Bitter Springs on the Salt Lake Road, about 50 miles from Camp Cady." [Actually Bitter Springs is between Afton and the L.A. Bureau of Water and Power transmission line, far closer to Cady.]

These early reports were accurate as far as the water supply is concerned. Cady is at the Mojave River bottom where today's Cady Ranch has numerous lakes and artesian wells. A large underground stream of pure water issues from the mountain at Soda Lake. In it are thousands of little minnow-size blind fish. The water is now used for baths at the health and retirement resort with the impossible name of Zzyzx Springs. At Rock Springs water was not too plentiful but was soon supplemented by government sunk wells a mile or so to the west, at a spot still bearing the place name of Government Holes. Enough water flows at Piute Springs to make a sizable creek which sinks into the thirsty sands a half mile or so away.

During the Civil War period, these outposts were manned by California volunteers who kept watch for persons trying to slip through and reach Texas or other parts of the Confederate States. Thus it may be noted that the Northern California-Nevada band of Confederate sympathizers, with whom Charles C. Breyfogle traveled struck south from Austin, Nev., determined to reach Texas via Arizona, a path that ended in their massacre near today's Shoshone.

When the vocal Dan Showalter of Mariposa raised his irregular cavalry and started out from Visalia he shunned the Government Road and headed south from Cajon Pass and eventual capture near today's Lake Hinshaw. Of course, it is known Showalter expected recruits at Belleville in the Holcomb Valley diggings but when his emissaries returned well supplied with drinks but not recruits, Showalter headed south rather than follow the road east that passed his camp in Cleghorn Canyon, off Cajon Pass.

It may be noted that, in addition to the small resident garrison, the Second California Cavalry under command of Capt. John Cremony was sent to clear the road after large Indian bands had been noted camping near the springs. Evidently the Cremony expedition in 1864 had only a temporary effect for it is noted that, in 1865, Capt. Edward Bales was sent out from Drum Barracks with Company D, native California cavalry, on a similar mission.

The little garrisons were drawn down until they were little more than squads in the later years of the war. Carleton, who rose from major to general, called for more and more men as he advanced from Fort Yuma to retake Arizona and New Mexico from the Confederates.

As the Civil War ended the California volunteers returned to civilian life, leaving the Mojave forts unmanned, an economy bitterly denounced by the press of San Bernardino and Los Angeles. Typical was an April 13, 1866 editorial in the *Los Angeles News*, which asserted:

"If General McDowell had sought to purposely injure the trade of this section of the state, he could not have found a more effective way of doing it than to remove protection from one of the principal thoroughfares of trade."

The protests were heeded. The forts were again garrisoned, this time by regulars who changed the name of Hancock Redoubt to Fort Soda. Fort Beale became Fort Piute. The camp at Rock Springs was moved to Marl Spring. Camp Cady itself was moved nearly a mile west to higher ground where adobe structures were erected though the older rock buildings, including the hospital, were retained at the original site.

Gold in quantities was being extracted from placer mines at La Paz, Arizona Territory. Travel moved to and from La Paz over the Government Road to Fort Mohave then went by pack train over a trail that approximated a route some 15 to 20 miles east of the Colorado River passing through today's Yucca and the now tiny settlement of Signal.

Regular soldiers were no improvement, it would seem. Lieutenant Eyre noted in one report that a private had deserted at Fort Soda "taking the best horse at the post." The soldier evidently knew his horseflesh and wanted to make his getaway certain. Some six weeks later the reports noted that he was caught mining gold in Eldorado Canyon, Nevada, up river from Fort Mohave.

Lieutenant Ord, one of a family steeped in military tradition, had his name perpetuated on a mountain range where he and a squadron were besieged by Indians. Another officer barely escaped with his skin when ambushed in Cady Crater. In 1867 Dr. M. E. Shaw, the surgeon, was slain while riding in an Army ambulance between Cady and Soda. His mounted escort escaped and reached Soda and reported fifteen Indians in the band of attackers. The same year Indians stole a horse from Lafayette Mecham at Fish Ponds, a station located at the site of today's Barstow Marine Corps depot.

Five men were killed when a punitive expedition headed by Lieutenant Hartman ran into an ambush at Aztec Spring, south of today's Daggett.

So the story of the forts along Old Government Road ran through the 1860s. In 1868 the Bradshaw Road was broken out from Dos Palmas across the Chuckwalla Desert to the Colorado River at Bradshaw's Ferry north of Blythe.

It was a quicker and far easier way to reach La Paz. Garrisons were withdrawn from the Mojave Desert route the last time. In 1871 the deserted buildings were sold and the last soldiers—the caretakers—departed. Final years had seen soldiers break into the sutler's store at Cady but apparently without punishment other than that inflicted by the Army. The San Bernardino County Sheriff refused to intervene. Possibly he didn't like the sutler.

After the Army left the desert the fort in Arizona was supplied by river steamboat. The Old Government Road declined in importance but continued to be a recognized route of travel until the 1880s. Then in 1883 the Southern Pacific laid rails from Mojave to Needles and in so doing carved out construction roads paralleling its tracks. Overland travel simply moved over to the railroad where supplies could be obtained at the frequent stations.

Since the 1880s the narrow pass between Fort Piute and Lanfair Valley has washed out as has the Afton Canyon line. Only from Lanfair Valley through to Kelso does a present day highway follow the old wagon route. In the lengthening shadows of late afternoon, however, one may still look across several sizeable stretches of desert and note the winding ruts carved more than a century ago by covered wagons and Army supply trains. They mark the route of the pioneer trans-Mojave route.

At Camp Cady the 1938 flood wiped out the adobe ruins. Parts of log barracks and store remain and downstream a crumbling stone wall marks the hospital site.

The barracks are the ones Coues, in 1867, described as "A Botany Bay sort of place" referring, of course, to the Australian convict colony of that name.

At Soda Lake parts, the lower parts, of the stone walls remain and can be identified from upper tiers added later. A soldier's name, "Stewart, 2d Inf.," can be noted carved on the cliff at Rock Springs where an outpost redoubt has also been preserved.

Excellent rock walls at Fort Piute still stand shoulder high complete with loopholes for rifle fire and an emplacement for artillery. Old buttons, bottles and occasionally an ancient cartridge shell can be found by visitors. A few graves dot the area but their origin is unknown to today's desert residents. Aside from an inquisitive historian the old Army forts sleep untroubled by the passing of time.

THE DESERT WAS OUR BEAT *by* Randall Henderson

A VAST DESERT wasteland! This was the image of southwestern United States quite generally shared by Americans a hundred years ago. At the time of the Gadsden Purchase in 1853, Kit Carson was quoted as saying the land was so barren "a wolf could not make a living on it." Editorial writers of that period referred to it as "Uncle Sam's cactus garden" and "Rattlesnake Heaven."

Five years later, in 1858, Lieutenant Joseph C. Ives was sent out by the U.S. War Department to explore and report on the Colorado River and its contiguous territory. In his notes he wrote: "The region last explored (the Grand Canyon of the Colorado) is of course valueless. It can be approached only from the south, and after entering it there is nothing to do but return. Ours was the first and doubtless will be the last to visit this profitless locality. It seems intended by nature that the Colorado River along the greater part of its lonely and majestic way, shall be forever unvisited and undisturbed."

Today—well, the people of seven states are fighting for the water and power resources of the Colorado River, and over a million visitors sign the registers of the National Park Service at Grand Canyon annually.

True, the average annual rainfall over much of this region is less than four inches. But along the courses of occasional stream-beds are fertile valleys which needed only the alchemy of water to transform them into productive farm lands.

Then came Teddy Roosevelt and the Reclamation Act of 1902, and a new era in desert history began. Construction of Elephant Butte dam in the Rio Grande, Roosevelt dam in the Salt River and Imperial dam in the lower Colorado in the early years of this century started a migration of farmers to the Southwest. Following them came craftsmen and merchants, schools and roads.

It was the technology of an industrial age which finally dispelled the image of a desert wasteland. Came the automobile and paved roads, air-conditioning and radio and virtually all the conveniences and comforts of metropolitan living. Within the span of a quarter of a century, "Uncle Sam's cactus garden" began to acquire a new image. Here was a land of far horizons, easily accessible for both transportation and communication, with clean air, unclouded skies, remote from the pressures and traffic congestion of metropolitan living. Here indeed, was an invitation to relaxation and recreation. The response during the last three decades has been an explosive growth of population and enterprise in such cities as Tucson, Phoenix, Albuquerque, Las Vegas, Palm Springs and scores of less publicized communities. And, with the influx of more people, soaring real estate values.

It was during the initial period of this new migration to the desert, in the depression years of the early 1930s, that the idea of a *Desert Magazine* was born.

I was publishing the *Daily Chronicle* at Calexico, California, in that period. One of my associates on the Chronicle staff was Wilson McKenney, a young graduate just out of journalism school. Wilson had an old jalopy, Ol' Breezy he called it, and spent his weekends exploring the desert of the lower Colorado. For each Monday edition of the newspaper he wrote a column about his camping adventures in out-of-the-way places. His column brought more favorable comment than any other feature in the newspaper. Often I accompanied him on his camping trips and, as we sat around the evening blaze and discussed his desert column and the reader reaction to it, the thought occurred: If folks like this kind of copy so well, why not give them a whole magazine of it—a monthly periodical devoted to the desert, its people, wildlife, arts and crafts, minerals, history, lost mine legends, ghost towns, Indian life and lore, and its travel and recreational opportunities with photographs and maps, and as much human interest as we can pack into it.

It was just a dream at first; but gradually, as we camped together in remote canyons where the silence was broken only by our own voices and the occasional call of a coyote, we began to discuss seriously the feasibility of such a publication and the details of its production.

We would define the region of our desert as the states of Arizona, Nevada, Utah, New Mexico and the desert portion of California. The guide lines for the format and content would be simplicity, readability, human interest, reader participation—and always, the feel of the desert. We would seek to dispel the image of a desert our forebears had feared and shunned. Our new image would be a desert endowed with health-giving sunshine, a breeze that bears no poison, a sky studded with diamonds, a landscape of pastel colors, thorny plants which through countless ages had clung tenaciously to life through heat and drought and the depredations of thirsty animals, and yet each season had sent forth blossoms of exquisite coloring as a symbol of courage that triumphed over terrific obstacles.

Back at the print shop we worked up a dummy of the first issue, the index of which included phantom articles on desert ghost towns, homesteading on the desert, hobbies of desert people, a bit of natural history, a motor trip to a scenic area with map and pictures—and finally, a page of poetry and two short stories with desert plots.

To provide initial capital for the project I sold a half interest in the *Chronicle* to a partner who would become its publisher, and bought a going printing business in El Centro, which we felt was a more advantageous location for the new publication. When we pooled our resources we had $6,000 and a printing plant.

With 618 paid subscribers, the first issue of *Desert Magazine* was published in November, 1937. Several hundred additional copies were placed on the newsstands in Southern California and Arizona.

An editorial in the first issue defined the purposes, the editorial formula, and the goals of the publishers. Quoting from the editorial:

"This is to be a friendly, personal magazine, written for the people of the desert and their friends—and insofar as possible, by desert people. Preference will be given to those writers and artists—yes, and poets—whose inspiration comes from close association with the scented greasewood, the shifting sand dunes, the coloring of desert landscapes, from precipitous canyons and gorgeous sunsets.

"The desert has its own traditions—art—literature—industry—commerce. It will be the purpose of *Desert Magazine* to crystallize and preserve these phases of desert life as a culture distinctive of arid but virile America. We will give character and personality to the pursuits of desert people—create a keener consciousness of the heritage which is theirs—bring them a little closer together in a bond of pride in their desert homes, and perhaps break down in some measure the prejudice against the desert which is born of misunderstanding and fear.

"It is an idealistic goal to be sure, but without vision the desert would still be a forbidding wasteland, uninhabited and shunned. The staff of the *Desert Magazine* has undertaken its task with the same unbounded confidence which already has brought a million people to a land which once was regarded as unfit for human habitation."

During the 21 years I remained as editor, we adhered very closely to our original formula—with one exception. Several months before the first issue was to be printed I announced plans for the publication in the monthly *Writers' Digest*, and invited free lance writers to submit manuscripts, including short-story fiction. The pay rate was to be one cent a word.

The announcement brought a deluge of mail. The western pulp magazines fictionizing the wild and wooly days of cowboys, outlaws, gunmen and vigilantes, were having their heydey. It seemed to me that every frustrated writer of western fiction in the land immediately dug up his rejects and mailed them to *Desert*. Some of the manuscripts were yellow with age. I can guess what they were thinking. "Here is a new publication. The editor wants fiction. Maybe he'll like this story which the others turned down."

Well, the first issue of the magazine went to press without any fiction. *Desert* was to be a slick magazine, and Mac and I agreed we were not going to clutter its pages with cattle rustlers, faro dealers and barroom girls. We wanted to create a different image of the Great American Desert.

The mail was not all hell-raising fiction. It brought letters of inquiry from writers who later became regular contributors, men and women who were qualified to write authoritative material on many aspects of past and contemporary life on the desert. Bylines which appeared frequently in the early issues of *Desert* included those of Arthur Woodward, then curator of history at the Los Angeles County Museum; Lon Garrison, then a park ranger in Death Valley National Monument; Mrs. White Mountain Smith, wife of the superintendent of Petrified Forest National Monument; John Hilton, the desert artist; Charles Kelly, historian of Utah; John D. Mitchell, dean of the lost mine authorities; Walter Ford, a school teacher in San Diego; and a little later, Jerry Laudermilk of Pomona College and Nell Murbarger, the roaming reporter of the desert. Occasionally we got a manuscript from Barry Goldwater of Phoenix, whose father once had a trading post at old Ehrenberg.

During the first year of publication we received no fiction we felt worthy of our pages. The only exception to this was Lon Garrison's tall tales of Hard Rock Shorty, a fictitious old jackass prospector of his own creation. During the second year of publication I mentioned casually on the editorial page that we still planned to use some fiction as soon as we could get suitable material. But the readers did not want it. The fan mail brought so many protests that we gave up the idea.

From an editorial standpoint, our first lucky strike was Norton Allen the artist. Norton was an amateur archeologist whose hobby was tramping the desert in quest of old Indian sites—until an illness left him so crippled he could walk only with crutches. He was a fine cartographer with a thorough knowledge of desert geography. He could work only two or three hours at a stretch, standing at his drawing board, and then would rest by lowering himself to his cot with the aid of a rope suspended from the ceiling.

Norton worked at his home in La Mesa, California, or in a trailer when he was on camping trips with his parents. He knew the desert so well that when errors occurred in the instructions from which he was working, he would correct them. I dare say that during the 21 years I was at the editor's desk and since then, for he continues to draw maps for *Desert's* present publishers, literally millions of motorists and hikers have found their way unerringly to the destination he mapped for them.

Our most controversial writer was Marshal South of Ghost Mountain in San Diego county. Marshal had once served as an officer in the British army. He came to the United States after World War I and hoped to win a place for himself as a writer and dramatist in Hollywood.

But he was a non-conformist whose radical views often antagonized associates who might have helped him. During the 1920s he made a meager living at various odd assignments. Then the Great Depression came and he became a private in the army of the unemployed.

Marshal became a rebel against a society which could not provide work for its people. He persuaded his bride, Tanya, to share a great adventure with him. They would turn their backs on civilization and go out on the desert and live as did the Indians of this region before the white man came.

They took off from a coastal city in an old jalopy and headed into the mountainous back country of San Diego county. They followed the unbeaten trails, and late one afternoon came to the base of a low range of mountains overlooking the old Vallecito state station of the Butterfield days. They climbed to the top of ridge above with their blankets, spread a tarpaulin between two juniper trees and camped there for the night.

This was in the early 1930s, and this mountaintop remained their home until Marshal's death in 1948. There was neither shelter nor water at the top of Ghost Mountain—the name they gave their retreat—but they built a crude camp with the materials at hand and carried their water from a spring at the base of the hill. In the years following they built a comfortable adobe house, and later a cistern in which to store the water which drained from the roof of the house.

The water for the adobes, cement, roofing, materials for doors and windows, building hardware and crude furniture were all packed up the steep hillside trail to the site. They cultivated the friendship of their wildlife neighbors—kit foxes, rabbits, reptiles, chipmunks, rodents. All life on the mountain was sacred to them.

Occasionally Marshal would make a trip out to Julian for salt, sugar, flour, coffee and seasoning, but they sought always to harvest their food from the desert and nearby mountains as prehistoric Indians had done. They learned to roast the buds of the mescal or agave. They gathered acorns, pinyon nuts and mesquite beans and harvested what seed they could from the chia sage. After the cistern was completed and the winter rains came, they were able to grow a little garden with water they drew from the well.

Three children were born during their sojourn at the home which they named Yaquitepec. As the time approached for the arrival of each of the children Marshal would take Tanya out to a hospital in the nearest coastal town for proper medical care.

My first acquaintance with the Souths was in 1939 when the *Saturday Evening Post* carried a feature story written by Marshal, giving many details of their experiment in primitive living.

Richard Van Valkenburg, Desert Magazine *writer, and the Navajo medicine man Ayoo'anlh nezi.*

On the occasion of Desert Center's twenty-ninth birthday celebration, author-artist John Hilton, left, presents an "old man" cactus to Desert Steve Ragsdale.

The *Post* article was vague as to the location of Ghost Mountain, and I wanted to get the mailing address. Here was a writer who was a natural for *Desert Magazine.* My quest for clues to the location of Ghost Mountain and its nearest post office came to an unexpected and happy ending when I received a letter from Marshal asking if he might write something for *Desert.* Of course the answer was yes, and I asked for directions so I might go to Yaquitepec and discuss some ideas I had in mind. This was in later 1939. The adobe house was not yet completed, but the Souths were occupying it, and at the end of a well-concealed trail to the top of the mountain I found two healthy youngsters scampering among the rocks, a neat motherly woman weaving a basket, and Marshal excavating the hole which was to be the cistern. Here was an intelligent American family imposing upon themselves disciplines which few civilized people would endure—but wholesome and happy. The reward for their self-exile was a degree of independence which few Americans know—and for which fewer would pay the price.

They told about their plans for the future—the garden they would grow when there was water in the cistern, the outdoor fireplace, exploratory expeditions into the surrounding desert in search for ancient Indian campsites, and for seeds and herbs which would add to their food supply. Theirs was a busy life, but it was never drudgery because tomorrow's dreams would make Yaquitepec more habitable. They had goals—and enthusiasm. They were sustained by a faith that held the promise of better days ahead.

During my two hours on the mountaintop, it was arranged that Marshal would become a regular writer for *Desert.* During 1940 he would write a serial—a monthly diary of life at Yaquitepec, detailing the problems and the satisfaction of their lonely existence on a remote desert mountain.

Marshal wrote well, and soon the readers of *Desert* were sharing with Tanya and Rider and Rudyard the thrills which every rising sun brought to this little family. We were receiving an increasing volume of fan mail. *Desert* readers were interested, but by no means in accord. Some of them admired the courage of Tanya and Marshal and regarded their experience as a noble experiment in human adventure. Others fretted about the lack of schooling for the children and were apprehensive that, growing up in this isolated environment, they would be misfits in the society to which they must return eventually.

But the readers need not have worried. Tanya was a fine teacher and, following Marshal's death in 1948, she moved to a coastal city where the children entered school well advanced in their studies and readily adapted themselves to the social complex of community life. One of the teachers once wrote that Victoria, youngest of the three children, was the brightest and prettiest girl in the senior class at high school.

Since desert history was to have an important place in our editorial coverage, I was delighted when I received a letter from Arthur Woodward of the Los Angeles County Museum. He suggested some historical subjects on which he had done research, and for ten years was a regular contributor to *Desert*. I soon gained a high regard for the range and accuracy of his historical reports. At various times he recalled for our readers the story of old Fort Mojave, the reclamation of the Palo Verde Valley by Thomas Blythe, early-day steamboating on the Colorado River, the explorations of Father Kino, the founding of old Ehrenberg, and scores of other courageous and sometimes tragic episodes in man's conquest of the desert Southwest.

Arthur was also an archeologist, and one summer he invited me to spend a month with him locating and recording with photographs and sketches some of the best preserved petroglyphs and pictographs left by ancient tribesmen on thousands of rocks widely scattered over the Southwest. Our trek included parts of Colorado, New Mexico, Utah and Arizona. The petroglyphs, incised in the rock faces with stone tools, are still very sharp and clear in some instances. The pictographs, painted on the rocks with pigments and preservatives known only to the tribesmen, have retained their form and color only in caves and sheltered places.

It was easy to identify some of the glyphs—the coyote, the sun, rain, reptiles and other symbols representing wildlife or the natural elements. Arthur hoped that by comparative studies of widely scattered examples of this prehistoric art it might be possible to deduct patterns which would give significance to this phase of Indian culture.

This probably was the most intensive study ever made of this subject. And yet, a year later when I asked Arthur what his research had revealed, he replied: "I do not know yet whether those glyphs express the artistry of the tribal poets, the wisdom of the medicine men, or the doodlings of aboriginal morons."

Indian life and lore had an important place in the editorial formula of *Desert* during the years I occupied the desk. I had spent some months among the Chemehuevis and Mojaves of the Colorado River country soon after leaving school, and it was my good fortune to enlist the cooperation of two writers especially well qualified to interpret the life and culture of other tribesmen.

Mrs. White Mountain (Margie) Smith, whose husband was then superintendent at the Petrified Forest National Monument in Arizona, had spent many months on the Hopi reservation in northern Arizona. She was very fond of these people and knew the intimate details of their religion and home life. I had the privilege in August, 1938, of accompanying Mrs. Smith and White Mountain to the annual Hopi snake dances. It is a deeply religious ceremony, and as I came to know these people as revealed to me by Mrs. Smith I gained a deep respect for them.

Their reservation is surrounded by the lands of the Navajo—but the two peoples are as different in many respects as the Eskimos differ from the Fiji Islanders. The Hopis are shrewd traders, and the story is told about one of their tribesmen going into the Navajo reservation one day with a basket of peaches and returning that evening with a Navajo pony.

While Mrs. Smith wrote knowingly about the Hopi Indians, and also contributed interesting personality copy about some of the white traders on the reservations, the Navajo also had a loyal friend on our staff of free lancers in the person of Richard Van Valkenburg. Van was an ethnologist in the service of the U.S. Indian Bureau, stationed at Ft. Defiance, then the Bureau headquarters on the Navajo reservation.

He and Mrs. Smith often met each other as they traversed the Indian country—and they would invariably engage in a friendly argument as to the comparative virtues of the Navajo and Hopi. I believe it was Mrs. Smith who first suggested to Van that he submit copy to *Desert Magazine*.

His first manuscript recounting an interesting episode in Navajo history was a welcome subject. But Van had never written for the press and his narrative was strangled with meaningless detail. Here was a writer worth cultivating, for he had access to the historical records of the largest and most colorful tribe in North America. He was learning their language, knew them well, and had their respect.

Van was eager to be a writer, and I was confident he had the talent and the material to write acceptable copy for our readers. After much correspondence his initial article was revised to meet our standards. His next effort was better, but further coaching would be necessary.

He wrote me that a Navajo medicine man had reported the discovery of an ancient cliff dwelling in a remote canyon on the reservation. The Indian was unable to scale the cliff to reach the mud and stone dwelling, but the walls seemed well preserved and were decorated with three large pictographs of wild turkeys.

I had planned to take a trip into the Indian country within a few weeks and asked him to wait and let me accompany him to the ruins. On the hike to the canyon we camped overnight at the hogan of the medicine man who was to be our guide, and our host butchered a lamb that evening as a special treat for his guests.

Next day we reached the prehistoric dwellings, but the sandstone cliffs had eroded to such an extent we were unable to follow the finger and toe steps which the ancient dwellers had used to reach their dwelling in a recess far up in the sidewall. The three turkeys were a conspicuous landmark, well preserved in black and white pigment.

Much of our two-day trek together was spent in suggesting to Van how this story should be written. He was an apt pupil, and after that his stories required very little editing. He became one of our most popular writers until 1952 when he was stricken with a heart attack. The Navajos gave him a burial ritual worthy of a tribal chieftain.

The mail was bringing increasing numbers of manuscripts from free lance writers as *Desert* became better known. But hardly one in 20 of them was acceptable material. Too many of them were tainted with the tenderfoot image of the desert—a land swarming with rattlesnakes and venomous insects, of untamed Indians and gun-toting frontiersmen, a land of intolerable heat from which there was no escape, of lone prospectors with burros panning the sands for yet undiscovered gold, and of cactus storing an every-ready supply of water for the thirsty traveler. Also, there were scholarly essays, very correct, but without a spark of human interest. Gradually, we became convinced that it would be easier to make writers of desert people than to instill the feel of the desert into professional writers whose manuscripts were plotted in the more sophisticated regions beyond the far horizons. Once I wrote to a woman whom I knew quite well, but who had only a casual acquaintance with this arid land: "If you want to write for *Desert* you should move out here and stay long enough to get some sand in your hair and some cactus spines in your shirt tail." Fortunately she had a sense of humor—and we are still friends.

In my role as a literary coach, one of my most apt pupils was John Hilton, now recognized as one of the West's finest landscape artists. John is a very versatile fellow. He is a botanist specializing in cactus, a gem collector and lapidary, and an entertaining musician. He was then residing at his little art and gem shop on Highway 99, fourteen miles south of Indio. He had seen the first issue of *Desert* in Valerie Jean's date shop across the road, and he drove to El Centro to query the possibility of becoming a contributor.

John was well acquainted with the semi-precious gem and mineral fields in the California and Arizona deserts, and he suggested writing a monthly travelog for the rockhounds.

Here was another natural for *Desert*, and for eight years Hilton wrote about a field trip, with maps by Norton Allen, for nearly every issue of the magazine, excepting the war years when there was no gas for field tripping. He alternated occasionally with biographical sketches of desert artists with whom he had a wide acquaintance. His subjects included Jimmy Swinnerton, Clyde Forsythe, Paul Lauritz, Burt Proctor, William Krehm, George Frederick, Fritioff Persson and many others.

John's first manuscript was an editor's nightmare. But I was not dismayed, for it revealed a rare sense of drama which is a feature writer's most important asset. I was sure he would develop the technical skill to make a good reporter, and my confidence was well justified. John has the knack of seeing the drama in every situation, and he soon added a very readable writing style to his other achievements.

During the first few months when the mail failed to bring enough suitable material for the next issue, Wilson McKenney and I would fill in the gap. For some issues, he or I would write two or three feature articles, using pen names for by-lines.

We were fortunate in our selection of an associate to carry on the office detail—typing, proof-reading and other clerical duties. Several months before the first issue was to appear we employed Lucile Harris who had been doing newspaper reporting for a weekly paper. Competent, faithful and enthusiastic, Lucile attained such an important role in our publishing venture that in 1942, when as a reserve officer in the Air Force I was called back to active duty, she took over the editorial desk in my absence. During this period, with Lucile as editor, Bess Stacy, a long-time bookkeeper and cashier for my printing business, and my daughter Evonne in charge of the circulation, the magazine prospered, and with the boss no longer on the payroll the books for the first time showed a black ink balance.

Soon after World War II ended I received a query from Harold Weight, a linotype operator, who had just received his discharge from the army and did not want to return to his trade. Harold had long been a student of Southwest history, had built up a fine personal library, and he hoped he could write acceptable magazine copy. I liked the tone of his letters, and when I learned he was also a gem and mineral collector, I asked him to write a field trip story for the rockhounds. John Hilton already had covered most of the gem fields with which he was familiar, and perhaps Weight could supply this material for us.

Harold needed no coaching. His copy was well organized, and accurate, and during 1947 he supplied eight feature stories for our readers.

Desert had shown steady growth. Our pressrun now was over 20,000 copies each month. The time had come when we needed and could afford another editorial associate and I asked Harold to join our staff. He would continue to write monthly field trips, and would occupy the associate editor's desk in the office.

Within a year Harold and Lucile were married, and we knew

it would be a congenial companionship for here were two studious and highly competent associates who had a common interest in both the history and contemporary life in this land of the pastel hills. They spent as much time as possible out in the field, following the desert trails, exploring the ghost mining camps, the gem and mineral fields and delving into the lore of legendary lost mines.

Eventually the time came when Harold told me frankly that he preferred the freedom of a free lance writer to the tedious detail of the editorial desk—and in their departure we lost two associates who had made contributions of inestimable value to the pioneering of a successful magazine of the Southwest.

Harold and Lucile, working as a team, as do Josef and Joyce Muench of Santa Barbara, continued to write for *Desert*, and for *Westways* and other publications, and Harold has published two books on the lost mines of the Southwest.

Nell Murbarger became a contributor to *Desert* in August, 1949, when her first manuscript—featuring the ghost mining camp of Shakespeare, New Mexico—won instant acceptance. In the following years she became a regular and popular contributor to our pages.

Like many other magazine writers, Nell began her journalistic career on a country newspaper. But towns—and even cities—were too small for the gypsy spirit of this young lady who had grown up on the midwestern plains made famous by Wild Bill Hickok, Calamity Jane and Deadwood Dick. She gave up a promising newspaper career to roam over the western country and write magazine articles about its history, frontier characters, ghost towns, landmarks—and always about people. Her special interest has been the abandoned mining camps. She travels alone much of the time and camps wherever she happens to be when the sun goes down.

Nell is a master of the art of portraying human character—and eccentricities. She invariably finds a lone survivor or two in the vicinity of every ghost camp, and these become the actors in history that otherwise might be dull and statistical. She has written three books about the ghost camps in the desert Southwest, the latest being *Ghosts of the Adobe Walls* in which she has brought life and interest to the abandoned ruins of mining and prehistoric

Indian occupation in Arizona. This volume was published this year by Paul Bailey's Westernlore Press.

Nell and her mother have spent the last four winters on gypsy tours in Mexico and Central America. They travel in a camper and much of the time follow the back roads to remote settlements where life is still very primitive. She loves to write about people. Her book, *30,000 Miles in Mexico*, is a day by day record of one of these trips.

Artists and poets have played an important role in dispelling the image of the desert as a grim and desolate wasteland. Everett Ruess was one of these. His name, like woodsmoke, conjures far horizons, and mystery.

Everett left Kayenta, Arizona, November 11, 1934 to write, paint and explore some of the ancient cliff dwellings of the canyon country in Arizona and Utah. His last letter to his parents in Los Angeles stated that he would be unable to communicate with them for ten weeks. Alone with his paints, books and burros, he disappeared into what at that time was the most uninhabited region of the United States. He never returned.

Poet, artist and adventurer, the desert trails were his roads to romance. His paintings captured the black-shadowed desolation of aboriginal homes high up in recesses of the cliff walls. His poetry told of beauty and wind, and the artifacts of prehistoric people. He sang of the wasteland's moods. Everett belonged to the desert, and in the end it claimed him.

I first learned about the saga of Everett Ruess in early 1938, soon after *Desert Magazine* appeared on the newsstands. Hugh Lacy, a Los Angeles writer, sent a letter of inquiry in which he outlined briefly the strange gypsy life of a young man who for four years had wandered the desert wilderness and then dropped from sight. The story, Lacy wrote, would be written serially in the notes and letters and poetry Everett had written to family and friends during his nomad life in the wilderness.

This would be welcome copy for the pages of *Desert*, for it would give the readers a glimpse of arid America through the eyes of an intelligent young man who had written: "I prefer the saddle to the street car and the star-sprinkled sky to the roof, the obscure and difficult trail leading into the unknown to any paved highway, and the deep peace of the wild to the discontent bred in cities."

Hugh Lacy's stories of Everett Ruess appeared serially through 1939, and later we published them in book form with the title *On Desert Trails With Everett Ruess.*

Everett's last journey was into the canyon country along the Colorado River east of Escalante, Utah. When they failed to hear from him after a few weeks, his parents spread the alarm, and search posses spent weeks combing the region of his last known campsite. They found his two burros in an improvised corral along Davis Creek, a tributary of the Escalante River, but no trace of Everett or his bedroll, artists' supplies or notes ever came to light. In my book *On Desert Trails Today and Yesterday*, I wrote what I have always regarded as the most plausible explanation of his disappearance—that he probably met death at the hands of cattle rustlers operating in the area, who suspected him of being an agent of the law seeking evidence which would incriminate them. But there is no confirmation of this, and as water rises in the new Lake Powell being formed behind Glen Canyon dam, the region of Everett's last camp will be inundated and likely clues to the mystery will be forever lost.

During my years as editor and reporter for *Desert* I spent as much time as possible in the field. With a competent staff in the office, it was possible to be absent for as long as a month at a time. These trips gave me contact not only with those who were writing for our pages, but also personal acquaintance with many rugged men and women who were playing leading, though often obscure, roles in the heroic drama being enacted on the desert stage of this period.

Just to mention a few of them: Harry Goulding and his wife Mike, veteran Indian traders in Monument Valley; Bill and Katherine Wilson at Rainbow Lodge, of which Barry Goldwater of Arizona was a part owner at that time; Cozy McSparron, colorful trader of Canyon de Chelly; Shine Smith, the big-hearted free lance missionary on the Navajo reservation, loved by Indians and whites alike; Chee Dodge, for many years the stalwart chief of the Navajo; Art Greene, lodge-keeper and boatman who now has a Park Service boating concession on Lake Powell; Desert Steve Ragsdale of the Chuckawalla Valley in California; Ross Musselman, veteran guide on Utah trails; Death Valley Scotty and Ray Goodwin, first superintendent of Death Valley National Monument; Nellie Coffman of Palm Springs, John and Louisa Wetherwil, Indian traders at Kayenta; Charlie Brown, state senator from Shoshone; Dr. Clarence Salsbury of the Ganada mission in the Navajo country—the list could go on and on.

I mentioned an evening I camped at the hogan of the Navajo medicine man Ayoo'anlh nezi. During the 24 hours Richard Van Valkenburg and I spent with Ayoo and his wife and two children I got an intimate picture of the family life of a Navajo long-hair.

White parents would marvel at the industry and obedience of these Navajo children. One of the reasons for this discipline is the gentle manner in which the Navajo address each other. During the time I was at the hogan I never heard a voice raised in impatience or command—not even when a battle-scared old rooster annoyed the 11-year-old girl with its persistent efforts to rush in and grab a bit of the dough from the pan in which she was making bread. She shooed him away with a soft-spoken Navajo word that I would have taken for a term of endearment under any other circumstances.

I have cited some of the highlights of a half century of experience as editor and reporter on the American desert. They have been good years. The desert has not changed during that period—only the popular image. Pampering civilization has come to the wasteland. Tucson, Phoenix, Palm Springs, Las Vegas, Albuquerque and scores of smaller communities now offer all the swank and luxury of the ultimate in sophistication.

To the old-timers, the desert was a challenge, its summer heat something to be endured, horses and buckboards quite adequate for our transportation needs. For recreation we explored the canyons, tramped the hills and mesas in quest for rare minerals, and played poker by the light of kerosene lamps. We lived close to the good earth and it was no hardship.

For a majority of those who come today the lure is golf courses, temperature-controlled swimming pools, floor shows in swanky dining rooms, and speculation in zooming land values.

I'll confess, there is a bit of nostalgia in what I am writing. But the desert has lost none of its natural charm. There are still thousands of remote canyons to be explored, trailless mountains to be climbed, rare species of plant and animal life to be identified, and lovely places where there is solitude for those who are aware of the tonic value of close communion with the natural world.

As one of the old-timers, I do not resent the coming of golf carts and heated pools, cocktail parties and fabulous profits in real estate. I can live with these things. But I do object to the chamber of commerce fiction that they are a gauge of progress. For me, the desert has confirmed what the professor in my philosophy class of long ago said to us: "True progress takes place only in the human heart and mind—in the broadening of understanding and vision, the maturing of the qualities of tolerance and generosity and humility."

SLAVERS *in the* MOJAVE

by Paul Bailey

THE MOJAVE DESERT is a big place. For Walkara, the infamous Ute horse thief and slaver, it was big enough to support a staging base for his repeated raids on the ranchos of Southern California, big enough in which to run away from pursuers, big enough to hide in it, a perfect place to secrete the stolen horse herds and the slaves. And to strangers the Mojave desert was an inhospitable place and barren, grim enough to discourage prolonged pursuit.

On his raids out of the Mojave Desert into the San Bernardino and San Gabriel Valleys the Ute chief Walkara took full advantage of the desert country. He had to share the desert with almost no one. Between 1835 and the coming of the gringo in Southern California, Walkara and his mounted thieves and slavers operated out of the Mojave with impunity.

There is no evidence that Walkara and his band ever made a permanent camp in the Mojave. But there is reason to believe that some of his camps—perhaps individual raid bivouacs—have been located by patient modern Mojave Desert explorers.

Piles of bleached horse bones have been found at places like Resting Spring in the Resting Spring Range near Tecopa—bones that could have come there easily as a result of a bloody and monumental 5000 horse raid that Walkara once staged. Seep Spring, out near Black Mountain in the Mojave wasteland, has been called a possible Walkara camp by archeologists.

Walkara knew the country, knew the waterholes and the natural tanks where water could be found all year. Water was important to Walkara. You couldn't take a herd of horses and slaves across the desert without water.

Some experts feel that Walkara's route from the Cajon Pass country—the funnel through which he struck at Southern California—was through Lucerne Valley, into the Newberry country, north beyond Yermo and thence, via a route that would become known as the Mormon Trail, into Nevada. Others feel that Walkara would have been more apt to follow the Mojave River for a way, at least, before striking northeast toward Nevada and Utah. He was always, of course, following a line that could be drawn from watering place to watering place.

But neither pursuers nor the desert completely stopped Walkara from raiding . . . other elements decided this. The Mojave

Desert, big, unmapped, friendly only to those who knew and understood it, was Walkara's ally from the beginning to end. The Mojave was Walkara's undisputed domain and he moved through it as he wished. No single military man—and since all his raids were war raids, he must be considered a military man—used this land to such an advantage. What brought Walkara to the Mojave in the first place may not have been entirely of his planning, but he took full advantage of the uncommon opportunity.

For call the Ute chief what you will, he was a shrewd man.

When Cortez landed the first horses at Potonchán, and with their aid made real and certain his conquest of New Spain, he changed the western world. The horse became the symbol of wealth and power. And as this strange, mighty, beautiful creature spread itself northward—tame or wild—it was coveted beyond any earthly possession. In North America, it made a mighty warrior of any Indian lucky enough to tame or straddle one. Those tribes which took to the horse became the conquering tribes.

No greater cavalry ever was put to the field than that of the Sioux, the Utes and the Navajos. Once the Apaches straddled the horse, they became the most cunning and invincible of foes. There were never enough horses to fill the demand. The horse, in the Americas, became the measure and symbol of wealth and power—a thing essential and wanted by Indian, Spanish and Anglo alike.

The horse came early into the Spanish Southwest, and remained to thrive in unbelievable numbers from New Mexico to the Pacific. On the lush coastal plains and high deserts of Southern California, under the baronial rancho system, the proliferation of horses and cattle had by the 1830s reached such proportions that few of the owners of these vast landed estates ever bothered to take even a head count of the thousands of animals that grazed the hills and the valleys. It was only natural that the horse-hungry Indians and mountain men of the Far West should cast greedy and covetous eyes upon this nimble treasure. The first horse raids were made by the nearby desert Indians upon the missions and *asistencias*, prior even to the great and golden era of the ranchos. But in the sixteen years from 1830 to the Mexican War and the coming of the gringo, the horse raids, particularly upon Southern California, became systematic, artful, and increasingly and incredibly daring.

In the procurement of horse flesh by either of the devious methods of bartering or stealing, no man's record has ever remotely equaled that of Walkara, the Ute. War chief, military strategist, opportunist, and implacable foe of the land-grabbing Americans, the reckless audacity of his raids into Southern California, and the harvest he reaped, ranks him unquestionably as the greatest horse thief in history. Second, he was a callous slave trader—and feared greatly for this talent.

Unparalleled as a leader, versatile as a man, Walkara is remembered for a lot of things. The Mormons of Utah remember him as their irascible, unpredictable thorn in the flesh. The humble Paiutes and walking tribes of the desert knew him and feared him, because he murdered their men, stole their women and children, and sold them into slavery. To the *Californios*, who saw their horses vanish in herds of thousands, he was the scourge of the desert—the ubiquitous ghost, who with his loyal and fearless band of fellow thieves (known to the Mexicans as *chaguanosos* or *chaquetones*) appeared, vanished—but always with enough of their horses to mount an army.

For a brief and meteoric period of time, this Ute war chief was lord and master of the vast desert area between the Sierra Nevadas and the Rockies, and southward from the Great Basin to the Spanish settlements of California, Arizona and New Mexico. His matchless cavalry, predominantly Ute, but made up of reckless adventurers from other tribes, were hellions of terror wherever they struck. Gwinn Harris Heap, in 1854, had this to say of Walkara:

"Having an unlimited supply of fine horses, and being inured to every fatigue and privation, he keeps the territories of New Mexico and Utah, the provinces of Chihuahua and Sonora and the southern portions of California in constant alarm. His movements are so rapid and his plans so skillfully and secretly laid that he has never once failed in any enterprise, and he scarcely disappears from one district before he is heard of in another. He frequently divides his men into two or more bands which, making their appearance at different points at the same time, each headed, it is given out, by the dreaded Walkah in person, has given him with the ignorant Mexicans the attribute of ubiquity."

While the life-span of this tempestuous, mysterious Ute war chief was comparatively short, never reaching into senility, his unparalleled record of lawlessness continued up to the hour of his death. He is one Indian that history is not likely to forget.

Known by a variety of names—Walkah, Wakara, Wauk, Walker, and Wah-ker—he rose to Ute chieftainship by his acts and courage, rather than by the primogeniture rights of birth. His father was an obscure clan chief rather than tribal chief, and his mother was reputed to have come from another tribe—some say she was a California mission Indian, acquired as a captive or by barter—giving rise to the claim that Walkara was not fully a Ute.

Walkara is believed to have had three brothers by this mother, but a host of half brothers by his father's other polygamous wives. Captain John W. Gunnison, before the tragic massacre of him and his surveying party by the Paiutes, wrote that Walkara was one of a family of thirty sons—the daughters were not counted. Of Walkara's brothers, not all are known. But those who are known are remembered as prominent chieftains, warriors and troublemakers by mountain men, explorers, and Mormons. Four of the brothers—Arrapeen, Sanpitch (San Pete), Ammon and Tobiah (Tabby)—eventually gained chieftainships for themselves—and are remembered for their part in the troubled resistance to white pioneering in the Great Basin. Others, like Sowiette, Tobiob, Hankiter, Tanterbus, Yankawalkits, Antonguer, Caloechipe, Nephi, and Kanosh, settled more peacefully into the new pattern of a white man's world after Walkara's demise. But, while Walkara's dusky cavalry scourged the west, a fair share of this unholy brotherhood was riding with him.

Walkara was born about 1808, in Utah Valley, on the Spanish Fork River (known then to the Indians as Pequi-nary-no-quint, or Stinking Creek). This was very close to the spot where Escalante, on his visit to Utah Lake in 1776, preached to the Utes, and planted his farthest north cross. Walkara's earliest rides to battle glory was with his father, uncles and brothers against the Snakes, or Shoshones, the hereditary enemies to the north. R. W. Young, as recorded in *The Contributor*, states that "When he [Walkara] was about twenty years old, a part of his own tribe deserted and joined the Snakes, among them being one of his own uncles and a number of other relatives. This small band of seceders even joined the Snakes in their warfare against the Timpanogos, then located on the Timpanogos or Provo River [Walkara's own tribe]. Walker's father and about forty of his relatives, entertaining scruples against fighting their own kindred, withdrew from the Provo River and moved over to Spanish Fork to live. But this did not meet the approval of the tribe and they attacked the little band of dissidents and killed Walker's father, whom Walker and his brother Arrapeen . . . buried about a mile south of Spanish Fork in Rock Canyon."

Walkara's spectacular career had its real beginning when he and Arrapeen, under cover of night, crawled into the camp of the Timpanogos Utes and cut the throats of the four braves who had to do with the murder of their father. Taking command over his father's band, Walkara turned his back upon the Ute nation, and, along with his father's harem of wives and numerous progeny, the whole clan went to live with the Paiutes.

The peace-loving Paiutes soon wearied of their adopted and troublesome cousins. The young Walkara was a terror; ill-tempered and quick to kill. He was soon universally detested by the kindly people who had given him sanctuary. Among the Paiutes it was agreed that he deserved death, but few of the Paiute men had the courage to attempt it. And those who did died by the quick knife of this hot-blooded and fearless young Ute.

Out of the ferment of this dislike and fear, and about the hard core of his family of cruel and clever brothers, Walkara gathered his band. Renegades and unwanted fighters from any tribe were welcomed, provided they possessed the hardihood to render unquestioned fealty to their young and ruthless leader. Walkara has gone down in history as the great Ute war chief—but Ute, Paiute, Shoshone, and even such white adventurers as Thomas L. (Pegleg) Smith and the mulatto Jim Beckwourth, were known to have ridden with him. And it was precisely this interest in and fraternization with the white race to which Walkara owed both his success and his undoing.

From the beginning, Walkara's band was a war party. His war was solely for booty—and the most important part of that booty was horses. Of horses, he could never get enough—not only for

Courtesy Huntington Library, San Marino, Calif.

Hutchings' California Magazine drawing of Pegleg Smith.

Courtesy Huntington Library, San Marino, Calif.

Early portrait of mountain man James Beckwourth.

the incessant demands of his fast-moving cavalry, but because horses were a mobile form of wealth—with quick and ready market to white and Indian alike. It was always worth killing a man to take his horse. From Bridger, Wolfskill or Smith came guns, ammunition, saddles, blankets and bright baubles for the horse herds Walkara could move into their corrals. With these helps and fighting tools, horses came easier, raids became more successful, and this source of wealth was made ever more certain. The whole west became their hunting ground.

From the Spanish slaving parties, which in the 1800s had penetrated deep into the northerly reaches of the Great Basin country in search of women and children to be sold at Santa Fe and the California pueblos, Walkara was taught another source to wealth. Other than occasional kidnaping, these slaving parties traded on the destitution of the desert tribes for the necessary women and children to fill the long caravan of human chattel they sent southward for sale as menials in the households of the wealthy Mexicans and *Californios.* Women and children were readily traded off for guns, horses, trinkets, and Mexican dried beef. But in this insidious traffic, which flourished for decades in the great west, it took Walkara the Ute to work it into a real business. Scientists have long pondered the puzzle of what became of certain "vanished" Mojave Desert Indian peoples. Some feel now that these small, peaceful bands were completely captured and enslaved by Walkara leaving no clue of their disappearance.

In addition to exacting tribute upon any parties traveling the Spanish Trail, it was his happy discovery that any woman, any strong or healthy girl, or boy, was worth one horse in even trade —not only from the procurers but in any Spanish settlement large enough to support this traffic. Not only that, but many Indian tribes to the east, as well as the Navajos to the south, used slaves and wanted them—and they, too, had horses for ready trade against the human chattel.

To Walkara it seemed stupid to barter with Paiutes, Piedes or any of the Digger tribesmen for their children or unwanted wives. It was easier and cheaper just to swoop down, take the captives, and shoot and scalp any of the men so foolish as to resist.

Through the energies of Walkara and his band, aided and abetted by the Mexican slavers, this traffic in human chattel grew ever more flagrant as Walkara grew in affluance and power from the horses and guns that were his through these nefarious dealings. Long caravans of horses down the southward curves of the Spanish Trail, with from one to three women and children roped astride the gaunt beasts, was a common sight. Their ankles tied with buckskin thongs passed beneath the horses' bellies, with no thought as to their comfort, and with little provision for their needs in food or drink, these hopeless prisoners were sent on to a life of servitude in the settlements of New Mexico and California.

But even this barter in human flesh was not enough for the avaricious Walkara. It outfitted his cavalry, and armed it superior to any striking force on the Great Western plains, including that of the Mexican garrison themselves; yet with Walkara and his riders, it only whetted desires for wider conquests, and a hunger to tap the resources of the rich lands from which flowed this trickle of wealth in guns and horseflesh.

By 1835 Walkara's name was spoken of in fear and whispers by every Indian village in the Rockies. Good horses, in quantity, were his. He had two hundred weather-and-battle-hardened braves who rode in Spanish saddles and were armed with the best American guns. He was feared, and he was famous. Already he was known as Hawk of the Mountains, and the Napoleon of the Desert. And, like the conquering Corsican, he fretted for a new world of spoils.

It was Pegleg Smith and James Beckwourth, a pair of trappers and mountain men, who were now emerging as two of the most infamous opportunists ever to turn traitor to their kind, who guided Walkara the Ute into the happy hunting grounds of the white man. To these mentors in the fine art of horse thievery, Walkara owes his greater fame.

Smith, who had lost a leg in an Indian ambush on the Platte, had made several trips into California, and had come out with enough stolen horses to more than make up for his losses in the *cantinas*. He also knew Santa Fe and the Mexican colonies to the east.

With dependence on horseflesh for locomotion Pegleg Smith became a sharp trader and unscrupulous procurer of animals. The first two years after donning his wooden leg found him trapping the Utah country as far south as the Virgin and Santa Clara Rivers, and living with the Utes and Paiutes of the high valleys in which Walkara was now coming of age. With Pegleg now was William Wolfskill, another trapper of renown, with whom he continued on to California. On this journey to Los Angeles, Pegleg was reputed to have discovered and lost the fabulous gold mine which was to make his name legendary in the annals of the west.

William Wolfskill bought Spanish horses with the returns from his peltries; driving them over Cajon Pass and back up to the Utes for trade at Jim Bridger's fort on the Green River. Pegleg squandered his beaver profits.

It was the intention of Pegleg to remain in Los Angeles, but *El Cojo*, "the Lame One," who loved to fight as much as he loved to drink, was soon recognized as a menace to the pueblo. The *alcalde* of Los Angeles ordered Pegleg to leave the town forthwith—which he did—taking four hundred of the pueblo's best horses.

Back again in the Rocky Mountain fur country, two important people now had eyes on the enterprising Pegleg as a man intimately and profitably to know. The first was Jim Bridger, who promptly formed a trapping partnership with himself, Sublette, and Pegleg Smith. The other man who courted the knowledge, experience, and horses of Smith was Walkara, who by now had made a clean break of tribal allegiance, had gathered his two hundred impatient cut-throats in his brother San Pete's (San Pitch's) valley, and was anxious to draw fresh blood for name and plunder.

Smith, ever the warm and sympathetic friend of the Utes—a friendship going back to the time of the loss of his leg when Utes had helped him—was not at all averse to a meeting with the rising young Ute war chief. Such a meeting was held and Walkara took this wild and pugnacious white man into his confidence regarding his aspirations toward independent chieftainship and, in turn, Pegleg filled Walkara's ears with the wonders of California.

In that land, Walkara was told, were tens of thousands of horses. Unguarded, and in vast herds, they grazed the verdant leagues of coastline. It would be no problem, he was told, for any clever raiding party to drive these animals over the mountains, and into those deserts which only trappers and Indians knew intimately enough to traverse in safety.

Walkara was immensely pleased with his new friendship with Wa-he-to-co, the fearless white man with leg of wood. In the spring, on the Green River, they would meet again. Out of it would come great plans to separate the *Californios* from their horses.

The years of his petty raids and slaving had already taught Walkara and his band all the secrets of the sun-scorched deserts of the Southwest; the isolated canyons, defiles, creeks and waterholes so essential to the preservation of man and beast; the Colorado crossings; the secrets of the Mojave; the canyon passes to the coastal plains of California. It had taught him also something of California itself, where Spanish *rancheros* lived in happy indolence amid soft climate, leagues of land, and the endless treasure of horseflesh which Pegleg had talked about. Every mile of the ancient trails to Los Angeles and Santa Fe already were clearly and cleanly stored in the alert and receptive mind of Walkara. All the mountain country from the Timpanogos of his homeland, east to Bridger's Fort and north to the tribal lands of the Blackfeet and Shoshones, and all the flat desert west to the California mountain wall would be his, for tribute and for gain. The Paiutes, the Piedes, the Tonoquints, the Shivwits—already were his to use according to the dictates of his desires. They were his because they had no horses. Without horses, any man who chose to do battle was already dead.

In 1835, before winter had broken its grip upon the highland valley of the Rockies, Walkara's first joint expedition with white men asembled itself in San Pete's valley for the pushoff toward Southern California. Jim Beckwourth, the winter's trapping partner with Pegleg Smith, insisted the expedition be strictly a trading venture, with the horses to come from their heavy load of peltry. The women and children Walkara had for his own share of trade loot. Whatever profit accrued was to be justly divided among Smith, Beckwourth, Walkara, with a smaller share to the four other white trappers who had joined up, and Walkara's cavalry. Walkara, who would much rather steal than trade, reluctantly agreed to the arrangement.

It was an impressive expedition that took off from Walkara's winter camp at "Little Salt Lake," and swung southward on the Spanish Trail. At the camp, Walkara left his own women, children, and elderly members of his clan. The horse-train was loaded heavy with beaver pelts. Tied to dozens of other animals were the women and children Walkara had previously seized from Paiute villages in the Great Basin. With it, alert and silent, rode Walkara's men.

It was Pegleg's plan to get their horses out of California by way of San Gorgonio Pass and to take them by way of the warm weather route across Arizona and New Mexico to the traders of the south and east who supplied the horse markets of Louisiana Territory.

Six weeks later, at Los Angeles pueblo, they had disposed of their pelts and slaves, and had added some horses and a fair sum of gold to their ledger of gain in the transaction. But the *Californios* proved cagey traders, and drove a lot harder bargains than had been anticipated. Sullenly Walkara followed his white friends from rancho to rancho while they haggled for some share of the riches in horseflesh everywhere about them. Up in one of the canyon pockets of Cajon Pass, his men chafed for action as the days of stupid bargaining dragged on. Walkara bought himself a tall beaver hat, drank firewater with Smith and Beckwourth, and waited moodily for them to garner enough horses to make worthwhile the long desert trip southward. After a week, with only fifty horses gained, and most of their gold squandered for *aguardiente*, Walkara decided to put a stop to such useless dawdling away of time. He simply told his brothers Arrapeen and San Pete to fetch the Utes down from the hills, and, in the night, to run off all the Spanish horses they could get.

When Smith and Beckwourth learned of Walkara's defection in favor of expediency, they were furious. So were the Spanish *rancheros*. The six hundred horses Walkara's Indians drove into the foothills went out through Cajon Pass, instead of San Gorgonio—with a posse of Spaniards in hot pursuit.

They never managed the white man's idea, and original plan, to drive their herd to eastern markets. Instead, they made the hastiest sort of return to Utah, and San Pete's valley. From there Pegleg and Beckwourth took their own horses and squaws north to Bear River, and Walkara and his band remained that spring and summer in their own lodges.

Walkara knew Smith and Beckwourth were displeased with the course events had taken on their trip south, and with the part he had played in upsetting their plans. To him it was all a little baffling. They had gotten horses. That was enough.

He saw the white men no more for three years, but through the Indian grapevine he knew full well where they were, and what they were doing. First they were at Fort Bridger; next they were at Taos and Santa Fe; finally Pegleg had settled on the Bear River with his squaws and his traps. Then in the late summer of 1839, after one of Walkara's slave-trading junkets across the Colorado, both Pegleg and Beckwourth rode into the circle of Walkara's campfire.

Walkara cared little for the shriveled, dark-skinned Beckwourth, but he had genuine affection for the big-hearted, roisterous, impulsive Pegleg. Happily he welcomed them to the camp. They had firewater in plenty. He offered them shelter, food, tobacco, and his best women. When all were well-fed, mellow and jovial, the proposition was made.

This time, the white men proposed, they would go to California. It had been a bad year for trapping. This time there would be no pretense about trading. They would take the horses, and be damned to the Spaniards. It would be a big haul. And this was the kind of thing that made sense and meaning to Walkara.

So Pegleg revealed the plan. Jim Beckwourth, whose reputation for trouble and thievery was not so blatantly recorded on *Californio* memory, would precede the expedition by at least thirty days. He would spy out the situation, locate every likely horse herd, and lay groundwork for a horse haul that would make them all rich.

While Beckwourth headed down the Spanish Trail toward Los Angeles, Smith hurried northward to Bear River, and thence to Bridger's place to outfit himself with a few trusted white helpers, and to complete arrangements for disposal of the coup once they had taken it safely away from the Spaniards. A month later he again appeared at Walkara's camp, with three other tough-looking mountain men, and his own belongings and retinue of squaws, all of which he left in custody of their brown sisters in the Ute camp. By now Walkara, too, was ready. The vicious and eager troop of riders followed southward on the tracks left earlier by Jim Beckwourth.

After leaving their armed retinue at Cajon Pass, and cautiously dropping down to the coastal plain, the two leaders quickly discovered that Beckwourth had done his job well. He had set up a sort of headquarters at the great Chino rancho, accepting freely of the traditional *Californio* hospitality. To allay suspicion as to status and intent, Jim had declared his intention of engaging in the then profitable business of hunting sea otter. Beckwourth, when he met Pegleg and Walkara at the foot of Cajon Pass, had notations ready for them on every Spanish horse herd from San Luis Obispo to the Santa Ana River.

The strategy that came out of this counsel was flawless. Walkara was to execute the mechanics of the great raid. This was the thing in which he excelled. With Indian cunning, he divided his band into small and maneuverable groups, each to handle one definite objective, all to strike on one specific night. Because of the dramatic familiarity given them on the previous raid, Cajon Pass was to be the point of convergence, where all the stock stampeded could be funneled out of the mountain onto the great and little known desert which stood before them and their security and sanctuary in the mountain valleys of the Utahs. Rendezvous point, and mountainous route of exit, was captained and guarded by Pegleg Smith and his fighting trappers.

For magnitude and sheer audacity there has never been anything comparable to that night's Walkara-Pegleg raid on the *rancheros* of Southern California. At least five thousand horses were sent thundering through Cajon Pass—of which less than two thousand were recovered by the aroused and fighting *Californios*. Walkara himself captained the group which made the greatest single coup—from Mission San Luis Obispo—a thousand of the finest blooded horses in California. Walkara took pains to include the silvered and brocaded saddles that went along with many of the animals. Rather than face certain battle with the *Californios* in and around Los Angeles, this herd was pushed out through the Tehachapis, to join with the others coming out to the high desert through Devil's Canyon and Cajon Pass, under the prod of Pegleg Smith, the trappers, and the running units of Walkara's *chaquetones*.

They had, in total, gotten out more than three thousand horses, but deathly close behind them rode the Spaniards—this time sworn to a war to the finish with the raiders.

The running battle that followed was vicious and merciless, and the gouging brunt of it was felt by Pegleg and those of Walkara's band who were forced to ride guard at the rear.

Ten years later, during Horace Bell's visit to Pegleg's Bear River rendezvous, the old trapper still had vivid recollections of that bloody fight through Cajon Pass. "They [the horses stolen] cost me dearly," Pegleg soberly recounted to Bell. "Three of my squaws lost brothers, and one of them a father, on that trip, and I came near going under myself. I lost several other braves [these from Walkara's band], and you can depend on it that I paid for all the horses I drove away. Them Spaniards followed us and fought us in a way that Spaniards were never before known to do."

With Walkara's arrival in the Mojave, the fleeing and bloodied trappers and Utes took new heart. Not only were the horses from San Luis Obispo added to their own grand coup, but Walkara had plans for revenge on the Spaniards who were taking such heavy toll on the fleeing raiders.

One-half of his band Walkara set to furiously driving the great herd of animals as fast and as far into the desert as possible. The remainder of his force, with Pegleg and the trappers, Walkara secreted in the willows about the Mojave water-hole where he was certain the Spanish posse would find it necessary to make their first desert stop. It proved a shrewd gamble.

Unaware of the trap, the Spaniards dismounted to water their animals, and to catch their own moment's respite from the chase. With blood-chilling Ute war cries, Walkara and his braves rushed the camp. In an instant the Spaniards' horses took to the desert in full stampede. Spanish guns spoke, and so did those of the attackers; but Walkara had no intention of tarrying to prolong the fight. Like the cunning savages they were, they followed the fleeing horses. An hour later they had rounded up the Spanish mounts and had added them to the vast herd already safely out of reach of their former owners. The Spaniards were forced to return to their California ranchos afoot.

* * *

As with the other more modest raids, there was no difficulty in disposing of the loot that went out of California in the big raid. Pegleg used his riches to underwrite a journey in style to Taos and Santa Fe, lively with booze, women, and the gaming he loved. After a series of sensational escapades, he returned to Bear River, set up a sort of trading post, and disposal center for stolen horses, and might have equaled the fame of his friend, Jim Bridger, as trader to the west. But Smith lacked Bridger's stability and persistence. He craved excitement, dreamed of gold mines, and eventually returned to California.

When the excitement of the big raid had died down, and after another half-hearted attempt at trapping, Jim Beckwourth likewise drifted on down the Spanish Trail to the California settlements. History attests that none of these supreme horse thiefs were ever strung up by the *Californios* they robbed. Instead of hanging for their crimes, they both enjoyed a modest amount of fame for their accomplishments in other fields. But neither of them again shared any grand raids with the Desert Napoleon.

But as a horse thief and slave trader Walkara still remained very much in business. His wealth went into outfitting his *chaquetones* with the best American guns, the finest accounterments, the fastest horses, instead of dissipating it away in frivolity, as had his paleface companions. Raiding, fighting, thieving, was his way of life, and he knew no other.

With the *Californios* now fully alert and vigilant, there no longer was the possibility of running five thousand horses out at a time, but Walkara's raids on the Southern California ranchos continued for over a decade, with monotonous regularity. He took horses, and plenty of them. And so successful was he at this perilous occupation that the trail across the Mojave came to be known as "Walker's Trail."

But the relentless movements of history already were ringing down the curtain on this great savage and his wild and reckless career. Those first American pioneers over the Oregon Trail were anxious and willing to bid for his stolen horses. But the Mormons, whom Walkara met in the very valleys of his homeland, were of a different breed. As a peace gesture, he offered them some of his land. Not only did they accept the modest offering, but immediately appropriated everything the Utes had once possessed. With maddening casualness, as though they owned it, the Mormons ploughed and fenced the ancient Ute homeland. They dammed the rivers, plowed the soil, and erected forts with guns pointed straight down Walkara's throat.

Perplexed and uncertain as to what was happening, but still not wanting to fight this Brigham Young and his strange people, Walkara offered them horses, which they apathetically bought. He offered them women and slave children, which they refused to buy. So he had Arrapeen, as an object lesson, dash the brains out of the children before the very eyes of the Mormons, to demonstrate to these people that they were too stingy and avaricious even to save the lives of the Piute children. From that point on, it was easier. Mormons bought children to save them from slavery and the cruel death that awaited them with refusal. But in Brigham Young, Walkara met his match.

Eventually Brigham was to exert a profound influence over the irascible Walkara, put a stop to his slaving, and even to baptize him into the faith. But this is another story entirely—of which it is sufficient to say that not even Brigham ever quite managed to tame this savage. Walkara became the wildest Mormon ever to don a breech cloth. His demands on Brigham for plural women, his thievery, and the "Walker War" he waged against them mark him as the greatest nonconformist on the Mormon roll of membership.

As if the problems of Mormon membership were not enough, there followed quickly the Mexican War, and the discovery of gold—and the profound changes that came upon California through this shattering epoch in history. Horse riding became a precarious business indeed, when American soldiers began guarding the passes, and straight-shooting frontiersmen harassed the retreating Walkara instead of the emotional and excitable Spaniards. With the coming of the gringo, a lot of the fun went out of the game.

American takeover of the Mexican-Spanish provinces of the west, and the stamping out of the slave traffic with the Spanish procurers by Brigham Young, now Utah Territorial governor, trimmed Walkara's once heavy trading in human flesh—though he did practice it in some degree up to the very end.

Had he lived another ten years, Mormon colonization, and the great western tide of American migration, would, by the very force of events, have blown the flame of this renowned Ute war chief into the oblivion it probably deserved. The end for Walkara came suddenly, while he still was a comparatively young man. Early in January of 1855 he was stricken with pneumonia, and before the month was out, the great Walkara was dead—at the age of 47 years.

His death occurred at Meadow Creek, near Fillmore, Utah. And his funeral, worthy of a great chief, was conducted as near as possible in accordance with his dying request. His two favorite wives were killed, to keep him comfort in the other land. And, since he'd been baptized into the Mormon faith, and had kept up an erratic friendship with Brigham Young, it was fitting that a Mormon or two share the grave with him, as friends and counsellors in the spirit land. Hunting parties were sent out to capture Mormons for the burial, but the Mormons, wise to Ute funeral customs somehow kept themselves vigilantly unavailable.

But, in spite of this lack, the funeral and its procession was still worthy of a great chief. In the shivering cold of Utah's January, the bodies of Walkara and his favorite wives were lugged high up the mountainside—so high that eternally he could look out over the great expanse of territory that once was his. At the foot of a great rock slide, visible for miles, the squaws, amid their lamentations, went to work in digging out the crevice for the huge grave. Gently, Walkara was laid facing the view. The women were placed beside him. Since no Mormons had been captured to share honors with him, Arrapeen and the riders did the next best thing. In his hands were placed the latest letter from Brigham. In with the food, arrow points, guns and ammunition, went the little gifts and mementos Brigham had given him.

Fifteen of his finest horses were slaughtered on the spot, for him to ride on the long journey, and to remind him of his unquestioned importance in the western dealings with this animal. The carcasses of these animals were carefully laid out in another mass grave alongside. Then the bodies—human and animal—

were covered securely with rocks. Nor was it to be allowed that his career as slaver should be forgotten. So, atop Walkara's grave, a circular rock cairn was built, and roofed stoutly and securely over with fresh-cut pine limbs. Inside were placed two live children—a little Piede girl, and a little Piede boy. The spacing of the rocks and limbs were such as to give the children air. Theirs, as the living, was to watch through the great transition of the noble dead beneath them.

And when it was over, and Walkara's people had sadly and mournfuly returned to the valley, the only live reminders of the great desert Napoleon, were the whimpering and frightened children, so securely rocked in their little prison above his grave.

KING *of the* DESERT FREIGHTERS

by Remi Nadeau

When Remi Nadeau was operating his mule-time empire in the 1870s, he used to ride over the California desert from one station to the next, inspecting the business. Once he came upon an outfit that had broken down when one of the iron tires had cracked. The rear wheels on his biggest wagons were six feet in diameter, with a tread six inches wide; it usually took three men to place one of the 150-pound iron tires on a wheel. Nadeau rode a number of miles to his next station, got a new tire, rode back with it slung over his shoulder and got the team and wagons started again.

This story is typical of the Herculean exploits that I have heard since childhood about my great, great grandfather. In our family, and even among many old-timers on the desert, he has taken on legendary proportions. As far back as I can remember, my parents and I were exploring mining camps served by his teams, looking for remnants of his way-stations, bumping over dirt roads he had surveyed and built, talking to "the oldest inhabitants" who remembered the white-bearded freightman and his jingling mule teams. I sat at the feet of family patriarchs and matriarchs who reminisced of magical places—Cerro Gordo, Panamint, Bodie, and Calico—and of exciting characters whom old Nadeau had encountered—Belshaw, the silver king of Eastern California; Banning, the early-day freighting competitor; and Vasquez, the bandit who terrorized desert roads.

In researching old newspapers for my first book, I made notes of every item I found on old Remi Nadeau. It was a detective job which sometimes confirmed, sometimes demolished the old word-of-mouth legends. I found to my delight that editors of the 1870s called Remi Nadeau "the boss teamster of Southern California," and "the Napoleon of inland freightmen." One correspondent in the Los Angeles *News* of September 5, 1871, wrote of him:

"He has given employment to more men, and purchased more produce, and introduced more trade to Los Angeles than any other five men in this city."

For years you could not pick up a Los Angeles newspaper without seeing a notice about the arrival or departure of Nadeau's teams. One weary reader charged that the item was kept in type from day to day at every newspaper, and when the compositor called for copy, the local reporter simply hollered, "Freshen up Nadeau's teams!"

* * *

The epic of Remi Nadeau began in the little Canadian town of Kamouraska on the St. Lawrence River, about halfway between Quebec city and the Gaspé Peninsula. One of fifteen children, he was born there in November 1819. It is said that his ancestors had been political exiles from France. Today the name Nadeau is not uncommon in French Canada, and in upper New England and the Great Lakes states.

Nadeau himself married a New Hampshire girl, Martha Frye, in 1844. Together they moved west to Minnesota and Illinois, where Nadeau plied the trade of millwright—one who builds mills. In 1860 he hitched two oxen to a small cart, said goodbye to his wife and seven children, and joined the Pike's Peak Gold Rush. Somewhere on the Platte River trail one of his oxen died. He found another man who was in identical trouble, but who was headed for California. With Gallic resignation, Nadeau yoked his ox with that of his new partner and headed for the Coast.

Wintering in Salt Lake, he arrived at Los Angeles in 1861. There he borrowed $600 from Prudent Beaudry, one of the city's pioneer businessmen and a fellow French Canadian. With this grubstake, Nadeau bought a wagon and six mules to enter the freighting business.

For several years he hauled mining camp freight in Northern California, Nevada, Idaho, and Utah, gradually building up his string of teams and wagons. Around 1866 he returned to Los Angeles and entered the rising commerce with the Owens River country.

Among his competitors at that time were Phineas Banning and Don George Alexander, who had pioneered the up-country trade. Apparently Nadeau had some kind of difficulty with them. Instead of using their dock at Wilmington, he established his terminus at Timm's Landing in San Pedro, where John J. Tomlinson had a wharf and warehouse. And in 1867 when Nadeau's wife and children came around Cape Horn, he refused to let them come ashore by Banning's regular lighter service to Wil-

Remi Nadeau freighting station in the Mojave in the late 1870s.

One of Nadeau's team and wagons crossing the Mojave desert country.

minton. Instead, the Frenchman chartered a boat and brought his family ashore to San Pedro without Banning's help.

* * *

In the late 1860s important silver strikes were made in the Inyo Range east of Owens Lake. Near the summit sprang a thriving new camp named Cerro Gordo (Spanish for "Fat Mountain"). By 1868 its output was largely controlled by two partners—Mortimer W. Belshaw, a San Francisco mining man, and Victor Beaudry, an Owens Valley storekeeper and brother of Prudent Beaudry. Together they owned the principal deposit of galena or lead ore, which was essential in smelting the silver ores. In the summer of 1868 each of them built his own smelting furnace to produce ingots of base bullion. Mostly lead, with some silver, they weighed eighty-seven pounds apiece and were worth about $35 at contemporary prices.

From that time on Belshaw and Beaudry's biggest problem was delivering these pigs to the Thomas Selby refining works in San Francisco, where the silver was separated from the lead and sold at the mint. The route involved a 250-mile haul by mule teams from Cerro Gordo to San Pedro, then a 400-mile steamboat ride to San Francisco. Surplus bullion was shipped around Cape Horn as ballast in sailing ships to the refineries of Swansea, Wales.

At first Belshaw and Beaudry shipped their bullion by independent freighters; but as the ingots piled up they sought a responsible contractor, and called for competitive bids to be made at the office of their San Francisco financial partner, Egbert Judson.

Remi Nadeau now saw his big chance. Operating against a number of competitors, he had to beat them to San Francisco. Fortunately he had a long-legged sorrel that was good for a strenuous ride. Named Hippy, for a slight limp in one hind leg, the animal nevertheless was celebrated for its speed and endurance. According to the story told by Nadeau's daughter, Mrs. Mary Bell, the old man mounted Hippy and pounded northward out of Los Angeles. On the first night he found one of his rivals sleeping alongside the road. Giving him a wide berth to keep from waking him, Nadeau raced on. After four hundred miles and four days, he pulled up at the Front Street office of Egbert Judson. He was coming out of the office with the contract in his hand when the first competitor arrived.

* * *

This remarkable ride—assuming it is more fact than myth—was made by a short, stocky Frenchman not quite forty-nine years old. It was to be the turning point in his life—for his most noteworthy career was still ahead of him.

The only photograph we have of Nadeau reveals an older man of full white moustache and beard—probably taken in later years. But contemporaries say that he was a man of endless energy, who talked in true Gallic fashion—rapidly, and with his hands as well as his tongue. One acquaintance called him "an agreeable, energetic little French gentleman." He was too absorbed in building up his business to be a model family man. According to his daughter, from the time he left Minnesota in 1860 his wife never heard from him until he sent for her and the children in 1867. He had a flair for elegance—as shown by the classic banquets he would later stage at his Los Angeles hotel. He was not unaware of feminine charms. After more than thirty years of marriage he and his wife were divorced and he married a young San Francisco belle named Laura Hatch. And he had a weakness for good horses. One of his competitors, John Delameter, gathered together a matched team of sixteen buckskin mules and made a point of driving them by Nadeau's house at Fifth and Olive, where the Biltmore Hotel now stands. Seeing them out his window, Nadeau could not resist; he bought them for a fancy price. They became his crack "Yellow Hammer" team, operating on the line north of San Fernando Pass, and driven by a privileged skinner named John D. Cage.

On another occasion Nadeau bought a fine matched pair of sorrel horses and proudly drove them through the streets of Los Angeles. When they were stolen he offered a handsome reward, which was soon claimed by a stranger who delivered them. Shortly afterward they were missing again, and were redeemed in the same manner from another reward-collector. Exasperated, Nadeau built a six-foot solid-board fence around the pair and guarded the gate with a vicious bulldog. This time he kept his team, and his temper.

Cerro Gordo, where the silver-lead came from. Photo was taken by author in 1939 when there was snow on the ground.

Photo by Russ Leadabrand

Beale's Cut, Fremont Pass, near Newhall, Calif., built in 1859, and used by Nadeau's teams.

Ordinarily occupied with business, Nadeau also had a mischievous streak. In 1876 a long legal contest over the ownership of Belshaw and Beaudry's mine was finally settled in their favor. Since the case had caused some shutdowns at Cerro Gordo, the whole town was caught up in a jubilant celebration. A bonfire was blazing in front of the American Hotel, the crowd gathered around, and the prominent men of the camp made rousing speeches. Nadeau was said to be in the thick of the celebrants, sitting on his horse, Hippy. According to one account, the merrymakers finally began throwing their hats into the bonfire. Nadeau shouted, "Come on, boys! Let's go help ourselves to new hats at Beaudry's store!" Since Beaudry had greatly benefited by the settlement and was helping to foot the bill for the party, nobody felt backward about raiding his store. In a few moments they reappeared wearing stovepipe hats, wide-brimmed slouch hats, even children's hats decked with gay ribbons; the late comers were outfitted with ladies' sunbonnets. Then they danced around the fire, and celebrated till daybreak.

* * *

It is not altogether certain when Nadeau first contracted to haul Belshaw's bullion. The earliest date recorded for his freighting to Cerro Gordo was in January 1869; the first contract let by Belshaw began December 1, 1868, and it is probable that Nadeau was the operator. Beginning in 1870 his name appeared regularly in the Los Angeles papers—first spelled "Nado" or "Nadaugh."

Originally his teams had ten mules each, drawing one large wagon with a four-ton cargo capacity. By late 1870 he had thirty-two teams of twelve mules and two wagons each. By the following spring he was experimenting with still bigger teams; one of them, probably using fourteen mules and three wagons, hauled in more than eight tons of bullion.

Nadeau was not necessarily the inventor of large mule teams. In the Comstock excitement of the early 1860s, the long grade into Virginia City required teams of as many as twenty mules. In his early career Nadeau probably saw such teams and may have operated some. Early in 1875 a twenty-mule team and two eighteen-mule teams from the Comstock passed through Owens Valley, and were hailed as the largest teams ever seen there.

But Nadeau was apparently the first to apply such teams in the California desert on a large, organized scale. By 1874 he had eighty teams, most of them with fourteen mules and three wagons each. In 1875 he had 100 teams, all of fourteen mules, which were increased to sixteen mules before the end of the year. These outfits regularly hauled ten tons of freight—the capacity of a narrow-gage box car. In the late 1870s the teams had eighteen mules, as shown in one of the accompanying illustrations, and by 1880 many of them had twenty and even twenty-two mules each.

Actually, the wheel span was composed of draft horses, which could handle the heavy tongue and take the shocks of the wagon better than mules. Thus a "twenty-mule team" really had only eighteen mules.

Such outfits hauled three blue-painted, high-sided wagons. The lead vehicle had rear wheels six feet in diameter, while the trailers, known as "back-actions" and "tenders," were smaller. Generally the outfits traveled in pairs, to help each other in case of trouble, and to double the teams up a steep grade. In this process both teams would be hitched in tandem (for a sixteen-mule team, this meant a string of thirty-two mules). They would haul one outfit of three wagons up the grade, then would be unhitched to return for the other three.

For convenience, each span of animals had its own designation. The next pair ahead of the wheelers were known as the "swings" or "pointers." Beyond them were the "sixes," the "eights," the "tens," and so forth to the front pair, known as the "leaders." While the wheelers were hitched to the wagon tongue, the rest of the animals were attached to a heavy chain extending beyond the tongue, and usually hanging about a foot above the ground. Each pair of mules saw to it that the chain extending ahead was kept tight, thus assuring that the pair in front was pulling its share.

The leaders each had a set of bells (five to seven in number) attached to the top of the collar, as shown in one of the illustrations. Since the teams plodded along at about two miles an hour, these bells were a warning to oncoming traffic that might suddenly burst upon them around a blind bend.

Each team was handled by a muleskinner who rode a saddle

An 1874 view of a Remi Nadeau team and wagons in front of the John Shepherd home, six miles south of Independence, Inyo County.

The Nadeau building in downtown Los Angeles at the corner of First and Spring Streets opened in 1883.

on the near (left) wheelhorse. He guided the team by means of a long rope known as a jerk-line which ran through harness rings to the halter of the near leader. A jerk on the rope meant a right turn, while a steady pull meant a left.

The skinner also had a long blacksnake whip which he could handle with the most remarkable accuracy. The expert skinner would claim he could knock a fly off the rump of a lead mule without touching the skin. Rarely did the popper of the whip actually touch an animal; usually, the crack of the blacksnake over his head was enough to stir him to greater effort.

Still another weapon of the skinner was a collection of rocks in the small bin at the front of the lead wagon; these he aimed with superior marksmanship at recalcitrant mules. One of Nadeau's teamsters, Pegleg Smith, would apply still more persuasion, if necessary. Leaping from his horse, he would run up to the offending animal and pound it with his wooden leg.

Accompanying these inducements was a collection of oaths which for sheer originality was unrivalled in the annals of profanity. The repertory of a muleskinner, with its marvelous juxtaposition of words, was a literary form which never has received due recognition. Ever since those freighting days the ultimate compliment to any oath is that it would "shame a muleskinner."

The driver also handled the brake on the lead wagon, and often walked alongside the teams rather than sitting in the saddle. Riding in one of the rear wagons was the driver's helper, known as the swamper, who handled the rear brakes, kept the rock bin filled with missiles, helped harness and unharness the mules, cooked the meals if they happened to camp in the open, and otherwise assisted the muleskinner.

* * *

These knights of the freight teams were not noted for their genteel manners. When Nadeau once said that it was very difficult to get good teamsters, he was referring to many necessary skills: the ability to handle a long string of animals on bad roads in the worst kind of weather; the responsibility to care for the animals and the freight as though they were the teamster's own; the honesty to keep from stealing cargo items and selling them; the fortitude to resist sampling the barrels of brandy and wine that went north from Southern California to thirsty mining camps; and the agility to stay out of trouble when in Los Angeles or any of the equally tough mining camps which they served.

Subject to sandstorm and cloudburst, the desert roads were often obliterated, and at best were full of deep ruts and chuck-holes. In dry washes, such as the stretch through Red Rock Canyon, the wheels ground through the sand up to the hubs and the brake-blocks dragged the surface. On downhill grades, there was real danger that the heavy wagons would bolt out of control and carry teams and teamsters over a cliff. The usual procedure was to unhitch most of the mules and tie or lead them behind out of harm's way, holding the wagons back by a combination of devices. These included chaining the wheels in place, fastening iron "shoes" to the rims to provide added friction, and even dragging trees behind. On the Yellow Grade, the seven-mile road from Cerro Gordo down to Owens Lake, one of Nadeau's skinners invented a double brake with blocks before and behind the main wheels, clamping them like a vise.

Despite such precautions, accidents were possible. One of Nadeau's competitors lost an outfit which rolled crazily over the brink of the Yellow Grade.

Even in Los Angeles, road conditions were hardly ideal. After one rain, a mule actually drowned in a mudhole on a main street. In 1872 Nadeau built the first road northward through the gap of the Los Angeles River to avoid the grade of Cahuenga Pass; but in flood times the mules had to swim across the Los Angeles River. In the wet winter of 1874 Nadeau had to hitch a pair of draft horses ahead of the mules to lead them into the water. In January two of his teams were stuck and were only prevented from drowning by the skill of the teamsters. As it was, one of the horses was lost, and the wagons were left stranded in the river till the water level subsided.

But from the heavy Los Angeles traffic of the 1870s, Nadeau's huge outfits had little to fear. When one of them encountered a buggy on Commercial Street, the Los Angeles *Herald* reported, "The wagon sustained no serious damage, but the buggy was slightly demoralized."

Nadeau's teamsters were equally capable of adventure when off duty. The Los Angeles newspapers of the 1870s reported numerous instances of them getting into barroom fights, dying in a knifing or shooting scrape, landing in jail, escaping from jail.

In February 1871, two of Nadeau's teams were camped at the mouth of Sand Canyon, south of Little Lake; in charge of the outfit was Nadeau's wagon boss, Austin E. Lott, a tall, sandy-haired frontiersman who had served as a post boy in the rebellion. In the evening they were joined at the campfire by a horsethief who was escaping from the Inyo County sheriff. Knowing his identity, Lott and his men let him bed down with them that night. After breakfast next morning they presented a double barreled shotgun at his chest. Tying him with a rope, they put him on top of a wagon and proceeded on their way. But through some miscalculation they left the shotgun in the same wagon. He untied himself, grabbed the weapon, and bidding them goodbye, disappeared up Sand Canyon. When the sheriff arrived Lott was embarrassed to tell him their story. But the officer followed the robber up to the snowline of the Sierra Nevada and captured him.

* * *

As in most desert freighting, mules were preferred to horses because they were hardier, less nervous, and more easily managed in the harness. They were also preferable to ox teams because they were faster and could go farther without water. But a good team required expert care. Nadeau kept his stations well stocked with hay and grain, and operated his own grist mills for grinding corn and barley. His animals were fat and sleek, but at times they were as obstreperous as the drivers. When leaving Los Angeles one of his wheel horses refused to budge. Alternately bucking and lying down, he was dragged through the city for nearly a mile, attracting a large crowd. Finally exhausted, he was heaved into a dray and hauled back to the corral in style.

Nor did the mules fulfil the popular conception of stupidity. On the trail, when a mule would go lame or otherwise give out, he was turned loose, and would invariably head for the nearest station. Expertly trained, the mules presented a beautiful picture of coordination when starting up, rounding a bend, or performing some other maneuver. As the teams moved out from a stop, the leaders would start first. As soon as the chain tightened behind them, the next pair would start, followed by the next.

The king of the desert freighters, Remi Nadeau.

Naturally, the longer the team the more difficult it was to assure that all the animals were pulling their share. When going around a bend, for example, the spans in the lead could not make their strength felt along a curving chain; the tendency was to pull the rear spans and the wagons off the road and across the corner. This might mean ramming the wagons into the hillside. Thus on passing such a bend the lead mules would step out of the trail and swing as wide as possible to keep the wagons going straight ahead up to the point of turning. After the lead spans had passed the turn the pointers and sixes had a special duty. The inside mule would jump across the chain and pull with his partner at right angles to the turn, so as to keep the wagon in the road and prevent it from cutting across the bend.

* * *

From 1869 to early 1882, Remi Nadeau was the leading wagon freighter of Southern California, and dominated the cargo traffic to the desert mining camps of Eastern California. To Los Angeles County he represented a market for all its surplus hay and barley crop, and a carrier of vast quantities of products to the desert towns. His delivery of silver-lead bullion from Cerro Gordo alone rose from 340 tons in 1869 to a peak of more than 5,000 tons in 1874.

At the same time, Nadeau's northbound wagons were hauling an amazing variety of goods to the mining camps—blasting powder, grapes, nuts, wine and brandy, corn, potatoes, bales of hay, crates of live chickens, billiard tables, water pipes, mining and milling machinery, even boats for the waters of Owens Lake. Some 2,500 tons of barley and 3,000 tons of hay, constituting respectively 27 percent and 40 percent of Los Angeles County's yield, were consumed annually by the Cerro Gordo teams. The combined volume of approximately 8,900 tons comprising the Inyo County trade of 1874 was practically half as large as the 18,000 tons Los Angeles exported through San Pedro the same year. Almost one third of that San Pedro export, too, was Cerro Gordo bullion. The value of the trade to Los Angeles may be determined by the following newspaper quotations:

"We know that Owens River trade . . . is the most important trade which comes to this town."

—Los Angeles *Star*, August 30, 1870

Loss of the Cerro Gordo and Owens River trade "would entail distress, if not ruin upon the community."

—Los Angeles *Star*, August 4, 1871

"To this city, the Owens River trade is invaluable. What Los Angeles now is, is mainly due to it. It is the silver cord that binds our present existence. Should it be unfortunately severed, we would inevitably collapse."

—Los Angeles *News*, Feb. 2, 1872

"It is the rich trade of the mining regions about us, and none more so than Lone Pine, Independence, Swansea and Cerro Gordo, that has encouraged the building of our elegant brick blocks, and furnishes tenants for our numerous stores and dwellings."

—Los Angeles *Express*, April 11, 1872

"These teams [Nadeau's], with all their wants to be supplied here, are in themselves enough to maintain a good sized town."

—Los Angeles *Mirror*, August 9, 1873

The feed consumption of Nadeau's teams "has been the great traffic of Los Angeles, and has perhaps done more to build up that city and develop the county than any other one enterprise."

—Inyo *Independent*, December 19, 1874,
quoting Bakersfield *Californian*

"The value, direct and indirect, of the 'Owens River trade' to the people of Los Angeles and San Bernardino valleys, as furnishing a market for the surplus products, is almost beyond computation."

—Los Angeles *Star*, January 16, 1875

Though Nadeau dominated the desert traffic in the 1870s, he had his competitors among the independent operators. Among these were Dan Hazard, W. A. Stewart, A. A. Cole, and Warren Matthews. Most important among the rivals of the early 1870s were William M. Osborne and E. Olinghouse, who offered alert competition for freight contracts. On December 1, 1871, Nadeau's contract with Belshaw and Beaudry expired; when they tried to lower his freight rates, he refused to sign. James Brady, a smelter operator at Swansea on Owens Lake, took the Cerro Gordo freight contract and sublet it to William Osborne. Nadeau kept his teams on the route as an independent operator but naturally his business suffered. He owed considerable money to the wholesaler, Harris Newmark, and offered to turn over the whole outfit in payment. But Newmark told him to keep his teams as busy as possible and pay when he could.

Meanwhile, another rival was looming in the shape of the Iron Horse. In the West of the 1870s, more and more the mule team routes became feeder lines to the railroads. From the beginning, Nadeau's operations were affected by the invasion of the railbuilders. When Phineas Banning completed his railroad from Wilmington to Los Angeles in October, 1869, Nadeau moved his southern terminus from San Pedro to Los Angeles. Gradually his expanding stables and corrals occupied the block bounded by Fourth, Fifth, Broadway and Hill.

While Osborne was hauling Belshaw's bullion in 1872, the Southern Pacific tracklayers were marching down San Joaquin Valley. The railhead reached Tipton, fifty miles north of Bakersfield, and all indications were that it would continue south to Tehachapi Pass.

Quickly the farmers and merchants of southern San Joaquin Valley reached for the Inyo trade. When Brady and Osborne's contract expired in December, 1872, Julius Chester of Bakersfield secured the business and turned the traffic over the Tehachapis to the Southern Pacific Railroad.

Foreseeing this change of route, Remi Nadeau had already contracted to haul the output of the flourishing borax camp of Columbus, Nevada. Thirty-four of Nadeau's teams left Los Angeles for Nevada on November 18, 1872, to haul on the route between Columbus and Wadsworth on the Central Pacific Railroad. While the Los Angeles editors bemoaned the loss, one citizen felt differently. To the Los Angeles *Express* he wrote:

> I am told Nadeau will remain, and will—horrible thought—possibly keep one team here to run short daily trips in and out of town, to make two items daily for each of the papers. Now I am frantic over that thought, and if Nadeau dares to keep that team here, I warn him fairly he must take the consequences.

But to the consternation of the Bakersfield people, the Southern Pacific railhead remained at Tipton for several months, making a longer haul than Chester had anticipated. Other problems, including a horse disease known as the epizootic, afflicted the Bakersfield freighter. As independent operators, Osborne and

Olinghouse continued to help by hauling bullion to Los Angeles. But by May 1873, 30,000 silver-lead bars had accumulated in Owens Valley. Along Owens Lake, miners were piling the ingots into brick walls and living in the silver-lined cabins. Belshaw and Beaudry faced disaster unless they could market their bullion.

Meanwhile, Nadeau was encountering difficulty in his borax freighting at the dry lakes of Columbus, Nevada. An early summer hot spell was preventing the borate crystals from rising to the surface of the ground. Recovery operations were suspended, and were not likely to resume until fall. In late May, 1873, Nadeau pulled off his teams and headed for Owens Valley.

Hearing that Nadeau was passing by, Belshaw and Beaudry went down to Owens Lake and met him. According to one account, they squatted in the sand and parleyed with him; they would cancel Chester's contract, they said, if he would put his teams back on the road.

Nadeau could see those mountainous piles of ingots and knew that the Cerro Gordo smelters were turning out 300 more bars per day. The only way to do the job, he told Belshaw and Beaudry, was for them to join him in forming a new freighting company and put up $150,000 to build more stations and buy new wagons and harnesses. He also specified that the Newmark debt be paid.

Desperate, they agreed to his terms. Together with their San Francisco partner, Egbert Judson, they formed the Cerro Gordo Freighting Company—an organization that would dominate the roads of the California desert for the next nine years. Retaining a half interest, Nadeau would serve as superintendent. With this agreement, he continued south with his teams, arriving at Los Angeles on the night of June 6, 1873. Explained the *Express*:

"Last night the old familiar sounds of Nadeau's bell teams rang out upon the air as the long strings of mules passed down Main street, dragging their long chains after them."

"It will give a wonderful impetus to trade here," wrote another editor, "and times will be lively again and money plenty."

Feverishly, Nadeau organized his new empire. Ordering new wagons and harnesses, he put eighty teams on the road by October. Another improvement had been in operation since the summer of 1872—a small steamboat named the *Bessie Brady*, which carried bullion across Owens Lake and saved three days' haul by mule team. With new stations and road improvements, Nadeau's teams were able to make the 230-mile haul from Cerro Gordo to Los Angeles in eleven days—a little more than twenty miles a day.

Over this route he operated his freight teams by an almost hourly schedule, like a stage line. While the loaded wagons went through from Owens Lake to Los Angeles, the teams and teamsters went back and forth each day over the same route between two stations. By August 1874 Nadeau had cleared the piles of 30,000 ingots and was keeping pace with the smelters.

Meanwhile, the railroad was still affecting his operations. In April 1874 the Southern Pacific completed a line from Los Angeles to San Fernando, at the north side of San Fernando Valley. Nadeau transferred the southern terminus of his line to the new railhead, which would remain there for nearly two years pending the construction of a long tunnel under San Fernando Pass.

Then from the north, the tracklayers in San Joaquin Valley passed Bakersfield and arrived at the foot of Tehachapi Pass in April 1875. There, during construction of the series of tunnels over the pass, the end-of-track would remain for more than a year.

Since this connection shortened the route to San Francisco by about eight days, Nadeau removed his entire establishment from Southern California and placed his headquarters at the Tehachapi railhead. First known as Allen's Camp, the new terminus soon took the name Caliente from nearby Caliente Creek, and became a thriving frontier town. When the Southern Pacific was finished over Tehachapi Pass in August 1876, Nadeau transferred his terminus to Mojave, where it remained for the next five years.

Though Cerro Gordo supplied most of his metal shipments, Nadeau sought new business at every desert strike.

In 1872 he sent his wagons all the way across Southern California to the new mining camps of Mineral Park, Cerbat, and Chloride in northern Arizona.

Late in 1874 he began teaming across the Mojave to Panamint, a new silver camp located in the Panamint Range bordering Death Valley on the west. On the return haul he picked up borax from John Searles' pioneer works at Searles Lake, now Borax Lake.

In 1875 he started serving Darwin, a new silver town southeast of Owens Lake. Two years later, after two adobe charcoal kilns were built on the west shore of Owens Lake, their product was carried by the *Bessie Brady* across the lake, and Nadeau's teams delivered it to Cerro Gordo and Darwin.

Beginning in 1876 Nadeau supplied the Minnietta and Modoc Mines (the latter owned by George Hearst) at the north end of the Argus Range. Next year he was loading charcoal at the ten new kilns in Wildrose Canyon in the Panamint Range, hauling it across Panamint Valley, and delivering it for the smelter at the Modoc. From the two furnaces he carried silver-lead bullion to the railroad at Mojave.

Starting in 1878 Nadeau's teams reached from Mojave all the way to the new camps of Bodie, northeast of Mono Lake, and Mammoth City, located near the present Mammoth ski area. Owens Valley towns and the mining camp of Benton in Mono County were also served on this route.

For a brief time in 1881-82 he freighted in and out of Calico, the silver town near the present Barstow, and for about a year in 1881-82 he operated at Tombstone, Arizona.

* * *

These far-flung camps, many of them located on mountainsides at the end of back-breaking grades, offered new challenges to Nadeau's teamsters. Among the classic frustrations was hauling a delicate cargo one or two hundred miles from the nearest railroad, only to have it smashed in unloading. Such, according to one story, is what happened to a large plate glass mirror for a saloon at Panamint. Again, in the summer of 1876 Nadeau was hauling machinery for the Modoc mine and furnace. One of the items was a cast-iron bed plate for a large engine. When it finally arrived from Mojave, his employees hitched a team to the casting and snaked it out of the wagon; sure enough, when it hit the ground, it smashed into little pieces.

Then around 1879 Nadeau hauled the machinery for the huge stamp mill at Mammoth City. Loaded with a huge boiler, a long team was struggling up the Sherwin Grade, just two days from the destination. The wagon tipped over, and the boiler crashed into the canyon below. Impossible to retrieve, it was still there at last report. Up from Mojave came another boiler, together with the other equipment.

One of the most remarkable cargoes was an enormous cast-iron flywheel, about twenty feet in diameter and a foot in width. It stands in place now at a clearing below the site of Mammoth City. In two places on the flywheel, still visible in white paint, are the letters: "M. M. Co. care of C. G. F. Co. Mojave." Clearly the mark of a railroad agent, the abbreviated letters stand for "Mammoth Mining Company" and "Cerro Gordo Freighting Company"—proof that the relic was hauled into this remote place by a Nadeau mule team.

Though most of Nadeau's hauls were over rough terrain, he was continually building new roads. Where most desert roads sprang up like cowpaths, following the contours of least resistance, Nadeau surveyed his roads and built them straight as a bullet across the desert. Typical is the Shotgun or Nadeau Road built in 1877 from the foot of the Slate Range crossing to the Modoc and Minnietta Mines. Today, viewed from the Slate Range summit, it still stretches before you straight up Panamint Valley. Another example was the Nadeau Road branching off from the main Antelope Valley route just north of the Soledad Pass summit. To cut twenty-seven miles from the Owens River route, Nadeau left the regular road before reaching Alpine Station; once on the desert floor, he drove a road straight to Buck Horn Ranch and Desert Springs, hitting the old trail again at the mouth of Red Rock Canyon. Finished early in 1872, this trail is still marked as the Nadeau Road on the Pearblossom Highway.

But despite his efforts, Nadeau's teams encountered many fantastic obstacles on the roads to desert camps. Some of the worst were the steep grade of San Fernando Pass, south of the present Newhall; the deep sands of Soledad and Red Rock Canyons; the road passing Searles Lake, where the wagon that strayed one inch off the trail might sink axle-deep in mud; the Slate Range grade into Panamint Valley; the Yellow Grade into Cerro Gordo—according to tradition, "You had to be drunk to drive it"; and of course such harrowing climbs as the Sherwin Grade above

Bishop and the Conway Grade beyond Mono Lake. Over these spots the stage passengers got out and walked, and sometimes pushed. Today one marvels that a mule team, with three wagons and a ten-ton cargo, could conquer those barriers at all.

* * *

Another hazard on desert trails was the irrepressible highwayman. Through the middle 1870s no stage road on the Mojave escaped his attention. Normally Nadeau's teams were carrying a cargo hardly worth the trouble of a holdup—silver-lead ingots as heavy as a sack of potatoes, but worth no more than an ounce of gold. When a wagon broke down these were often tossed aside along the road, where they were perfectly safe until they were picked up by the next team.

But from some camps Nadeau hauled pure silver. At Panamint, Senator Bill Stewart of Nevada fired up his furnace in the late summer of 1875 and begin turning out silver pigs. On hand for the first shipment by Nadeau's teams were two desperadoes—John Small and John McDonald—who had sold Stewart one of his Panamint mines. But Stewart was ready for them. While they watched, his men poured off the first metal from the smelter—into large molds each accommodating four to five hundred pounds of silver. Outraged, the two bandits turned on the grinning senator. He was, they said, the meanest man in the Panamints.

"Do you think it's right to play that game on *us*," cried one, "—and after we sold you the mine, too. Why, we can't haul away one of those boulders."

"You can't expect *me* to be sorry for you, can you?" returned Stewart.

Exasperated, the outlaws fell to struggling with one of the ingots, but it wouldn't budge. A few minutes later they brought a husky pack mule, but when they tried to put one of the pigs on his back he kicked and jumped till they had to give up. After all, where could they cash in a 500-pound chunk of silver? Nadeau's wagons rolled safely across the Mojave with the silver cargo.

But despite such precautions, Nadeau's teamsters and his stations were still vulnerable. On February 25, 1874, two other desperadoes appeared out of Walker Pass and descended on the station at Coyote Holes. They were Tiburcio Vasquez, California's arch-bandit of the 1870s, and his cutthroat lieutenant, Cleovaro Chavez. In a twinkling they seized the station, which doubled as a stage stop and an outpost for Nadeau's teams. Holding the occupants prisoners, they robbed the upstage from San Francisco when it arrived. Among their victims was M. W. Belshaw of Cerro Gordo, who was sitting on the box beside the driver when Vasquez halted them at gunpoint.

The bandits had hardly finished robbing the stage passengers when two of Nadeau's teams pulled in from the south. Vasquez and Chavez relieved the teamsters of their coin, then spurred southward with the stage horses. Belshaw appropriated four of the freight mules for the stage harness, and the travelers moved on northward without pursuing the bandidos.

But once out of cover, Vasquez and Chavez held carnival on their way south. After crossing the Mojave desert they robbed another stage and another of Nadeau's teamsters in Soledad Canyon. For the next three months they lurked in Southern California, emerging once for another foray near El Monte in April.

It was not the bandit's first visit to Southern California. The two previous winters Vasquez had come south to hide from northern posses in the mountains around Soledad and Tejon Passes.

On one of these excursions, according to Remi Nadeau's niece, Mrs. Melvina Lott, Vasquez was lying alongside a desert road, badly wounded. It happened that Nadeau came along in a buggy, making his customary tour of his stations to pay his employees. Under the seat, mixed in with grocery bags for camouflage, were sacks of gold coin. But Vasquez was in no condition for robbery. Nadeau took him aboard, drove him to the next freight station, and ordered the keeper and his wife to nurse him back to health. Vasquez recovered and left the station swearing never to rob Nadeau's teams.

On at least two occasions, according to stories passed down in the family, Vasquez had opportunity to test his vow. In the narrow Beale Cut at the top of San Fernando Pass, he and his gang were waiting for a freight team climbing laboriously up the north grade. But when it hove into sight through the narrow slit, Vasquez recognized Nadeau's blue-painted wagons. Astride the near wheeler was Nadeau's eldest son, George, who was a partner in his freighting business. Vasquez called off his men and let the team pass.

At another time Nadeau was driving on a lonely road, his buggy loaded with payroll money. Around dusk he saw a band of horsemen approaching. Hoping to elude them he drove into a clump of trees. The riders came up and the leader—Vasquez—called him to come out. When he appeared and was recognized, the bandit let him go.

In still another instance, Vasquez is said to have been terrorizing a desert saloon. Flourishing his six-shooter, he swore to kill the next man who came through the swinging doors. Knowing that Nadeau was in town, someone went out to get him, since he was believed to be the only one who could handle Vasquez. When Nadeau entered the saloon Vasquez saw him and hesitated. The little Frenchman took in the situation, walked up to the bandit, slapped him on the back, gave him a cigar, and walked out with him arm-in-arm.

According to Nadeau's niece, he made a point not to turn informer on Vasquez. When his wife berated him for this, he replied:

"Freighting is my business, and as long as my freighters are not bothered by Vasquez, Vasquez is not bothered by Nadeau."

While this attitude might be typical of the Frenchman's businesslike attitude, the fact that Vasquez captured one of Nadeau's stations and robbed three of his teamsters only three months before he himself was captured would tend to discount the Nadeau-Vasquez legends.

In any case, Vasquez was captured near the present Hollywood in May 1874, and executed the following March in San Jose. A few days later his lieutenant, Cleovaro Chavez, invaded the Mojave Desert again. On the 24th he and his gang robbed the stage and freight station at Little Lake. For the next four days they rode south, robbing teamsters and travelers. While Chavez was finally killed in Arizona Territory in November 1875, two other imitators took the road and robbed the tollhouse and a stagecoach on the Yellow Grade below Cerro Gordo. At the end of April they captured one of Nadeau's outposts, Water Station, which was located seven miles north of Trona and is now known as The Tanks. A few weeks later one of them was killed on the South Fork of Kern River, and the other fled to Mexico.

* * *

In 1881 the Iron Horse was again crowding Nadeau's empire. Building south from the Central Pacific in Nevada, the Carson and Colorado narrow-gage drew off Nadeau's Bodie trade. He sent twenty-seven teams to Tombstone, Arizona Territory, where he hauled ore to the nearest point on the railroad. With the remaining eleven teams he withdrew from Bodie and operated from Mojave as far north as Bishop Creek for the rest of the year.

In January 1882, after the Carson and Colorado reached Belleville, Nevada, it took away the Owens Valley trade. Nadeau transferred his remaining teams to Tombstone, where he sold them all in February. Others had already been sold to the Pacific Coast Borax Company in Death Valley, and to his wagon boss, Austin Lott, who teamed in the early 1880s between Calico and Daggett on the Santa Fe Railroad.

After two-score years in western freighting, the old man saw his empire disintegrate. Victor in more than one competitive contest, he could not withstand the onslaughts of the Iron Horse.

Now sixty-two years old, the little Frenchman still had plenty of business energy. He immediately put the money from his freight business into a hotel. Built at the corner of First and Spring Streets, where the *Times* building now stands, it was opened in 1883 as the first four-story building in Los Angeles and the first with an elevator. Since the center of Los Angeles was still the first two blocks south of the Plaza, Nadeau's contemporaries said the hotel was too far out of town and called it "Nadeau's Folly." But through the 1880s and '90s the Nadeau was the reigning hostelry of the city. According to tradition, some of the celebrities who stayed there were Benjamin Harrison and Theodore Roosevelt; Mark Twain, Hamlin Garland, and Henry M. Stanley; John L. Sullivan and Jim Corbett; Edwin Booth, Sarah Bernhardt, Nellie Melba, Anna Held, Lillian Russell, Lotta Crabtree, Adelina Patti, Lily Langtry, and Helena Modjeska.

At the same time, Nadeau was plunging into other ventures. As early as the mid-1870s he bought extensive acreage in the present Beverly Hills, where he raised sheep. In 1877 he leased large tracts of land in the present Hollywood area and started planting several thousand acres of barley for his mule teams. Later he raised 30,000 acres of barley in the vicinity of Inglewood. Beginning in 1880, he founded the sugar beet industry in Southern California on his ranch in the Florence area south of Los Angeles, and also on a large tract in the Ballona District, near Playa del Rey. In 1882 he launched the largest vineyard on the Pacific Coast (3,600 acres) on his ranch in the Florence area.

But adversity dogged these enterprises. Drought struck his barley fields. When he imported machinery from France to process his sugar beets, it arrived in an unworkable condition. Insects attacked his vines, and later a flood washed out the winery and much of the vineyard. Nothing, except his hotel, succeeded like those mule teams.

On January 25, 1887, Remi Nadeau died at his home on the corner of Fifth and Olive. Pallbearers at his funeral included some of the noteworthy names of Los Angeles history—Harris Newmark, Robert M. Widney, J. S. Slauson, E. F. Spence, and the man who had lent him his original grubstake twenty-six years before, Prudent Beaudry.

When Nadeau died the Great Boom of the 1880s was well under way. With speculation in the air, he was planning other vast enterprises, despite his recent reverses. To raise capital he had mortgaged his hotel and most of his other properties. He left an estate valued at about one million dollars, but due to the mortgages and a contested will, little of it reached his survivors.

But other evidences remained to mark the way of a pioneer. In Los Angeles, Culver City, San Fernando, and Mojave, streets still bear the name of Nadeau. Near his old ranch south of Los Angeles, Nadeau Junction remains a station on the Santa Fe Railroad. On lonely desert roads, crumbling walls reveal the sites of his way stations. In silent towns, where the window panes are broken and the doors bang crazily in the wind, one can listen and with a little effort hear the faint jingle of team bells and the pop of the blacksnake. Through the sagebrush on Main Street swings a ragged line of twenty mules, coughing and snorting, their chain clanking and dragging in the dust. Behind them roll three blue-sided wagons, groaning with the silver cargo of another day.

WAR *on the* COLORADO RIVER

by John Upton Terrell

LATE IN 1921, a group of men met in a lodge just outside Santa Fe, New Mexico. They came from the seven western States containing the enormous basin of the Colorado River. The Federal Government also was represented by a brilliant engineer serving his first year as Secretary of Commerce, Herbert Hoover. The purpose of the meeting could be simply stated, but the problems which the men hoped to solve were composed of many technical mysteries and geographical complexities.

One-twelfth of the land area of the United States is drained by the Colorado River—parts of Wyoming, Colorado, Utah, New Mexico, California, Arizona and Nevada. Down from the mountainous backbone of the West, across vast plateaus of forest and desert, through the deepest canyons of the continent, it flows some 1,600 miles to its hot delta in the Gulf of California.

Compared to other major American rivers, the Colorado is not large. In a state of nature, however—as it still was in 1921—no river was more violent, more unpredictable, more subject to devastating drouths and floods. If its precious waters were ever to be beneficially used, it had to be tamed. Without adequate and dependable controls any development would be imperiled and, therefore, any financial investment would be insecure.

Obviously an interstate agreement was necessary even before plans for costly dams and diversion systems could be formulated. No specific project could be proposed until it was known how much water was available for it. Nor could any of the seven States fully utilize its share of the river until the size of that share had been determined; until its water rights had been legally established.

Hoover was named chairman of the conference, and thereafter in a series of meetings spread over eleven months the commissioners argued and frequently engaged in bitter wrangling. At last, on November 24, 1922, they affixed their signatures to a document designed to serve as the basic law of the river. They called it the Colorado River Compact.

It was an historic day, memorable in the annals of water and power development in the West. As the compact signers departed from Santa Fe they thought they had conceived a pact that would insure an enduring peace on the wild and mighty Colorado.

In reality, they had written the script for the largest, longest and costliest water and power war in history.

The Colorado River Compact divided the river into two parts, an upper and a lower basin, to each of which it apportioned specific amounts of water. It did not apportion water to the individual states. Each basin was expected to negotiate a separate agreement under which its share of the river would be divided among the states it contained.

Things didn't work out as planned. Not until 1949, more than a quarter of a century after the Compact was signed, were the States of the Upper Basin able to complete an understanding acceptable to all four of them.

The Lower Basin States of Arizona, California and Nevada have never been able to agree, and as this is written in 1964 the violent fight they have carried on for forty-two years may well continue for some time to come. Although a few phases of the controversy appear to be nearing final settlement, new conflicts have arisen that make improbable a legally binding armistice in the near future.

Soon after the 1922 Compact was signed, six of the States ratified it. Arizona was the lone holdout, its political leaders demanding assurances of a water supply that California and Nevada considered unfair and not in accord with the provisions of the Compact. By this action Arizona blocked peace on the Colorado just as that goal was in sight. Without ratification by all seven States and approval by the Congress the Compact could not become operative.

However, the six States which had accepted the Compact did not propose to be thwarted by the uncooperative Arizona Legislature. Machinery was set in motion to have the Compact given life as a six-state agreement. It took six years to overcome Arizona's disruptive tactics.

Victory was finally achieved by the passage in 1928 of the Boulder Canyon Project Act, which Arizona had opposed successfully through five sessions of Congress. The legislation authorized construction of the largest dam in the world in the Lower Basin of the Colorado River. Under the terms of the act, six of the basin States had to be parties to a Colorado River Compact, and California, the fastest growing State, was required to pass a special law setting a limit on the quantity of river water it might divert for its own benefit.

These requirements were quickly met. On June 25, 1929, President Herbert Hoover proclaimed the Boulder Canyon Project Act effective, and so, as a six-State agreement, the Colorado River Compact did become the basic law of the river.

In approving Boulder Dam (later called Hoover Dam) Congress had been cautious and practical. Before any money could be appropriated, it decreed, contracts for the power that would be generated had to be signed by the public agencies and utility companies which would use it. These contracts had to guarantee repayment to the U. S. Treasury of the entire cost of the great project, plus interest, within fifty years.

It was the job of Secretary of the Interior Ray Lyman Wilbur to allocate Hoover Dam power to the States and to sign contracts with the purchasers. He called meetings for that purpose. All interested parties responded, except Arizona. It refused to attend, even though eighteen per cent of Hoover Dam power was reserved for its use.

Wilbur was left with no alternative but to sign the necessary contracts without Arizona present. When that was accomplished Congress approved the first appropriation for the dam. It amounted to $10,660,000.

Arizona made an attempt to block the money in Congress, and filed an objection to the expenditure with the U.S. Comptroller General, but these moves were futile. Next, on October 13, 1930, Arizona filed suit in the U.S. Supreme Court against the Secretary of the Interior and the other six basin States to halt construction of the dam. It also asked the court to declare the Compact and the Boulder Canyon act unconstitutional.

In dismissing the Arizona suit, the court declared: (A) Authority to construct Hoover Dam was a valid exercise of Congressional power. (B) The Boulder Canyon Project Act did not abridge the water rights of Arizona. (C) There was no threat to Arizona by Secretary Wilbur or the other basin States.

Twice more Arizona appealed to the Supreme Court, and twice more its pleas were rejected.

Arizona's next step was to threaten the use of military force to halt the development of the river. By this time (1934-35) Parker Dam was under construction 155 miles downstream from Hoover Dam. It would create the reservoir, Lake Havasu, from which Colorado River water would begin its long journey across the desert of California through one of the world's longest aqueducts to Los Angeles, Pasadena, San Diego and other Southern California cities. Parker Dam was being built by the Federal Government, but the funds for it had been supplied by the Metropolitan Water District of Southern California.

Arizona's next step was to threaten the use of military force to stop work on the dam, and it was stopped by the builders to avoid possible bloodshed. Quickly the Federal Government went to the Supreme Court, asking for an injunction to halt Arizona's acts of violence. The court did not grant the injunction because the complaint of the Government failed to show that construction of the dam was authorized by statute. This oversight was quickly remedied by Congress. Work was resumed, and the dam was completed.

On literally scores of occasions, Nevada, California and Arizona negotiators had struggled to reach an agreement for the division of the water apportioned to the Lower Basin, but every meeting had resulted in complete failure. Meanwhile, California had signed contracts with the Federal Government which called for the delivery of 5,362,000 acre-feet of water from the lower river. (An acre-foot is the amount of water necessary to cover an acre of land with water one foot deep.)

Under the contracts this water was allocated in California as follows:

For lands, principally agricultural, in the Imperial and Coachella Valleys, in the Palo Verde District and the Yuma Project on the California side of the river, a total of 4,150,000 acre-feet.

For the Metropolitan Water District of Southern California, a total of 1,212,000 acre-feet.

Nevada and California had reached an accord, but three main issues kept California and Arizona far apart. They were not difficult to explain or to understand, but they appeared to be insoluble.

Issue No. 1: Under Article Three, Paragraph A, of the Colorado River Compact, the Lower Basin States were apportioned in perpetuity "the exclusive beneficial consumptive use" of 7,500,000 acre-feet of river water per year.

The Upper Basin States received a similar amount.

This was known as "Three A Water."

Article Three, Paragraph B, of the Compact said:

"In addition to the apportionment of Paragraph A, the Lower Basin is hereby given the right to increase its beneficial consumptive use of the Colorado River waters by one million acre-feet per annum."

This was known as "Three B Water."

It was this "Three B Water" that was in controversy.

A million acre-feet is a great deal of water. It is enough for the irrigation of about a quarter of a million acres of arid land, or it would supply all the needs of about five million city dwellers.

The Limitation Act which California was obligated to adopt under the six-State Compact said:

"California agrees to limit its use of Colorado River water to 4,400,000 acre-feet of the waters apportioned to the Lower Basin by Paragraph A, plus not more than one-half of any excess or surplus waters . . . ."

From the beginning, California had maintained that the term "excess or surplus" included all "Three B Water."

The question to be settled, therefore, was: Does California share equally in the million acre-feet of "Three B Water?" California said *yes*. Arizona said *no*.

Issue No. 2: In a state of nature, the Gila River in Arizona was a "wasting" tributary of the Colorado. Especially in the last one hundred miles before it joined the main Colorado its bed was wide, sandy, flat, and subject to the intense heat of the desert.

The Bureau of Reclamation estimated that in a state of nature the Gila had emptied approximately 1,100,000 acre-feet of water into the main stream each year a short distance above the Mexican border. After the development of central Arizona, water from the Gila was used almost entirely in the Phoenix area. There about 2,300,000 acre-feet were taken from it each year, and used up—beneficially consumed.

The difference between the two figures, about 1,200,000 acre-feet, was, before the development of central Arizona, lost by evaporation, deep seepage and other causes, as the Gila flowed in its hot bed toward its junction with the Colorado.

The words "beneficial consumptive use," as they were used in the Compact, were important in this phase of the controversy. The Compact specifically apportioned water for "exclusive beneficial consumptive use."

Arizona contended that it should be charged for 1,100,000 acre-feet of Gila water, the amount which the Reclamation Bureau estimated had emptied into the Colorado from the Gila before the coming of man.

California contended that Arizona took, used and "beneficially consumed" 2,300,000 acre-feet of Gila water, and should be charged with using that amount. California did not question Arizona's right to use this water.

Thus, the second question to be answered was: Where and how must Arizona measure the amount of water it took from the Gila?

California maintained that this water should be measured where it was actually used. Arizona maintained it should be measured at the confluence of the Gila and the Colorado.

But the Gila did not empty into the Colorado as it did in prehistoric times. The Gila was all used in central Arizona.

Issue No. 3: Hoover Dam created Lake Mead, then the largest man-made body of water on earth.

There were immense evaporation losses in Lake Mead, as there were in any reservoir of the kind. Arizona contended that California was limited to the use of 4,400,000 acre-feet of water, regardless of its contracts with the Federal Government for 5,362,000 acre-feet, and that the evaporation losses at Lake Mead must be deducted from that 4,400,000 acre-feet.

It was California's position that the 4,400,000 acre-feet was a *net* quantity.

This was the question to be answered: Was the amount of "Three A Water" to which California was entitled a *net* quantity, or was it subject to reduction by reason of evaporation and other losses in Lake Mead and other reservoirs?

Through the years, while these major problems prevented the Lower Basin States from reaching an amicable agreement, development of the lower Colorado, nevertheless, went steadily forward. Hoover, Davis, Parker, Palo Verde and Imperial Dams controlled the floods, generated power, stored water for times of drouth, and diverted it to produce rich crops on hundreds of thousands of acres. The great All American Canal carried water to the Imperial and Coachella Valleys. The Colorado River Aqueduct took it over mountains and deserts to the coastal plain of Southern California.

Into the Southwest in these years poured an ever-increasing flood of people, forming the greatest migration in the world's history. Industry boomed, and sprawling plants rose where only orange trees, lush meadows and cactus-covered mesas had existed. The taxpayers of Southern California had invested more than half a billion dollars in projects to bring Colorado River water and power to their homes, farms, offices and shops. Moreover, installment payments with interest due were being made on schedule, and in some cases were paid ahead of time.

After years of fighting the 1922 Compact and forcing the other basin States to negotiate a six-State Compact, Arizona had a change of heart. In 1944 it decided that it would, after all, become a party to a seven-State Compact, an instrument that did not exist. The Arizona Legislature purported to ratify the original Compact.

Not a few distinguished lawyers held the opinion that the action was not legal. The Six-State Compact, which Congress had approved, and which was the basic law of the river then in effect, was a contract. Arizona was not a party to it, and they felt that Arizona could not be a party to it under any interpretation of laws governing contracts. The question has never been resolved to the satisfaction of all Compact signatories.

Arizona had a good reason for its belated attempt to become a member of the Compact. Plans were being drawn for the immense Central Arizona Project, which would require an enormous amount of Colorado River water. Now Arizona feared that its continued rejection of the Compact might militate against its demand for that water.

The situation was pointed up by the Bureau of Reclamation officials in several statements which stressed the need for settlement of the old Lower Basin controversy. Although the Bureau wanted to build the Central Arizona Project, it admitted that assurance of a water supply for it was a matter yet to be determined. Also, the Bureau declared that its plans for the project were being drawn on the assumption that Arizona's claims were correct. If the position of California was upheld, either by the Congress or a judicial decision, there would be no water supply for the Arizona project.

In 1946, the Reclamation Bureau issued a comprehensive study on potential developments in the Colorado River Basin. In this book the States again were urged to agree on their respective water rights. Governor Earl Warren of California, acting in accordance with this recommendation, wrote to Governors Vail Pittman of Nevada and Sidney P. Osborn of Arizona suggesting that they meet and endeavor to arrange for negotiation of a Lower Basin Compact or, failing that, agree either to arbitration of the differences or to take them before the Federal Court for legal adjudication.

Pittman was agreeable to the proposal, but Osborn replied that since Arizona's position was right there was nothing more to be done.

In 1947 the Central Arizona Project bill was introduced in Congress. California viewed it as an unprecedented menace, and prepared to wage an unrelenting fight against its passage. Nevada took a similar position.

The bill called for construction of eight dams. One of them, to rise in Bridge Canyon on the Colorado, would be nearly 700 feet in height. The other seven would be built in the project area. Bridge Canyon Dam would produce a large amount of power, and a third of it would be given free to Arizona to operate a gigantic pump lift. The pump lift would raise water out of Lake Havasu a thousand feet nearly straight up, from which point it would flow by gravity in an aqueduct more than 240 miles to the project lands. The other two-thirds of Bridge Canyon power would be sold to Southern California consumers. Ironically, they would not only have their water supply imperiled by the project but they would help to pay for it.

The estimated cost of the project was $738.4 millions, but that figure did not include necessary upstream dams and works without which Bridge Canyon Dam reservoir would fill with silt and be useless as a power producer in twenty-five years. The cost of these additional works was variously estimated between $350 and $450 millions. Thus, the total cost of the project would have been well in excess of $1 billion. Arizona said nothing about that in its bill.

Simple arithmetic demonstrated that if Arizona was allowed to divert more than a million acre-feet from the river for the project there would not be enough water remaining to serve the other Lower Basin projects for which rights had been long established, and in which enormous investments of public money had been made.

Besides the water rights question, California and Nevada had another strong argument against the project, one that attracted attention both in Congress and throughout the Nation. It involved economics that anyone could understand.

Figures in the Reclamation Bureau's plans showed that the farmers who would benefit from the project could not possibly pay more than an infinitesimal fraction of its cost. Inasmuch as Federal money was to be loaned to build it, this meant that the taxpayers of the Nation would have to pick up the immense bill. Moreover, the Bureau's figures showed that the persons who would derive the most benefits were some four hundred large landowners who owned fifty-five per cent of the project lands.

California and Nevada supported their contention that Arizona did not own the water needed for the project by pointing out that no agreement existed for a division of the Lower Basin's share of the river. The issues which had been in controversy since 1923 remained unresolved, and Arizona had refused to enter into further negotiations on them. Arizona was arbitrarily claiming it was entitled to the water, but it had no legal grounds on which to base such a claim.

Now California and Nevada sought to take the Colorado River controversy into the U.S. Supreme Court for final adjudication. Because of its great investments in projects on the river, the United States Government was an indispensable party to any litigation of this nature. It could be made a party only with the permission of the Congress. To obtain this permission, the four Senators and thirty-one Congressmen of California and Nevada introduced joint resolutions.

Arizona vigorously fought the Supreme Court resolutions. California and Nevada stood as firmly against the Central Arizona Project. For six years, through the 80th, 81st, and 82nd Congresses, the battle raged.

The most powerful man in the Senate was Arizona's Senator Carl Hayden. The Senate Majority Leader was Arizona's Senator Ernest W. McFarland. By logrolling, these two influential men were able to get the Senate to pass the Arizona project bill. Getting it through the House of Representatives was another matter. There Arizona had neither numerical nor political strength. California alone had thirty Congressmen, and they were united against the project. If they were unable to get the House to approve the Supreme Court resolutions, such influential members of the California delegation as Harry R. Sheppard, Clair Engle, Carl Hinshaw, Norris Poulson, Chet Holifield, Gordon McDonough and Cecil King were able to rally enough supporters to block the Arizona project.

The climax of the bitter battle came when the House Interior Committee announced that it would give no further consideration to the Central Arizona Project until the Lower Basin rights controversy had been settled. In other words, the project would be placed in legislative moth balls until there was a legal determination that water was available for it.

This action by the House committee killed Arizona's last hope of obtaining either a political or a legislative settlement of the water rights problem. Faced with this barrier, Arizona suddenly did what California and Nevada had long attempted to do.

On August 13, 1952, Arizona filed an original suit against California in the U.S. Supreme Court. It charged that California was using in excess of the amount of Colorado River Water to which California was legally entitled, "to the injury and damage of Arizona."

The court issued a show cause order, and California responded that it welcomed the suit. After three decades of fighting, the Arizona-California conflict at last was in a position to be adjudicated by the highest court of the land.

Ten more years passed during which there were long hearings before a Master and several sessions before the Justices themselves. When, in 1963, the court made its finding, the decision was not favorable to California. The best that California could hope for were the 4.4 million acre-feet of water it owned under the provisions of the Limitation Act, which the California Legislature had enacted so the six-State Compact could become effective and Hoover Dam could be built.

But the war for the Colorado is far from concluded. The decision of the Supreme Court brought only one phase of it to an end. A new *casus belli* has arisen. The Interior Department's name for it is "A Water Plan for the Southwest." Once more the legislative trumpets are calling the water and power armies to battle on Capitol Hill.

REFERENCES

Hearings, House Subcommittee on Irrigation and Reclamation, Feb., 1947, March, 1949, February, 1951.

Hearings, Senate Committee on Public Lands, June, 1947, March, 1949.

Hearings, Subcommittee Number 4 of House Judiciary Committee, May, 1948, March, 1949.

House Document 136, 81st Congress, 1st Session, 1949.

Senate Report No. 832, 81st Congress, 1st Session, 1949.

House Serial No. 37, Committee on Public Lands, 1950.

Booklet "The Nation's Most Fantastic Project," Colorado River Association, Los Angeles, 1951.

U.S. Geological Survey, "Water Supply of Central Arizona Area," Washington, D.C., August, 1951.

U.S. Supreme Court, Arizona vs. California, August 13, 1952.

THE MYSTERY *of* DEATH VALLEY'S LOST WAGON TRAIN

by E. I. Edwards

TO MY KNOWLEDGE, no definitive account of Death Valley's lost wagon train has ever been written; yet any serious approach to this desert's fascinating history cannot entirely escape consideration of it. The possibility of the one-time existence of a lost wagon train with its attendant horrors of suffering and death should not be shrugged off as mere sensational nonsense; neither should it merit credibility solely on the basis of its emotional appeal. After being ignored for well over a hundred years it is time the numerous references to abandoned wagon trains and bleached human bones receive intelligent evaluation, either to establish their absolute truth or to expose their inherent error. This paper is a documented study written in the hope of accomplishing that purpose. In its preparation some twenty-five early accounts have been selected and examined from among a hundred or more consulted.

Oddly enough, few episodes of comparable historic stature have been so extensively chronicled by such a large number of actual participants as has the now-famous Death Valley saga of 1849-50.[1] Rarely do we find such pronounced unanimity as is demonstrated by these source writers in their relation of what actually occurred. The absorbing details of that memorable Christmas week of 1849, and the month that followed, have been spelled out with dramatic clarity. The story is written for all to read and understand. Moreover the entire episode may be brought into sharp chronological focus as the result of contemporaneous reference to it in the writings of those who were in no way involved in the ill-fated venture.

Curiously, and despite this formidable array of factual data, all manner of bizarre and fantastic articles have been perpetrated upon a receptive public concerning mysterious ghost caravans whose members perished from heat and thirst, leaving their bones to bleach upon the hot desert sands of a desolate valley called Death.

[1]Among the published accounts of members of the original 1849 party of Death Valley emigrants, we note the following writers: Brier, Mrs. J. W. (1898; 1913); Brier, J. W. Jr. (1903); John M. Colton (1903); Asa Haynes (1938); W. L. Manly (various newspaper articles; book in 1894); Louis Nusbaumer (1944); John Rogers (1894); Thos. Shannon (1903); L. Dow Stephens (1916); Jacob Y. Stover (1937); Sheldon Young (1942). (Supplied dates refer to the publication, and not the writing, of the item.)

The authentic account of Death Valley's early history is quickly told. A group of emigrants—perhaps a hundred or more—defected from a slow-moving wagon train bound for San Bernardino from Salt Lake City. They headed west over unknown country, hoping to make their way to the California gold fields by a more direct route. After weeks of tortuous travel, they suddenly found themselves in a deep and narrow desert valley. Rising precipitously from its floor, and forming its western boundary, loomed an imposing mountain range.[2] This occasioned no special concern to the majority of those who were traveling on foot; most of them crossed directly over the valley, climbed the mountain barrier, and continued on their way. They experienced no unusual hardship nor suffering in the valley itself.

A few of the emigrants had wagons; and for them the mountains posed a very real problem. The wagons could not leave the valley; they were inescapably trapped and would have to be abandoned. It was these abandoned wagons that later gave origin and impetus to many of the fictive tales regarding lost wagon trains and bleaching human bones.

The wagons in this party of 1849 emigrants fell roughly into two divisions. Some eight or ten belonged to a group of young fellows who styled themselves Jayhawkers. Another group, consisting—in part—of three families, had seven wagons. The Jayhawkers descended into the valley through what is now known as Furnace Creek Wash. They turned north and made camp by a water hole presently referred to as McLean's Spring, or Jayhawker Well. Recognizing the futility of any attempt to haul their wagons over the steep mountain barrier, they decided to rest for a week (it was Christmas week of 1849) and dry the meat of their weaker oxen over fires kindled from the wood in their wagons. Having accomplished this, and driving the remaining oxen before them, they crossed the valley on foot, climbed over the mountains, and eventually arrived at their destination. Four reported deaths occurred among those who more or less regularly accompanied the Jayhawkers, and there were other fatalities in some of the splinter groups; but all these deaths took place on the intervening mountains and deserts be-

[2]The Panamints.

tween Los Angeles and the narrow valley where they had abandoned their wagons. Only one death is reported to have occurred in Death Valley itself.

The other seven wagons turned south after descending Furnace Creek Wash and made camp in the vicinity of what we now know as the Bennett's Wells-Tule Spring area. As an alternative to an immediate abandonment of their wagons and possessions, it was decided to remain in camp for a few days while two of their number went forward on foot in an effort to scout a feasible wagon route out of the valley. The saga of these two courageous young men—William Lewis Manly and John Rogers—is heroic and inspiring. Against almost insurmountable difficulties they crossed the unknown desert country into Los Angeles. Then, with commendable chivalry, they *returned* over the vast, threatening deserts and mountain ranges to rescue the men, women, and little children helplessly awaiting their arrival at the lonely water hole in that far-away desolate valley.

By the time Manly and Rogers returned, some four weeks following their departure from camp, three of the wagons had left the water hole. (It was later learned that one—perhaps two—of these had succeeded in working its way south and out of the valley to ultimate safety.)[3] There appeared no acceptable alternative but to abandon the four remaining wagons, carry out the children on ox back, and escape on foot across the intervening mountains and deserts to Los Angeles.

This is the story. And from it emerge certain facts:

1. Among all the several groups who comprised the historic Death Valley party of 1849, fourteen men are said to have died of fatigue or hunger or thirst.[4] However, and this is significant, with only *one known exception* these deaths occurred on the slopes of the Panamint and Slate ranges or on the Mojave desert. *Only one individual is reported to have died in Death Valley.* This was the elderly "Captain" Culverwell; and his death cannot truly be attributed to the desert. Its proximate cause was his own indiscretion in walking out from camp, sick and alone, finally to be overcome by exhaustion or—conceivably—by heart failure.

[3]The wagon of Schlagel and Nusbaumer; one, and perhaps two, wagons of Henry Wade and possibly the Earharts.

[4]Fish, Robinson, Isham, an unknown man whose skeleton was later found by the Indians with a bullet hole in his skull, nine members of the so-called Pinney-Savage group, and Captain Culverwell whose death occurred on the floor of Death Valley.

2. No one was "trapped" in this primitive wilderness. Even Manly's party, had they chosen, could have passed directly across it; did, in fact, prevail against it and ascend its western barrier. *All* of them escaped—men, women, children, oxen and dog.[5] All that remained "trapped" in Death Valley were perhaps a dozen wagons—the four abandoned intact (except for their canvas tops) by the Bennett and Arcane families in the region of the present Bennett's Wells-Tule Spring area, and the running gears of the wagons belonging to the Jayhawkers that were abandoned at a site presently known as McLean's Spring. As we know now, had these wagons and the wagons belonging to Bennett and Arcane followed a southerly route they might have escaped without sacrifice of oxen or the loss of a single wagon.

3. It must be conceded that Death Valley proved a most considerate host to its first white visitors. It was kind, or *tried* to be kind, to all of them. It provided beautiful desert weather for their pleasure. It supplied all the water they and their animals could drink. It made available, even though its offerings were not accepted, sufficient food to sustain them. It was not directly responsible for the death of a single individual, although one group of men, women and little children abided there for five long weeks.[6]

This is the story as revealed by the source accounts of actual participants. This is not hearsay evidence. This is not something conceived in the mind of an accomplished writer and brilliantly dramatized for the entertainment of his readers. It is a story told by ordinary men and women, none of them possessing scholarly attainments. The story of Death Valley's first emigrant party is a story builded upon unembellished and unequivocal fact.

Where, then, do we find inception of the portentous name that presently identifies this desert region? Are the remains of a dozen abandoned wagons and the death of one individual sufficient to fasten upon this kindly valley the melancholy name of "Death"?

In his book—*Death Valley In '49*—published in 1894 when the author was well advanced in years, Manly credits his own group (the Bennett-Arcane families) with naming the place. He tells us they had just climbed out of the desert into the mountains; and, before starting on their second day's trek, they turned for a farewell look at the place they had called home for five dreadful weeks. Then someone, probably Manly himself, remarked "Goodbye, Death Valley."

[5]Mr. Bennett's dog "Cuff," the only dog reported among all the emigrant parties.

[6]The families of Bennett and Arcane.

DEATH VALLEY

IN '49.

IMPORTANT CHAPTER OF

California Pioneer History.

—THE—

AUTOBIOGRAPHY OF A PIONEER, DETAILING HIS LIFE FROM A HUMBLE HOME IN THE GREEN MOUNTAINS TO THE GOLD MINES OF CALIFORNIA; AND PARTICULARLY RECITING THE SUFFERINGS OF THE BAND OF MEN, WOMEN AND CHILDREN WHO GAVE "DEATH VALLEY" ITS NAME.

BY WILLIAM LEWIS MANLY.

SAN JOSE, CAL.:
THE PACIFIC TREE AND VINE CO.
1894.

Title page from William Lewis Manly's Death Valley in '49.

Later, the honor of bestowing the name "Death Valley" was claimed in turn by—or for—the Jayhawkers and the Brier family.[7] The question of *who* named Death Valley is not so important as to know how it was possible for the name, once bestowed, to survive. The appellation—"Death Valley"—was a common one; at one time or another it was applied to just about every difficult desert area in the west. In fact, several of the Death Valley emigrants used this sinister designation to identify a desert one hundred miles east of the present Death Valley; and they again made use of it in referring to the Searles Lake country where, incidentally, they really suffered and really faced death. Why, then, did the name disappear from these others and continue to survive for the one desert area that perhaps least deserved it?

Of some interest in this connection is the fact that our first known appearance of the name Death Valley in print occurred over eleven years *after* Manly claims to have originated it. On April 12, 1861, we find mention of the name in an article published by a San Francisco newspaper—the *Alta California.* We note it again, on the following day, this time in the newspaper—the *Visalia Delta.* The usage in both instances was employed by the Boundary Survey group who entered the valley in the year 1861. Also, in a series of articles, one bearing the preparation date of February 24, 1861 and others listing preparation dates in March of the same year, the Boundary Survey writer makes frequent use of the name; but these articles did not appear in print until July 9, 1861, when they were published by the Sacramento *Daily Union.* In the year 1863 what is perhaps the first *book* mention of the name occurs in Hittel's *Resources of California.*

As prospectors and exploratory groups began entering the valley during the two decades following 1849, these weird tales of a lost wagon train—to which reference has been made—began coming out of the sand and creosote wastes of the Mojave. Reports were first circulated by word of mouth, later by printed accounts appearing in newspapers and books. Sensational tales they were, most of them having to do with a mysterious Ghost Train that entered Death Valley in mid-summer of 1850, only a few months

[7]For a detailed study of the naming of Death Valley see the author's *The Mystery Of Death Valley: How It Was Named.* (The June, 1962 issue of *The Branding Iron,* No. 61; published by the Los Angeles Corral of the *Westerners.*)

following the crossing of the original party. Although differing slightly in their non-essentials, the basic core structure of these elaborate yarns followed a more or less constant pattern that developed from the common thesis of a legendary wagon train whose every man, woman, child and beast perished from heat and thirst. Now and then some more imaginative narrator would inject the "Lone Survivor" theme. Others would add a human interest touch by creating a heroine role or by featuring the dramatic situation of wagons being lowered by ropes and chains over the rugged cliffs of the Funerals.[8] Invariably, in recounting the horrors of this catastrophic debacle, reference would be made to the lurid situation of human bones being left to bleach upon the burning desert sands. Nearly all these vague references to a lost wagon train managed to extract some little fact or incident from the true wagon train episode of 1849. With few exceptions the accounts readily acknowledged that the origin of the train was unknown, the personnel was unknown, and the destination was unknown.

That which contributed most significantly to the surge of lost wagon literature, and to the continuing credence accorded it, was the almost total reluctance on the part of the survivors in the original party to attempt refutation of it. Perhaps they preferred not to. There is reason to believe that some of them gave at least tacit support to these spectacular tales of a lost wagon train. The more terrifying the stories, the more pronounced became the inference of heroism on the part of the participants in the *original* wagon train. The fact that they were the first to pass through this dreadful region gave them something to talk about; something that would impel people to pause and listen to whatever they chose to say. A few, not so modest as William Lewis Manly, made the most of this unique opportunity to glamorize and glorify themselves. This tendency became all the more noticeable when these fugitive experiences, *as they related them*, were reduced to writing by such prominent authors as J. Ross Browne, Randolph Spears, Henry Hanks, and others, long before Manly got around to writing his epic account of what *actually* occurred.

[8]Although there was necessity for wagons being lowered by ropes and chains in certain areas as, for instance, at Mt. Misery, there is no reputable evidence that this practice was resorted to in bringing the wagons into Death Valley.

It was not until 1894, or forty-five years after the original crossing, that William Lewis Manly's *Death Valley in '49* was published. His was the first responsible relation of the basic story of the now-famous 1849 experience. This unfortunate delay in revealing the true facts permitted the lurid Ghost Train fiction to take firm root and capture the imagination of an eager and receptive audience.

Even after the publication of the truth, many refused to accept it. Many still refuse to accept it. They find it more pleasant and exciting to abide by the image already created in the public mind.

* * *

Henry G. Hanks' *Third Annual Report of the State Mineralogist* (1883) while chronologically not the earliest book account of Death Valley, is of considerable significance with respect to our study of the lost wagon train theory. Although denied the circulation normally enjoyed by most *non*-scientific publications, the Hanks' *Report* is included among the more important contributions to Death Valley literature.

Hanks' interest, in his *Report*, relates to borax; not to the desert's historical lore. He makes it clear that he knows little or nothing of Death Valley's history, and that he cares even less about it. There is no mention of a lost wagon train; and this despite the fact that he was present in Death Valley at a time when evidence of such a train, had there been one, might still have been discernible. Hanks was writing some eleven or twelve years *prior* to the Manly account which, it will be recalled, gave the first authentic report of what had actually occurred in Death Valley in 1849-50. Hanks writes that he *heard*, but does not *believe*, that a fellow by the name of Bennett discovered gold. He also has something to say of the origin of the elusive Lost Gunsight mine rumor.[9]

[9]One of the fables of the Lost Gunsight (and there are many available) tells of a member of the authentic party of 1849 accidentally falling, while climbing in the Panamints, and breaking the sight on his gun. He picked up a rock, nonchalantly carved a gunsight out of it, and proceeded on his way. Upon arriving in Los Angeles he found his gunsight to be of pure silver. Various members of the emigrant party have at one time or another been extended credit for this extraordinary discovery. True or false, the legend of the Lost Gunsight has lured—and continues to lure—considerable numbers into Death Valley in a fruitless search for it.

That which makes the Hanks' *Report* of primary importance to our determination of the existence or non-existence of a lost wagon train is the fact that he knew and interviewed men who had led exploring parties into Death Valley several years earlier. He candidly informs that he compiled his historical material on Death Valley from the notes furnished him by these early explorers.[10]

Here, as we shall presently see, are data of superlative value. Before examining them in detail, it is essential that we understand their peculiar impact upon the lost wagon train theory.

It must be remembered that the discovery of Death Valley by the 1849 gold seekers was not by design. It was both unpremeditated and accidental. These emigrants *blundered* into this desert valley; hadn't the faintest idea they were discovering anything, and could not have cared less even had they known. Their only concern, and it was an urgent one, was to get out and away from this dreadful wagon-trap at the earliest possible opportunity.

Within a very few years after the Forty-niners passed through, however, organized parties went into the region for the express purpose of systematically exploring not only the valley but its contiguous area. These groups were not under compulsion to get out of the valley; they were there to search for gold, or to conduct surveys, or to explore scientifically this segment of desert.

It is to be assumed, therefore, that these several parties investigated every accessible part of the valley. Had there been the slightest evidence of a lost wagon train the men in these early exploring parties would have observed and reported it. Thus it becomes patent that the findings of these separate groups are likely to confirm or deny the possibility of a lost wagon train having entered the valley prior to 1861. Their failure to observe and report such evidence would tend to point up the fallacy of such a contention.

One of these early groups is known as the Second Darwin French Expedition; and these men entered Death Valley in 1860, only ten years later than the Forty-niners. Hanks tells us they crossed

[10]Hanks writes that his historical references were "compiled from notes furnished by Dr. S. G. George, who visited the valley in 1860, William T. Henderson, 1860, Hugh McCormack, 1861, R. R. Hawkins, 1882, I. Daunet, 1883, and others."

". . . the head of Panamint Valley, thence by a rocky pass to a camp in Death Valley, *where the emigrants left their wagons,** twenty-five miles a little west of north from Furnace Creek."

We find, in this reference to the French Expedition, not the slightest allusion to a lost wagon train, nor to human bones bleaching in the heat of a desert sun. On the contrary, we can make immediate identification of the camp "where the *emigrants* left their wagons." Ostensibly, the reference is to the camp of the Jayhawkers, north of Furnace Creek, where they abandoned the running gears of their wagons at a place known today as McLean's Spring.

The second of these early groups mentioned by Hanks is the Dr. George Expedition who also came into the valley in 1860, entering during the month of October. This group, like the French Expedition, camped at the McLean's Spring site. Says Hanks:

"They followed the same general route of the French party, remained at the Emigrant Camp for some time, prospecting the hills in every direction . . . Although 10 years had passed, the tracks of men, women and children were distinctly seen, as fresh as if newly made; the irons of the wagons were where they had been left. The remains of ox yokes were seen, which had been laid out for use on the following day, with the chains extended on the ground in front of each wagon, showing the number of oxen to each, and traces of the old camp fires were plainly seen. While prospecting the hills, Dr. George and Mr. Thayer found the bones of white men within 300 yards of a spring of good water, believed to be those of the emigrant party."

The Dr. George report introduces perhaps the most favorable evidence of a Ghost Train available in the reports of the several exploring parties entering Death Valley during the decade immediately following the crossing of the original parties. Even so, we cannot equate the findings of this group with the published accounts of Death Valley's purported lost wagon train.

The visible tracks of women and children in the camp of the Jayhawkers are readily explained. One of the many component groups in the original emigrant party was the Brier family, consisting of the Rev. Brier, his wife and their three children. Manly,

**Editor's note:* Here and in other extracts the italics are the author's.

in writing of the Jayhawkers at their wagon-burning camp at McLean's Spring, states:

"The Jayhawkers were still making their preparations when . . . Rev. J. W. Brier and family came up to their camp."

And Brier, in one of his letters, writes:

"My family now fell in with the Jayhawks. We traveled with them a part of the time and generally camped with them on the same ground but were no part of their Company."

The reference to the finding of bones "while prospecting in the hills," is not conclusive, although it is our first mention of such a discovery in this general area. Mr. Hanks does not inform us as to the *number* of skeletons found; neither does he enlighten us as to just how they determined these were "the bones of white men." The words "prospecting in the hills" serve only to remove us from the Death Valley locale. Unfortunately, they do not pinpoint nor even approximate the distance from the Valley; neither do they indicate the general direction of the prospected area. The bones could have been those of some unnamed prospector or desert tramp; may perhaps have been those of the nine members of the Pinney-Savage group who, in 1849 or 1850, met death somewhere in the mountains west of Death Valley. (See reference to this group in the section on Alexander Majors' book.)

The next exploring group of record is the Hugh McCormack Party who entered the valley in March of 1861. They saw the wagons of the emigrants; and it would appear they, too, saw the wagons abandoned by the Jayhawkers at McLean's Spring. Says Hanks:

"He [McCormack] discovered and named McCormack's Wells, which may be found on some of the old maps [in the McLean's Spring area]. Six miles south of these wells he met with a spring that emitted sulphuretted gas. Here the old wagons of the emigrants were found. At Mesquite Springs he saw the shallow grave of a person supposed to be one of the emigrants, probably a woman, as a portion of a calico dress was found with the bones, left exposed by the drifting of the desert sands."

This is our only functional reference to this woman.[11] For that matter it is our sole reference to the body of anyone in the valley

[11]Reference is made to "bones in calico dresses" in the discussion of the Captain Colton *Interview* of February 4, 1903.

proper, among all these early parties, except—of course—the body of Captain Culverwell, the only one in the entire personnel of the original groups of forty-niners whose death is reported to have occurred in Death Valley. McCormack hazards the guess it was a woman because he saw a portion of a calico dress with the bones. A possible explanation is that the skeleton was that of an Indian who may have appropriated one of the brightly colored calico garments discarded by the Jayhawkers, or perhaps by the Briers. A possibility surely; but not a fortified conclusion. All we know for sure is that none of the original emigrant party is reported to have died in the Jayhawker camp at McLean's Spring.

* * *

The U.S. Boundary Commission Survey Group of 1861, while not included by Hanks in his early historical review, shares kindred importance with those of the French, George and McCormack groups. Here again we find a specially organized body of men entering Death Valley for scientific investigational purposes within less than a dozen years following the authentic, original party. The Boundary Survey Group consisted of fourteen men and three camels—the first and only camels known to have crossed Death Valley. Articles written by members of the Boundary Survey were published in issues of the 1861 Sacramento *Daily Union.*[12]

The Border Survey is perhaps best remembered for two reasons: they brought camels into this desert; they supplied us with the first known *printed* mention of the name Death Valley.

The men of the Survey explored portions of the Valley quite thoroughly—perhaps more thoroughly than any of the other early groups. Their entrance into the valley, as pointed out, was less than twelve years following that of the original party. During this interim the entire region had remained essentially undisturbed. Old tracks were still visible, discarded items were quite largely intact. Few people had passed through, other than the

[12]Printed references to this group may be found in the San Francisco *Alta California* for April 12, 1861; the Visalia *Delta* for April 13, 1861; and the Sacramento *Daily Union* for June 25 and 29, July 9, 11, 13, 31, August 7 and 10, 1861; and in Dr. Arthur Woodward's capable study—*Camels and Surveyors in Death Valley* (Publication No. 7, Death Valley '49ers, Inc., published at Palm Desert, California, by Desert Printers, Inc.).

exploring parties mentioned; and perhaps there were occasional unrecorded visits of itinerant prospectors. Beyond any doubt, the findings of the Boundary Survey Group have vital bearing upon our study of the possible existence of a lost wagon train.

In all probability their first camp was at the site of the Bennett-Arcane encampment in the Bennett's Wells-Tule Spring area where the four wagons were abandoned:

"We observe the faint track of the emigrant wagons of '49 . . . and this morning we came to a spot where they had camped. . . . It was strewn with the relics of their wagons—the spokes, tires and hubs of the wheels, and the iron of the running gear, chain, broken pots and other remains of camp equipment marking the abandonment and destruction of part of the train."

Exploring northward, they came upon the remains of the Jayhawker wagons at the McLean's Spring campsite; and here they saw the bones of the weaker cattle the Jayhawkers had slaughtered:

"Here again we find the traces of cattle in plenty, and the less perishable parts of their wagons [it will be recalled the Jayhawkers had burned the wood in their wagons], trace chains, broken pots, etc. It was here, *it is said*, that they lost some of their companions by death, and nearly all their stock, and all their remaining wagons left behind."

The most exacting scrutiny of this report will yield no gruesome evidence of human bones strewn over the desert sands. The words "it is said" are used by the writer to qualify his conjecture of human death. In the absence of a factual account of what truly occurred (Manly's book was still some thirty-three years in the future), it is plausible to suppose that anyone coming suddenly upon these abandoned wagons and quantities of cattle bones would immediately surmize that tragedy of great magnitude had once been enacted here.

Of one fact we may be reasonably sure. Had there been even marginal evidence of a lost wagon disaster the Boundary Survey would have discovered and recorded it.

Because the first known printed application of the name Death Valley is traceable to the Boundary Survey writers, most authorities are willing to concede them the honor of originating the name. This assumption is open to doubt. The very words of the

Boundary Survey people negate it. In their letter of March 24, 1861, they write:

> "Two or three miles from camp we crossed the faint trail of some emigrant wagons driving to the southwest, made in the year 1849 by a party on their way to California, who separated on the Salt Lake Road from a very large train coming that route, and attempted to get in this way near the parallel of 36. They drove through the pass in the Amargosa Mountains . . . and down Furnace Creek *into Death Valley*, where they lost their animals and several of the company from exhaustion, *from which incident the valley derives its name.* Here leaving their wagons, they rambled among the mountains of this desolate and terrible country for several weeks, finally straggling into the settlements in the most miserable plight."

Thus it appears logical to assume this desert had already received—and was generally known by—the name Death Valley for some time before the arrival of the Boundary Survey party in 1861. Incidentally, these men have supplied, in this letter, one of the most nearly accurate summations of Death Valley's early history to appear prior to the publication of William Lewis Manly's book.

This letter of March 24 removes any doubt to whom the Boundary Survey writer referred whenever he spoke of the "emigrants" and the "emigrant wagons." His reference was unequivocally to the original emigrant party of 1849; not to any mythical lost wagon train.

* * *

The Blasdel exploration group of 1866 is the last of the specially organized parties to enter Death Valley within the first two decades following the 1849 emigrant party. Blasdel was Nevada's first elected Governor. One of the members of Blasdel's organization was the eminent State Mineralogist—R. H. Stretch. Quite possibly it was Mr. Stretch who wrote the letters that were published in the newspaper *Territorial Enterprise.* The writer consistently signed his letters "Viator"; but in publishing one of them the newspaper states that "Viator" was "a gentleman of eminent scientific attainments and a graphic and elegant writer."

By the time Blasdel's group made their presence known in Death Valley an event occurred that completely disrupted the even tempo of this desert's here-to-fore placid existence and exerted incalculable influence upon the lost wagon train mystery. In the year 1860 the important silver ore diggings were discovered in the Coso range. One logical route to the Coso diggings passed through Death Valley.

The real impact of this sudden mass migration of prospectors did not assert itself until the spring of 1861. By that time hundreds of miners were pouring across the desert, funneling through Furnace Creek Wash into the once isolated valley called Death. Why this route? Like dumb animals they followed the lead of those who had gone before them. In complete ignorance of what had occurred, they pursued the wagon tracks laid down some ten or twelve years earlier. Understandably, they assumed they were traveling an accepted roadway to the Cosos.

Even during the days of the Boundary Survey's visit to the valley this on-rush of prospectors—although in its initial stages—was observed and duly noted:

> ". . . since the late Coso silver discoveries (1860), . . . eagerness and credulity have led several to trail these wagon tracks [those of the original Forty-niners] as far out on the desert as this."

Unfortunately, no record has been located of those who traveled this road to the Coso mines. At best, we can only read into this hiatus a conjecture of what probably happened. It is not unreasonable, surely, to suppose that at least a few of these early-day miners traveled in wagons. If so, it follows logically they would travel the road of the forty-niners all the way down Furnace Creek Wash into this narrow sandy valley, only to find their wagons hopelessly trapped by the uncompromising Panamints, as had the Jayhawkers before them.

Assuming this to be true, then from the middle of 1861 forward all identity of trails, abandoned wagons and even bleached skeletons would be difficult—if not impossible—to establish.

Six years following the Coso discovery, when the Blasdel party entered Death Valley, the character of the land had drastically altered. The influx of gold-seekers had continued at an accelerated pace. Men were now working the hills and mountain canyons bordering Death Valley in their determined quest for gold. The mythical Lost Gunsight lured many to prospect deep into the confines of the valley itself. Despite the fact that old tracks and old trails were quite largely effaced, or were no longer distinguishable from the infinite tracing of more recent markings, "Viator's" letter of April 21, 1866 to the *Territorial Enterprise* merits consideration:

"*Lost Wagons* is the name given to some little pools of alkaline water near the north end of Death Valley in memory of the early emigrants who on account of the cattle giving out were at this place obliged to abandon their wagons, the remains of which lie scattered around their old camping grounds. But few of the party are left to tell the story of their fearful journey; but those fragments of wood and iron speak more eloquently than words of the sufferings of those miserable wanderers, who footsore and weary, with thirst and starvation staring them in the face, were obliged to abandon their wagons on the desert, and trust themselves to a country where even the meanest of God's creatures can scarcely maintain a foothold. . . . Among so destitute a company, it is more than likely that some of them perished at this place from the debilitating effect of the water . . . but there were no monuments to show that any of them were buried there."

Although, as has been emphasized, almost anything could have occurred in Death Valley by the year 1866, and while the abandoned campsite "Viator" describes could have been that of some later wagon train that stalled here, in all probability he had come upon the 1849 camp of the Jayhawkers at McLean's Spring "near the north end of Death Valley." This conjecture is further strengthened by "Viator's" reference to "the *early* emigrants," indicating the campsite gave evidence of having been abandoned for some time.

Obviously, "Viator's" melodramatic surmise of the fate of these emigrants is a mere—albeit a natural—flight of his imagination. He is careful to qualify his ventured opinion by remarking that "it is more than likely that some perished . . . but there were no monuments to show that any were buried there."

"Viator's" observation, incidentally, illustrates how effectually one man's chance remark may escalate into the realm of established fact. Like those who preceded them, "Viator" and his colleagues in the Blasdel Party were not intimately conversant with what had *actually* occurred in Death Valley nor what had *really* happened to these early emigrants. Only Manly's factual record, to be published twenty-eight years later, could inform them accurately and intelligently regarding this.

While it may be impossible to assert with absolute finality that "Viator's" description relates to the abandoned campsite of the Jayhawkers at McLean's Spring, one can know with certainty that nothing in his letter gives even token support to the lost wagon train argument.[13]

* * *

Captain James Hobbs, in his *Wild Life In the Far West* (1872), provides a notable exception to the marked absence of eye-witness accounts in support of the lost wagon train contention. There is an episode described by Hobbs in which he states categorically that he actually *saw* human bones in Death Valley.

Hobbs may perhaps be considered an equivocal character in that his unqualified claims of having seen so much and having known so many are apt to engender doubt in the minds of his readers. On the other hand, there is so much in Hobbs that relates to known fact that one is hesitant to dismiss his entire book as spurious.[14] Concerning his Death Valley experience, Hobbs writes:

"During the year 1852, an emigrant train passed through this section, attempted to go by way of the valley, as they stood in great fear of the Indians who infested the mountains. But they ran from one danger into another. In crossing this desert they lost their way, and with one exception all perished."

Conveniently, just here, Hobbs explains it was this "one exception" who gave him his information. So this much of the report we can dismiss as hearsay. But Hobbs continues:

"On our arrival in the Valley, we found the remnants of the train and the skeletons of the party, in a locality which agreed with the description given us as did the location of surrounding mountains in the distance."

[13]It is outside the scope of our present study to explore the personnel, purposes and accomplishments of these several early groups who visited Death Valley during the fifteen-year period following the crossing of the original party. Mr. Carl I. Wheat, in his informative *Pioneer Visitors To Death Valley After The Forty Niners* (California Historical Quarterly for September 1939), provides an excellent summation of this phase of Death Valley history.

[14]According to the eminent authority, Mr. Robert J. Woods, the late Dr. Henry Wagner inclined to the belief that the Hobbs' narrative should be regarded as authentic.

Wild Life

IN THE

FAR WEST;

PERSONAL ADVENTURES

Of a Border Mountain Man.

COMPRISING

Hunting and Trapping Adventures with Kit Carson and others; Captivity and Life among the Comanches; Services under Doniphan in the War with Mexico, and in the Mexican War against the French; Desperate Combats with Apaches, Grizzly Bears, etc., etc.

By Captain JAMES HOBBS,

OF CALIFORNIA.

ILLUSTRATED WITH NUMEROUS ENGRAVINGS.

Published by Subscription Only.

HARTFORD:

WILEY, WATERMAN & EATON.

1872.

Title page from Wild Life in the Far West, *by Captain James Hobbs.*

Here, then, is our first eye-witness account of skeletons in Death Valley. Authentic? Possibly. But extremely vague. Hobbs gives no indication of the number of skeletons, nor does he supply data concerning the train itself.

Irrespective of Hobbs' veracity or the absence of it, if he saw skeletons they may well have been from groups entering the valley enroute to the Cosos. Hobbs' visit to Death Valley was in the very late sixties or the early seventies. The skeletons he saw, *if* he truly saw skeletons, were not—certainly—from any lost emigrant train attempting to cross the valley "during the year 1852" nor, for that matter, prior to the year 1861, when the name Death Valley first appeared in print. Had this been so, then one of the early exploratory groups would have commented regarding them. Also, one familiar with Hobbs' style will recall that he usually elaborates when discussing any unusual incident. The fact that he barely alludes to his discovery of skeletons in Death Valley would indicate that he considers the episode to be merely a routine occurrence in his eventful life or, and this seems more probable, there were not enough skeletons to get excited about. Had there been a sizeable train, Hobbs would not have omitted one gruesome detail in recounting this extraordinary experience.

* * *

Oliver Roberts in his *The Great Understander*, written and published by W. W. Walter in 1931, offers a much more detailed and graphic account. In writing this book, Mr. Walter states he used "special care to preserve the wording of Oliver Roberts de la Fontaine's narrative."

Roberts came out upon the desert as a very young man, and for eleven years roamed the Mojave and the Owens Valley country during the 1870s. In 1887 he was appointed Assistant Adjutant General of Nevada, became a mining engineer, a Mason, a Shriner (Islam Temple, San Francisco), and—in his later years—became deeply religious. Mr. Walter was his religious teacher. *The Great Understander* adheres too rigidly to the truth in certain known areas to suggest any serious doubt that Roberts' descriptions of people and places and incidents stem from his actual participation in, or association with, whatever he chooses to describe.

THE

GREAT

UNDERSTANDER

True Life Story of

THE LAST OF THE WELLS FARGO
SHOTGUN EXPRESS MESSENGERS

COMPILED BY
WILLIAM W. WALTER

PUBLISHED BY
WILLIAM W. WALTER
AURORA, ILLINOIS

Title page from William W. Walter's account of Oliver Roberts, The Great Understander.

Roberts is implicit in his assurance that he not only heard, but actually *saw*, evidence of death in the desert:

"I had not gone far when my foot struck something very light and round and it rolled away. This startled and aroused me somewhat, and upon looking I found I was fairly surrounded with the bones and skulls of both men and beasts. The thing which had rolled when my foot struck it was the bleached skull of a human being. I stood spellbound, for I had heard of the place many times from miners who had passed it on their way to the Panamint mining excitement from Pioche, Nevada in 1874."

Roberts' discovery of human bones occurred in—or about—1877, some ten years prior to his appointment as Assistant Adjutant General of Nevada. He explains further that he had "heard" that these bones belonged to a party of nearly 400 emigrants who perished here about twenty-seven years previously for want of water. He continues:

"I moved a few yards and found the remains of the wagons. There was but little of them left now. The thick wagon tires were still bright from the pressure of the brake and some looked as though they had been run the day before, for there was no rust on the iron. I remember noting that the wagons had all fallen toward the east—the side most exposed to the sun."

Roberts' contact with his human bone pile occurred seventeen years following the discovery of silver in the Cosos. Again it should be stressed that, within a short time following the Cosos discovery, hundreds—perhaps thousands—of prospectors swarmed across Death Valley. It may well be that some of these gentlemen donated their skeletons and their wagons to Roberts' sensational find. As in the instance of the Hobbs report, we can be reasonably sure that the Roberts' skeletons did not decorate the sands of Death Valley prior to 1861 else their presence would have been duly noted in the writings of the early explorational parties.

In fact, the greatest deterrent to the truth of Roberts' claim is the complete absence of substantiation from any source, at any time. It is impossible to correlate it with the known facts relating to this desert area. Aside from Hobbs' brief mention, Roberts and only Roberts claims to have seen this spectacular array of skeletons and abandoned wagons. Had a sizeable wagon train or, for that matter, *any* wagon train—irrespective of size—met with such appalling and calamitous disaster in Death Valley, the news of it would have spread over the entire country within a matter of days. Subsequently to 1861 Death Valley was a well-publicized desert. Prospectors were exploring every remote sector of it.

There is another facet to this astonishing discovery, and this relates to the conditions under which Roberts admittedly made it. Astride his faithful horse "Injun," he arrived in Death Valley on this memorable occasion both hot and thirsty. Poor old "Injun" managed to partake of a few bunches of choice loco weed and went suddenly berserk. Heat crazy. Roberts had to shoot him. "Injun" accidentally fell on the canteen that contained a few cherished swallows of water which Roberts was zealously guarding. To sustain life, he was forced to drink "Injun's" blood. Then *he* went berserk. It was during this stage of his delirium that he saw, or *thought* he saw, the human bone pile and the abandoned wagons. He saw something else, also. He saw "a thousand dancing skeleton forms."

Concluding his eerie account he continues:

"I now stood where the wagon train had come to its last stop. Here was the place where the oxen and horses had refused to go any farther and none of the party had strength to retrace their steps. The men, women, children and stock had perished in this land of furnace heat, and around me lay the bones picked over and scattered *for miles* by the coyotes and buzzards—those scavengers of the desert."

Could it be that Roberts, in his advanced state of delirium, was standing in the midst of the abandoned Jayhawker wagons and the piles of ox-bones at McLean's Spring? This would appear to be a sensible explanation of this enigmatic account. Roberts informs us it was quite some time before he fully recovered from this almost fatal ordeal and the illness that followed his ultimate rescue from the horrors of Death Valley.

* * *

Still two years prior to the release of Manly's definitive account of the experiences of the Forty-niners in Death Valley came a remarkable book by John Randolph Spears. *Illustrated Sketches of Death Valley* (1892) is one of our truly great desert items; and

ILLUSTRATED SKETCHES

OF

DEATH VALLEY

AND OTHER

BORAX DESERTS OF THE PACIFIC COAST.

BY

JOHN R. SPEARS.

CHICAGO AND NEW YORK:

RAND, MCNALLY & COMPANY, PUBLISHERS.

1892.

Title page from John R. Spears'
Illustrated Sketches of Death Valley.

few would question an assessment ranking it second only to the Manly in the importance that attaches to its Death Valley interest. Spears was a newspaper man, with a newspaper man's penchant for dramatization. His reference to Death Valley's early history, together with the Rinehart monstrosity that copied it (and which we shall presently consider), did more than all else combined to fix the lost wagon train legend in the public concept. Death Valley's early history, as preserved in *Illustrated Sketches*, is a confused jumble of the actual experiences of the authentic party of 1849 with those of a legendary lost wagon train. In a masterpiece of melodramatic hogwash, Spears writes, in part:

> "Fires were made from the scant fuel of the desert—the grease brush—supper was cooked and eaten with little or nothing to drink, and then all prepared for the most pitiful experience that comes to the traveler, the passing of a night in a dry camp—a camp without water—a camp in which the cattle bawl, the men toss about, and mothers with breaking hearts vainly strive to soothe the little one's wailing for want of drink."

How, then, shall we evaluate the Spears' relation of Death Valley's historic heritage? Happily, we encounter no difficulty in determining the extent of its credibility. Happily, too, this evaluation need not be predicated upon the tenuous premise of mere personal opinion. Spears himself has provided the basis for a true assessment of it. He prefaces his historical summation with these words:

> "The history of Death Valley is found only in tradition. *As I have gathered it*, here it is . . . the *facts* we don't know about that party would make an interesting book, no doubt; but this much *tradition* tells!"

Spears might profitably have employed Edna Brush Perkin's candor, as she expresses it in her delightful book—*The White Heart of Mojave* (1921): "It is impossible to get the details of the stories from the old-timers; each has a different version and no one is very clear about his own."

* * *

More than Spears, Robert E. Rinehart in his *The Naming of Death Valley* in *The Illustrated Weekly* magazine of the Los

Angeles *Times* of August 16, 1908, influenced public opinion. He was—and is—the lost wagon train legend's super salesman. Even today, although the details of his fantastic yarn are quite generally unknown, the idea is firmly entrenched that some frightful disaster, some horrible and sinister tragedy, befell a huge wagon train that had become lost in mysterious Death Valley.

The inevitable query persistently confronts us—*Why did they name it "Death Valley?"* Were a dozen abandoned wagons and only one recorded death sufficient to fasten this ominous name upon such a lovely and peaceful valley?

Rinehart didn't think so. As much as we may censure him for his imaginary conclusion, we should not too severely criticize his reasoning. It must be remembered that of all the accounts we have thus far examined, the Rinehart is the *only* one to appear subsequently to the publication of Manly's book in 1894. And, strange as it may appear, Rinehart was familiar with the Manly. Furthermore, he became convinced from the reading of Manly's intimate record of the original party that some other group had entered Death Valley after the forty-niners and had met with tragic disaster. On the basis of this assumption, he reasoned that this second group had been lured into the desert as the result of following the tracks laid down by the forty-niners. And he concluded that it was because of the terrifying experience of this second group—this purely imaginary group—that the awful name of Death had fastened upon this desert. Rinehart pondered, back in 1908, the inescapable truth which has since confused so many of us, that no recorded incident nor circumstance nor experience relating to the original party could even remotely justify branding this quiet and friendly desert with the irrevocable stigma of Death.

Rinehart erred, of course, in his arbitrary insistence that another train—a mysterious Ghost Train—had penetrated and given name to the valley. His position is untenable because it represents something he manufactured out of thin cloth. It has justification, but it lacks substance. It is a myth.

By 1908 there was developing an awareness of Death Valley that was largely non-existent prior to 1900. Rinehart was a capable writer and a convincing one. His imaginative genius elevated his chosen subject to the loftiest heights of fantasy and sheer newspaper nonsense. He created in the minds of his wide circle of readers a new and fascinating image of this far-off mysterious land. More than Spears, more than Manly, perhaps more than any writer before or after him, he popularized Death Valley and made it a beckoning symbol in the minds of people everywhere. Even today this symbol persists. Death Valley is one of our last remaining frontiers of mystery and high adventure.

While it is true that Manly's classic revelation of Death Valley's true and unembellished history had been off the press for nearly fourteen years before Rinehart's chimerical account appeared, the Manly books were collecting post-publication water stains in a damp basement while Rinehart's popular article was catching the fancy of thousands of avid newspaper readers.

With naive candor, the author admits that "the lost wagon train and the victims of (this) christening party have never been identified." He prudently explains that "little is known about the doomed wagon train . . ." Therefore, because no one can refute his theory with a more sensational one, he supplies a baroque description of it:

"Death Valley gained its name back in the overland days from the ill-starred attempt of a wagon train to cross the dry, deep-set hollow that sinks, as a monster's cupped hand, between the burnt-red mountains of the Funeral and Panamint Ranges. The entire party perished, man and beast. Such wholesale loss of life awed even the pioneer prospectors of the Argonaut time, and they fastened on the Valley its somber name and spread about the desert the unsavory reputation it can never outlive."

Then, immersed in the vagaries of his own mischievous creation, Rinehart continues:

"In the gamut of desert hardship there is no horror such as the horror of a camp without water. Horses whine pitifully, and cattle bawl hoarsely in their effort to make known the unspeakable thirst torture they do not understand. Fantasy plays with the restless nerves and minds of men and women, and drives them to delirium. Thirst-maddened, men and women shriek for water. On that dreadful night Death Valley's christening party drank the bitterest cup of human woe.

"Men and women in frenzy fled the camp, and scattered at random over the trackless sand waste in search of water. Some too weak to

Photo by Floyd B. Evans, FPSA

It was country like this—salt flats close at hand and the snowy Panamints before them—that finally stopped the Death Valley emigrants.

leave their wagons, abandoned by their fellows, perished miserably in camp . . . Others, crazed, came to Salt Creek and in their delirium gulped down the brackish, poisonous water. They died beside the stream. Lone wanderers, lost among the sand dunes, dropped in their steps and passed over the Great Divide. All around the somber camp were strewn the shining skeletons of man and beast."

Curiously, Rinehart acknowledges and extends full credit to his source. Who inspired him to write his article, and who gave him the requisite material for it? *Spears*. Disregarding all the truly credible sources among the *actual participants*, he chose a fellow-newspaper man who, according to Rinehart, "gave the first genuine treatment of that region." Yet it will be recalled that Spears disclaims all responsibility for the truth of what he writes; informs us his material derives solely from hear-say, and is "as I have gathered it" and "the history of Death Valley is found only in tradition."

Thus we have the interesting manifestation of a veritable chain reaction among these early writers. Rinehart *lifts* the Spears' version; Spears deliberately *steals* from Hanks; Hanks acknowledges complete and absolute credit to his three infallible sources—Darwin French, Dr. George and Hugh McCormack.

Rinehart's feature article received unqualified support from a popular writer of that day—the versatile, but gullible, George Wharton James—in the latter's *Heroes of California*, published some two years following Rinehart's *Naming of Death Valley*.

* * *

J. Ross Browne, in his *Adventures in Apache Land* (1869), was perhaps the first to publicize Death Valley by including some account of it in his widely-read book. Although Hittel is believed to be the first to mention the name of this desert in a book, Browne devotes several pages in an attempted relation of its early history. This accomplished writer had no empirical knowledge of Death Valley; had nothing, in fact, but the crudest of hearsay information disseminated by word of mouth that grew more eloquent upon each successive telling.

Browne wrote well. Absence of dependable source material did not inhibit him; and it is remarkable how closely he adhered

ADVENTURES

IN THE

APACHE COUNTRY:

A TOUR THROUGH ARIZONA AND SONORA,

WITH

NOTES ON THE SILVER REGIONS OF NEVADA.

BY J. ROSS BROWNE,

AUTHOR OF

"YUSEF," "CRUSOE'S ISLAND," "AN AMERICAN FAMILY IN GERMANY," "THE LAND OF THOR," ETC.

Illustrated by the Author.

NEW YORK:
HARPER & BROTHERS, PUBLISHERS,
FRANKLIN SQUARE.
1869.

Title page from Adventures in the Apache Country, *by J. Ross Browne, 1869.*

to the truth. His is no fictionized account of lost wagon trains and human skeletons. Although there is considerable variation from the actual facts as we know them today, Browne is plainly attempting description of the original train; not a hypothetical one. He places the date in 1852, rather than 1849; says there were sixty wagons, when actually there were one hundred seven; classifies the personnel as consisting "chiefly of Mormons, but among them were some gentiles," whereas he should have reversed his estimate; informs us that the train "left the Mountain Meadows for San Bernardino," although he probably meant to say it was near Mountain Meadows that the defecting groups withdrew from the train and headed for the gold fields. Later he places the point of defection "at the Amargosa," and says that seven wagons "started out to explore Death Valley." It will be recalled there were seven wagons in the Bennett-Arcane group. Browne reports a Methodist minister and his wife in the party; and this we know to be true. Only thing—Browne named his preacher "King." The correct name was "Brier."

In his story, Browne takes up the old refrain that echoes down the corridors of time into almost every tale told of Death Valley—the lost mine episode. Browne names three men—Farley, Cadwallader and Towne—who broke away from the train and discovered a rich vein of silver. As invariably happens, before the mine could be located it became lost. Farley succeeded in getting himself killed; Towne died; Cadwallader was always too drunk to be useful as a guide. Now we know something of two of these men—Farley and the one called Towne. The former was a cartographer with the Darwin French expedition in Death Valley; the latter figured prominently in the original party of 1849. In any event, Browne qualifies what he has to say concerning this unsuccessful mining venture: "I tell the story," he says simply, "as I heard it."

* * *

Although making its first printed appearance in July, 1928, *A Tragedy of the Desert* was actually written by James H. Martineau in 1910. Its publication in the July, 1928 *Improvement Era* occurred seven years after the author's death. He must have been well along in years when, in 1910, he wrote—or perhaps dictated—*from memory* concerning events that had occurred fifty-two years earlier (1858). Moreover, the events of which he wrote were not experienced by him personally, but were related to him by another.

The Martineau item has at best only a tenuous claim to reliability. It was published seven years after Martineau's death, and eighteen years after it was first written. It was prepared from memory fifty-two years after the story was told to him by another who had experienced the events he described some nine years prior to the time he related them to Martineau. Now if this explanation doesn't make sense, then what hope exists for the article itself?

Irrespective of this, the item deserves objective evaluation because of its peculiar relation to the original Death Valley party of 1849 and also because of its possible application to the lost wagon train theory. This is attributable to Martineau's statement that the man who had revealed this incredible experience to him was his old comrade and friend—"*Mr.* Bennett." Instantly, at mention of "Mr. Bennett," our interest is kindled; and the James Martineau item cascades into prominence.

The story finds its inception during the activities of the "White Mountain Mission," in 1858. During this year relations between the Mormons and the United States Government were sufficiently strained to cause Brigham Young to take a dim view of the future of his people in Utah. The diabolical massacre at Mountain Meadows in 1857 had greatly intensified these strained relations. President Young sent out several groups to scout possible escape routes and future places of abode should his flock be expelled from Utah. One of these groups—the White Mountain Boys—made their way into the region of the present Panaca, Nevada; quite probably followed what has generally been considered the emigrant route into Nevada's Pahranagat Valley, particularly around the present area of Crystal Springs and Hiko. Martineau was a member of this group. So was the enigmatic "Mr. Bennett." The writer informs us there were sixty men in this company, under the leadership of Col. William H. Dame. Martineau was appointed its historian.

Now among these sixty was one with whom Martineau avers he became "personally intimate." Says they were "comrades" in the mission. Oddly enough, he does not appear to recall his "intimate" friend's first name. Merely refers to him as "*Mr.* Bennett." This may bear some weight in support of the contention that Martineau—presumably in his seventies or even his eighties at the time of writing, or dictating, "Mr. Bennett's" narrative—was lacking in mental acuity or, at best, was depending upon a faulty memory to recall what actually had been told him.

Despite its irregularities and inconsistencies, the story—as Martineau relates it—cannot be dismissed as entirely fatuous. There is too much of unquestioned accuracy in it to justify our regarding it lightly. Only an actual participant could have known—as far back as 1858—many of the detailed experiences related by "Mr. Bennett." In 1858 no books, and few—if any—newspaper accounts, could have come into the narrator's possession to supply him with first-hand knowledge concerning these experiences. Only direct participation could have produced such an intimate understanding of them.

"Mr. Bennett" relates that his group defected from a California-bound wagon train against the advice of their Mormon guide. He mentions that one of their members had a map depicting the proposed cut-off route. He speaks of entering "what is now appropriately known as Death Valley." Incidentally, if "Mr. Bennett" actually referred to this desert as "Death Valley" back in 1858, then his is our first recorded use of that name and perhaps gives support to Manly's claim of naming it. He speaks of a rain storm supplying the water that saved the life of every member of their group (Manly says it was a *snowstorm* that providentially spared their lives). He tells of being forced to abandon their wagons in Death Valley; even mentions the singular incident of a woman, dressed in her finery, being bucked off one of their oxen when she tried to ride him out of Death Valley, and is explicit in explaining how the incident provoked merriment and laughter among members of the saddened and despairing group. Manly relates this entire experience in absorbing detail. And he names the woman. She was Mrs. Arcane.

Up to this point in "Mr. Bennett's" strange narrative we are reading almost precisely what did—in fact—occur; even to a relation of some of the minor incidents and personal details.

Again it must be stressed that only one actually present when these details were enacted could be informed of them back in 1858, less than nine years after they occurred. The only source record we have of them today is that given us by William Lewis Manly, himself a participant. And his book—*Death Valley In '49*—was not published until 1894, or thirty-six years later.

Now, unfortunately, a purely imaginative touch is injected into the narrative and we are confronted with situations that are absolutely at variance with the true experience of the authentic party. Says Martineau—relating that which Bennett supposedly told him:

"But there was no time for sentiment. All fatherly, brotherly or motherly love seemed lost–a selfish desire–each for himself. One becoming too weak longer to proceed was left behind to die alone, for weakened men were not strong enough to carry anyone else. Thus husbands or wives abandoned their companions, mothers their children, and children their parents, leaving them sitting down fainting, but alive, to linger a few days–if not sooner torn in pieces by wild animals–then to die alone.

"Finally as we reached the eastern foothills of the Sierra Nevadas, but seven were left of all the company, six men and one woman. Admiring her plucky fight for life we had helped her all we could, until she told us not to try to save her any longer. She might as well die here and now as tomorrow. That seemed true. She sat down upon a stone, bade each goodbye and we left her alone. But we had not been more than an hour in camp when here she came, seemingly as well able to travel as others. She said she had felt resigned to die, until the thought came –what if a wolf should find her and tear her in pieces? Deadly fear gave her renewed strength. She rose, staggering at first, but finally gained her comrades and camp. The following day we were discovered by a white man out hunting for game and he conducted us to his camp where we found food and safety."

Such is the ridiculous finale to an otherwise sensible tale. We cannot but admire the fortitude of this one gallant little woman who bravely turned away from the envisioned horrors attending her possible meeting with one little coyote to rejoin these six *human* wolves whose lack of chivalry and courage impresses us as being far more dangerous to her welfare.

Who *was* this mysterious "Mr. Bennett?" Was he the true Asabel Bennett of the authentic Manly-Bennett-Arcane group

McLean's Spring (or Jayhawker Well), where Jayhawkers abandoned their wagons.

Sunset view of the old Eagle Borax site in Death Valley.

of 1849? I think he was.[15] Quite indirectly, Manly himself substantiates this belief. In the beginning of his article, Jim Martineau states: "The writer was personally intimate with one of the survivors of that party, a Mr. Bennett, who afterwards joined the Mormon Church . . ." etc. At one point in his book—*Death Valley In '49*—Manly speaks of attending the funeral of the first Mrs. Bennett, the brave lady who—with her husband and three children—remained at the lone camp in Death Valley while Manly and Rogers were out scouting a route for their escape. Manly continues this statement by telling of his return to the gold country following the funeral. Says he entered into the business of purchasing gold dust from the miners and that he followed this business for "about two years," selling it in 1859. This places Mrs. Bennett's funeral in or near 1857. Manly further states that, in the same year he sold his business (1859), Bennett returned *from Utah* and they saw each other for the first time in two years. He said that following the first Mrs. Bennett's death "Ase" gave away their youngest child, moved to Utah with his other four children, married a Mormon girl, lost his property, blamed it onto the Mormons, and returned to California without his Mormon wife.

Thus, from a disinterested but eminently qualified source, we may construct evidence in support of the identity of Martineau's inscrutable "Mr. Bennett." From this independent source we know that the Asabel Bennett of the authentic party was in Utah during the year 1858 when James Martineau says his "Mr. Bennett" told of his harrowing experiences. We know, from Manly, that the true Asabel Bennett became a Mormon, just as Martineau said his comrade had done.

We cannot coordinate the latter portion of Martineau's narrative with the known experiences of the Manly-Bennett-Arcane group in Death Valley. We can only assume that Mr. Martineau —or the party responsible for the composition of his story—

[15]My opinion, in this instance, has altered considerably from that expressed in *Desert Voices* (Los Angeles; Westernlore Press; 1958). A more intensive study of the Martineau article, and perhaps a more knowledgeable evaluation of it, have conclusively identified the abstruse "Mr. Bennett" as the real Asabel Bennett of the original Death Valley party. In the preparation of the comment in *Desert Voices,* I was not entirely familiar with all the facts—including the Manly reference—presented in this immediate study; or, perhaps more accurately, I did not intelligently utilize all the facts with which I was familiar.

yielded to an understandable urge to dramatize. Either this, else —as has been suggested—Martineau in his old age was victim of a tricky memory and confused the narrative Bennett had related with other stories he had heard during the fifty-two years intervening to the preparation of his article.

In any event, it is reasonable to conclude that "Mr. Bennett" was not alluding to any lost wagon train. Whether he was truly the Asabel Bennett of Death Valley fame or another Bennett entirely, whether he existed in flesh and blood or was merely a creation of Martineau's vivid imagination, the truth remains that the wagon train he *attempted* to describe was the one that actually blundered into Death Valley in the winter of 1849.

* * *

Captain John Colton, one of the original Forty-niners, was interviewed in February 1903, when a very old man, by a brash reporter from the San Francisco *Bulletin*. This reporter has been criticized, and deservedly so, for the liberties taken in reporting what the estimable Captain Colton is supposed to have said as well as the mannerisms employed in the saying of it. Captain Colton is plainly confused in his alleged comment:

"About a dozen stragglers, who had followed our train down from Salt Lake, got lost in Death Valley and all died of starvation and thirst. Soon after another train of about thirty people, including a number of women, lowered their wagons into the Valley by means of ropes, and scattered in search of water, all dying but two or three, some of them within 100 feet of a spring. Their bones—some still in faded Calico dresses—and ox yokes and wagons and even tracks in the sand were found there twenty years later."

Here we find reference to Spears, relative to the wagon-lowering episode; to Dr. George's mention of death near a spring of water; and to Hugh McCormack's discovery of bones in a calico dress. The reference value of the Colton material is attenuated by the suspicion that it is the reporter, and not Colton, who supplies the substance of the interview. At best, the Colton item is of apocryphal value only.

* * *

Arthur J. Burdick in his *The Mystic Mid-Region* (1904), who managed to err in almost everything he attempted to write of a historical nature, runs true to form in his imaginative comment on Death Valley:

"Death Valley has been rightly named. It was christened with blood and has ever lived up to its title. Sixty-eight out of seventy Mormon emigrants who wandered into that dread region in 1849 gave their lives to its christening. The story of their terrible death from torture of thirst and agonies of heat is too horrible to print."

One cannot escape the very obvious, if impertinent, observation that Burdick's final sentence introduces a subtle method of avoiding facts when we know of a certainty there *are* no facts. Also, it should be mentioned that Mormons, as an organized group, did *not* enter Death Valley. At least, the records of the Church fail to disclose any such venture.

* * *

Alexander Majors' account of "The Jayhawkers of 1849," from his *Seventy Years On the Frontier* (1893), is of relatively minor importance; but it is of interest for three excellent reasons: first, it is an early Death Valley item, preceding Manly by a year; second, it does not once mention the name Death Valley; and third, the substance of the narrative or—more precisely—the inspiration for it, was in all probability supplied by Jayhawker John S. Colton. Of some further interest is the fact that, while not implementing its substance with stupid lost wagon train propaganda, Majors' record candidly discusses one incident that other writers have touched upon but lightly. He describes this singular occurrence in these words:

"Here thirteen of their number branched off, on New Year's Day, taking what jerked beef they could carry and started due west over the mountains . . . Of these thirteen, but two lived to get through, and they were found by ranch Indians in a helpless condition, and brought in and cared for. They had cast lots and lived on each other until but two remained. When questioned afterward in regard to their trip, they burst into tears and could not talk of it."

Reference to cannibalism among these men—there were actually eleven, and not thirteen, of them[16]—appears in the Jacob Y.

[16]In John B. Goodman's helpful publication "Over The Salt Lake Trail In The Fall Of '49" (1957), he presents the letter of W. B. Lorton, dated Jan. 30, 1850. This letter resolves for all time the problem of determining the personnel of the strange group that has baffled Death Valley historians. There were *eleven*, not *nine*, men in the party; and Lorton names them: Chas. McDermot, Savage, John Adams, G. Wiley Webster, T. Ware, J. Ware, Baker, Samore, Allen, Moore, Pinney.

Stover *Narrative*, but with an entirely different construction placed upon it.[17] Says Stover:

"I met Pinney and Savage (the two survivors) in Nevada City. They gave me the history of those travels . . . 'We went over the mountains and travelled through a rough country, nothing to shoot, not a living thing to be seen, till our horse meat was all gone, and we came one night into a camp on a big desert. The boys said we would have to draw cuts in the morning who should be killed to eat. As we did not want to be killed to be eaten or eat anybody, when we thought they were asleep we got up and travelled all day; then we took our butcher knives and dug holes in the sand and covered up all but our heads till night when we could come out and travel all night again. By this time we did not fear them and were recruited. This sand was what saved us.'"

Significantly, Stover is silent in regard to these two men bursting into tears and being unable to talk. From other sources we learn that, several years later, nine skeletons were found huddled behind a little barricade of brush.[18]

Manly, however, partially supports Majors. He does not directly accuse Pinney and Savage of cannibalistic intentions; nor does he imply such a tendency on the part of the other members of the group. He does make this rather cryptic comment; and from it the reader may draw whatever inference he chooses:

". . . it will be remembered that one party of eleven started out on foot before the wagons were abandoned by the rest of the party (at Mt. Misery). Nothing was heard of these for several years, but long afterwards nine skeletons were found at the remains of a camp, and the other two were afterwards seen in the gold fields. When spoken to about this party, they burst into tears and could not talk of it."

[17]From Dr. John Walton Caughey's "Southwest From Salt Lake In 1849."

[18]*The Pacific Historical Review* for June 1937. L. Dow Stephens in his "*Life Sketches Of A Jayhawker Of '49*" (1916) states that in 1864 a man from the Slate Range said members of his party "had come across the remains of nine men all together behind a little barricade of brush." Mention of the discovery of nine skeletons "some years later" may be found in the Rev. John Wells Brier article, "*The Death Valley Party of 1849*," *Out West* magazine, March and April 1903. The egocentric Charles F. Lummis, a man of fixed opinions and deplorable prejudices, writes in his *Mesa, Canon and Pueblo* (1925)—"Nine young men, stronger than the average of the wasted band, reached this terrible trough ahead of the others and perished with thirst. Years later, their bones were found, cuddled there in a little volcanic bowl to which they had crawled to escape the cold winds of the night, by Governor Blaisdell and his surveyors, and he gave the name 'Death Valley' from this circumstance." Lummis had the temerity to write this even though he was familiar with Manly's version of the naming.

I have purposely stressed this incident of suspected cannibalism, because it effectually points up the wide spectrum of emotional conduct that exerted such a peculiar influence upon the entire Death Valley saga of 1849. This one relatively small emigrant party—it was essentially a splinter group from the parent Sand Walking Company—had its brave men and its cowards; those who were courageous and those who faltered; those who were strong and those who were weak. There were those among them who would steal food from women and little children to satisfy their own selfish needs; there were others who would pour out the last few drops of water from their canteens to sustain the life of a comrade. The structural fibre of this pioneer group was of a texture and pattern designed to encourage the emergence of unrestrained emotions, whether for good or for evil. With some—as with the group Majors describes—the fear complex completely dominated thought-processes and ravaged judgments.

Elsewhere, Majors deviates slightly from dependable accuracy, perhaps for theatrical effect, thus again providing grist for the lost wagon train fiction-mill. "Many died," he tells us, "from exposure, hunger and thirst, and were buried in the drifting sands where they fell." Actually, this statement does not stray too far from the avenues of truth. At least four of the Jayhawkers, or those who accompanied them, are definitely known to have fallen in death. And certainly Majors was justified in continuing: "those who were left moved on, weak and tottering, not knowing whose turn would be next."[19] He further states that "there were thirty-four of the party who lived to reach that valley;" that is, who succeeded in making their escape to safety. We think this a sensible estimate; perhaps a surprisingly accurate one.

* * *

R. S. Dix's article "Death Valley," in the *Chautauquan* of August 1891, is of a piece with Rinehart's ornate article. Emotional and

[19]A year later Manly expressed it in much the same way when he wrote: "The thought came to everyone that perhaps it would be his turn next to sit down and see the others pass on. In fact the probability of any more of them living another day was very poor, for they all grew weaker and weaker with every hour, and no one knew how many hours must pass before they could hope for water."

sometimes mawkish by his very eloquence, Mr. Dix failed to exert an influence comparable to that precipitated by Rinehart; neither did he reflect the latter's recognized literary ability. The item is of more than collateral importance, however, largely because of its age. It bears a date three years in advance of Manly; one full year prior to that of Spears.

It is evident that Spears and Dix drew heavily upon common sources, one of them indubitably the Hanks' *Report* of 1883. Like Hanks who preceded him and Spears and Rinehart who followed him, Dix fixes the date of the lost wagon party as mid-summer of 1850, or about half a year following the crossing of the authentic party.

"This," he writes, "is the Death Valley of miners' tale and travelers' dread; the Death Valley which got its name from the direful fate which, in 1850, overtook all but two of the thirty immigrants who first explored it. The following is the story of their sufferings as told by the two survivors."

It is understandable that Mr. Dix would neglect to supply the names of these "two survivors," or in what circumstances the story was obtained from them. We can attempt only a conjectural approach to the source of his equivocal reference to "all but two of the thirty immigrants." Thus far we have discovered only two other accounts that speak of but two survivors—the Burdick (1906) and the Colton (1903).[20] Burdick's reference appeared several years *later* than the Dix article. Similarly, only Spears and Colton—beside Dix—insist upon a personnel of exactly thirty members; and the Spears, like the Burdick and the Colton, appeared *after* the Dix *Chautauquan* article.

It becomes increasingly difficult to rationalize these fugitive references to the over-all pattern of lost wagon train literature. Elsewhere I have discussed the probable recourse of early writers to some common source that is presently lost to the knowledge of students of Death Valley history.

In reading the Dix narrative, it becomes apparent that he is alluding to the original emigrant train of 1849. For example, his reference to their defection from the parent company out of Salt Lake tallies with the factual background of the Forty-niners.

Dix continues his eloquent discourse:

[20]Colton, less specific, states: "all dying but two or three."

"The flaming ball of the setting sun lay low in the west. The reflection of its red glare illumined far to the east the azure sky, and touched with golden paints the second range of mountains which loomed up just beyond. And between the mountains upon which they stood and the second range, in a chasm five thousand feet deep, lay a valley of marvels like unto those of the Arabian Nights. As far as the eye could reach, there was nothing but gleaming white splendor; not a trace of vegetation, not a creature to break the solemn silence which pervaded the place like a benediction; nothing but white everywhere, dotted here and there with twinkling pools of water . . . At last in despair, starving and thirsting, they abandoned their teams and in small parties of about five men each endeavored to find their way out of the death trap, but all perished save the two whose tales of struggle and misery gave the valley its name and furnished substance for the stories which, for many a long day, turned the back of any wise traveler upon its salt splendor. . . . Burning salt marsh at its bottom, pathless tracts of salt and borax just above, then the thorny bush, and yet higher the mournful stunted pine, all under the glare of a blazing sun, unrefreshed by brook or pond, and enlivened only by scorpion and snake; and last of all, the bones of hundreds of lost travelers bleaching in one's path."

Then our grandiose author includes a direct quote from another, but fails to extend credit for it:

"Such is the Valley of Death. One does not need burial, for the body will not decay, but will simply be shriveled up to a mummy, and lie there to an eternity, imperishable, staring up at the burning sky. Here and there over the awful plain of salt and alkali are scattered the dead bodies of men and animals preserved for all ages to come."

Mr. Dix chooses to ignore the slight inconsistency of telling us in one line of "the bones of hundreds of lost travelers bleaching in one's path"; and, almost in the next sentence, assuring us that "the body will not decay, but will simply be shriveled up to a mummy, and lie there to an eternity, imperishable, staring up at the burning sky." Bones or mummies; it makes little difference. Anything can happen in Death Valley.

Intolerable as his style becomes, and untenable as we know some of his statements to be, his article cannot be ignored. He does not impress one as being a writer who would initiate an idea or construct an immutable premise out of thin air; therefore, one fact emerges crystal clear. Mr. Dix—and, for that matter, Burdick, Spears and others—drew upon a source unknown to us; a *lost* source we have thus far failed to locate.

Photo by Floyd B. Evans, FPSA

Beauty and desolation, these are the main qualities of Death Valley; and from these two features has grown a monumental amount of apocryphal stories about the first white visitors here.

Other accounts of relatively minor importance, and there are many of them, have appeared in the past and continue to appear even down to the present. For example, as late as 1959 a graduate engineer came out with an excellent book on early mining towns; but when he writes on the subject of the Lost Gunsight Mine he—of all people—sadly confuses his reference to early Death Valley history.

In 1956 a capable book on lost mines and hidden treasure came off the press. Unfortunately, the passage on Death Valley history smacks suspiciously of Browne's 1869 account. We can understand why Browne, at this early date, should err; but what excuse has a modern-day writer for such careless inaccuracies?

Incidentally, the latest edition of the Encyclopaedia Britannica leaves much to be desired in its reference to Death Valley. This is not only unfortunate; it is inexcusable.

George Q. Cannon, a member of the original Salt Lake train from which the Death Valley groups defected, writes—in his 1869 *Narrative:*

> "Around the valley they wandered, and the children, crying for water, perished at their mothers' breasts. The mothers soon followed, and the men, with parched tongues, tottered and raved and died. After wandering for some time, *it is said*, the survivors found water in the hollow of a rock in the mountains, and a few finally succeeded. I have heard it stated that eighty-seven persons, with numbers of animals, perished in this fearful place, and since then it has been called Death Valley."

G. C. Pearson, another member of the Salt Lake train who did not join the Death Valley groups, recalled, in 1894, that it was reported all died of thirst except one member—a colored man. Pearson continues: "For the correctness of this I cannot vouch only as to the party being lost. It is more than probable that it was as reported."[21]

* * *

Reference to lost wagons is commonly found in Death Valley literature. Dane Coolidge, in the chapter on "Burnt Wagons" in his

[21]*Overland In 1849*, by G. C. Pearson; edited by Jessie H. Goodman with an introduction and notes by John Bartlett Goodman III; 1961.

Death Valley Prospectors (1937), informs us the emigrants abandoned several wagons "about seven miles northwest of Death Valley Junction, on the old road that follows the railroad." Fellow by the name of Herman Jones told Coolidge about locating these wagons "two hundred feet to the right of the main wash going up, and a little over three miles from Nelson's Well." Naturally, Mr. Jones had no difficulty in finding the wagons, for he got their location direct from an old man in San Bernardino who got it from a map that came from a dying man down Mexico way. It was all that simple.

Then there's the story an old Indian told "Dad" Fairbanks of a party of white men burning their wagons in the lower foothills of the Funerals because of an Indian attack. It is only natural that the sight of burned wagons would immediately suggest Indian attacks; and it is possible Indians may have attacked and burned some of the original emigrant wagons, although we have no dependable source proof of this. In the majority of instances the burning was done by the emigrants themselves whose wagons provided fuel to cure the meat of the weaker of their oxen.

Manly, in a letter written to his former trail-mate A. C. Clay in 1894, speaks of the "old camp a 100 miles east of Death Valley . . . This camp is where Jim Martin left his wagons, if you remember."

Dr. Margaret Long, in her conspicuously important Death Valley work—*The Shadow Of The Arrow*—expresses the belief that twenty-seven of the wagons of the original party camped for the last time together at Papoose Lake, in Nevada. Says Dr. Long: "Those of the Briers were abandoned in Fortymile Canyon; those of the Bennetts and most of the Jayhawker wagons, in Death Valley itself. A few were destroyed at Burnt Wagons (near Death Valley Junction), and the Martin party left theirs behind somewhere between Emigrant and Amargosa Valleys."

Chalfant, in speaking of one of the Pacific Coast Borax wagons abandoned by C. B. Zabriskie in 1889 about twenty miles northwest from Stovepipe Wells or more than forty miles from Furnace Creek, writes: "Lost Wagons is now shown far from the camp of '49, miles from where the wagons were burned. It marks a place where a wagon was abandoned many years later."

It remains for Mr. L. Burr Belden, recognized authority on

Death Valley, to give us our most sensible—and informative—account of the "Lost Wagons" episode. Writes Mr. Belden:

"He (F. M. 'Borax' Smith) sent his first lieutenant, Christian Brevort Zabriskie, down to Harmony to haul off salvageable stuff to Columbus Marsh. He loaded it on borax wagon and trailer and started up the valley with a twenty-mule team. There was no grain and the mules weakened under the heat and straight desert hay (wild hay) diet. There was just a sandy track up valley to the west and lower than today's road. Near Mesquite Spring Zabriskie cut loose the trailer wagon when convinced he couldn't pull the train up the sandy canyon beyond Ubehebe to Oriental Wash. It wasn't worth going back to salvage. It stood there twenty years, gradually being raised on an island as sand around it washed—or blew—away. Scotty and Bill Keyes both carved their names on it in 1908. Around 1930 Bob Eichbaum went up and hauled it down to Stovepipe Wells (he first called his resort Bungalow City) where it can be seen today between the lobby and dining hall buildings. The wagon began to get on maps as 'Lost Wagon' or 'Lost Wagons' over the years."[22]

* * *

On the basis of the source material examined, it is difficult to relate the lost wagon train episode to the known facts of early Death Valley history. The inescapable conclusion is that no lost wagon train ever existed except in the errant imagination of those who spoke or wrote of it. Despite his convictions, however, the careful historian will not pragmatically assert his conclusions unless they are fortified with irrefutable facts. And this, where Death Valley is concerned, is not always possible. Death Valley's mysteries are too numerous and too tightly incapsulated within their own obscure origins to tolerate any quick, unsupported solution in the academic mind of the self-assured student. There are too many unanswered questions, too many variants among dissident interpretations and explanations.

Much of this uncertainty stems from the essential nature of the original Forty-niners themselves. We know so much about them; yet, curiously, so very little. This discovering party of unattached men and family units was not a compact body marching resolutely over the desert sands to a fixed destination. They more closely resembled a disorganized horde of frightened children. In the complete absence of competent leadership, each be-

[22]From L. Burr Belden's letter of February 27, 1964, to the author.

came a law unto himself. To regard these widely-scattered and divergent groups as one closely integrated party is to have an erroneous concept of their true status. They were composed of an indeterminate number of groups; and within these individual groups there was no designated leadership. Occasionally some one member would nominally be regarded as "Captain" by others in his outfit; but even in this capacity he exercised little or no authority and formulated no decisions. From its very inception the original Death Valley emigrant party *thought* as individuals, *acted* as individuals, *lived* as individuals. At no time was there any effective concert of opinion and action among them.

Manly alludes to this when, in writing of the Jayhawkers' exit from Death Valley, he says they "came across a dead ox left by some party *that had gone before them*." Again he makes reference to this prevalent lack of organization when he writes:

"They [the Jayhawkers] saw [on the summit of the Panamints] a small firelight at a little distance and went to it, finding a poor lone camper, taking care of himself . . . It seemed there were many men from the various parties scattered around the country, each one seeking out the path which seemed to suit best his tender feet or present fancy, steering west as well as mountains and cañon would permit, some farther north, some farther south, and generally demoralized, each thinking that as a last resort he would be able to save his own life."

Perhaps one day a diary or letter or newspaper clipping, telling of some of these unknown wanderers, will be discovered in a forgotten attic trunk. Perhaps, too, the original notes of Darwin French and Hugh McCormack and S. G. George may sometime be found; or the book in a limited edition of only one hundred copies, reportedly authored by Sheldon Young, may be uncovered in some dusty basement or in a neglected storage bin of a second-hand book shop. Persistent rumors would have us believe that Mormon prospecting expeditions entered the Valley in the late 1850s. The Church may eventually find trace of documents in support of this. Mexicans almost certainly crossed the Valley and conducted mining operations in the Amargosa until—so tradition states—they were murdered by the Indians. The San Bernardino Meridian Survey was supposed to have entered Death Valley around 1854; but, if so, no authenticated document supports it. Interesting, also, would be more detailed information concerning the 1850 expedition of Dr. E. Darwin French. The San Francisco *Bulletin* of February 10, 1869 informs only briefly of it. There is reason to believe the Buel-Todd party of 1864 prepared a written report; but, if so, this too is a lost document.

These are the *known* instances of possible visits and incidents relating to Death Valley. Unquestionably, other groups and lone individuals entered the valley during the early years of its history. Of these, too, we may some day discover supporting documents.

Hopefully, in the time to come, we may learn more concerning the legend of the mysterious lost wagon train.

There is a viable belief current among those who claim an interest in lost wagon train narratives that a missing source, common to several of the earlier writers, exerts a dominant influence upon the subject. It may be only a verbal source that has never been reduced to writing; but, oral or written, its impress is clearly demonstrable in early Death Valley literature.

A similar situation has long been apparent to students of the Bible with respect to the New Testament Gospels. There is noticeable evidence of the three later Gospel writers copying from Mark; but there is also discernable evidence of all four Gospel writers drawing from a common—and unknown—source that was at one time available to them. The technical designation for this lost material is "Q," representing the word "Quelle," which is German for "source."

The writer has been interested for many years in the effort to locate and identify this "Q" of Death Valley literature if, in actual fact, such a lost source exists. That it was available at one time there can be little doubt.

We have elsewhere noted the unmistakable use of Spears by Bob Rinehart, and of Hanks by Spears. Hanks, of course, depended upon the notes of McCormack, George, Henderson and others for the historical section of his *Report*. Hanks is unquestionably the source for other writers besides Spears. Dix, Spears and Rinehart follow his lead in selecting the year 1850 as the date of the Ghost Train's entrance into Death Valley; also they derive much of their technical and scientific data from him.

But Hanks is not our lost common source. Perhaps the "lost"

historical notes of McCormack, George and Henderson would qualify as the mysterious lost source common to the early writers; but this could be ascertained only upon meticulous examination and comparison. The "party of thirty" bit was not extracted from the Hanks *Report*; yet, Dix, Spears and Colton utilize it. The "two survivors" story is not to be found in Hanks; yet Dix, Burdick and Colton use it to advantage, while Spears ignores it and tells us there were a dozen who survived. Both Spears and Browne name Towne as one of the survivors. From the information Spears disseminates with respect to the McCormack and George parties, one would suppose he had access to their now-lost historical notes. While no one would have reason to doubt the honesty and accuracy demonstrated by Hanks in transcribing these missing notes, it could well be they contained additional material of peculiar value to us, whereas Hanks may have found no purpose in copying them in their entirety.

Such a source, if it exists, would have at best only a specious claim to accuracy and authenticity. The object in calling attention to the possibility of a lost source is not to suggest its infallibility nor to arouse the hope that its discovery would irrevocably establish the certainty, and perhaps the identity, of a lost wagon train. The most we have a right to expect from a lost document of this nature is the satisfaction of having solved a mystery that has intrigued many of us for a long, long time.

Readers are aware that it is impossible, and would serve no beneficial purpose, to assemble all the material written on Death Valley's lost wagon train. It is chiefly in the earlier items that we develop our greatest interest, and this quite largely refers to those written prior to the publication of Manly's book in 1894. Evidently there were many such accounts in circulation. Spears, in his *Illustrated Sketches* published in 1892, remarks:

"Surely the story of Death Valley should have been preserved, but, unfortunately, although *scores of articles* have appeared in print on the subject, they have usually been imaginative. . . . The history of Death Valley is found only in tradition."

* * *

To have influenced in any way the naming of Death Valley, a lost wagon train must have entered this desert prior to April of 1861, the date when the name *Death Valley* first appeared in print. In point of fact, the name was probably in common use at a much earlier date.[23]

In this study, primary emphasis has been placed upon the reports of those organized groups who entered the valley during the 1860s for purposes of prospecting or scientific exploration. At the time of their visits little, if anything, had occurred to disturb the physical appearance of this desert area. Everything was much the same as when the original emigrant party crossed over in 1849-50. Their wagon and ox tracks were plainly visible; even the foot prints of their men, women and children were distinguishable. The abandoned wagons and camp equipage remained where they had been discarded, and in much the same condition except for some little disturbance by Indians and occasional prospectors.

Had there been evidence of a lost wagon train these early groups would undoubtedly have observed it. The fact they did not mention such evidence is significant. They saw abandoned wagons; and they saw cattle bones and discarded equipment. They also saw human footprints. *And all these they identified as belonging to the emigrant party of 1849.*

For our immediate inquiry, however, their reports omitted one piece of essential information. They neglected to mention the *number* of wagon remains they saw. In the circumstances it would have been possible for a second wagon train to enter Death Valley in the summer of 1850, or even as late as 1858, without the exploring parties being aware of it. During the 1850s the gold fever was raging at a brisk tempo. Another wagon train, heading west, could have turned into the tracks of the original emigrant party and hopefully followed them to their ultimate entrapment in a desolate, sand-choked valley. When these tracks abruptly terminated amid the remains of abandoned wagons and bleaching cattle bones, then whatever forlorn hope this second group may have cherished would likely have died within them. Conceivably, they would have ventured no farther into this uncharted wilderness with their wagons, but would have abandoned them along with those belonging to the party that had preceded

[23]The Boundary Survey Party (1861) indicate that the valley had already received its name before they applied it in its first printed appearance.

them. The sight of abandoned wagons would have signaled the utter futility of attempting further passage. The exploring parties of the 1860s would likely have no knowledge of a second wagon train, and would naturally assume all the wagons belonged to the original emigrant group.

The paucity of information relating to the actual or even approximate number of abandoned wagons seen by the exploration parties is, in this instance, deplorable. Had they seen only four abandoned wagons at the Bennett's Wells-Tule Spring area, and only eight or ten at McLean's Spring, then we would have known definitely that no wagons from a later train had been abandoned with those belonging to the original party.

Helpful in this connection is an item appearing in the Reese River *Reveille* on October 2, 1865 regarding the Buel-Todd visit to Death Valley in January, 1864:

"Here they found the remains of the unfortunate train. The iron work of *eight* wagons, which had doubtless been burned by Indians—gun-locks, trunk locks and hinges and broken glass and earthenware were lying scattered about on the ground!"

The speculation that the wagons were perhaps burned by Indians is obviously in error. Also, we are not told specifically to whom these wagons belonged. In February of 1865, Todd returned to Death Valley with a party of five men, entering from Lida Valley into the northern part of Death Valley. This time they camped:

". . . at the head of the salt marsh in Death Valley . . . 12 miles north of the remains of the 'lost wagons' of 1852."

If we discount the understandable discrepancy in the 1852 date, the position and the number of abandoned wagons check out accurately. There would probably have been some eight or ten wagons abandoned by the Jayhawkers. Certainly, had the wagons of a later party been abandoned with them, the number would have been substantially greater.[24]

[24]This very important item from the *Reveille* was called to my attention by George Koenig of Van Nuys, California, one of our more reliable authorities on Death Valley. Mr. Koenig informs the writer that "I agree with the wagon tally: 7 for the Jayhawkers and 1 for one of Young's 'Independents.' " (By "Independents," Mr. Koenig refers to one who was not a member of any particular group, but traveled independently with the party of emigrants.)

For whatever it may be worth, further support—although somewhat indirect—is supplied by George Miller's account of his visit to Death Valley in the spring of 1869. Accompanying Miller was W. H. Rhodes (or Rood), one of the original 1849 party. Says Miller:

"We went on into the mouth of Furnace Creek. There we found the tracks of the emigrants' wagons, and the cattle tracks, plain to be seen. Following these over alkali flats you could see them for hundreds of yards ahead of you. We followed on until we came to the Poison Springs—some call them the Salt Springs—about 15 miles West of Furnace Creek in Death Valley. That was the place where Rhodes' party left their wagons. The Indians had burnt the wagons, but the irons, logchains, skeins, staples from their ox-yokes, and linch-pins from their wagon axles were there."

This, of course, refers to the Jayhawker camp at McLean's Spring where they abandoned—and burned—their wagons. The thought occurs that, had there been additional wagons to those left by the emigrants, Rhodes—a former Jayhawker—would have remarked about it and Miller would have mentioned it in his article.

Fortunately, the determination of the existence or non-existence of this hypothetical lost wagon train is not dependent upon a knowledge of the number of abandoned wagons observed by visitors in Death Valley during the 1860s. A much simpler, and more dependable, criterion is available to us. If such a train did enter Death Valley, then one of two end-results would be a concomitant to our unqualified acceptance of this fact: (1) All, or substantially all, its members would have perished; or (2), a considerable number would have escaped to safety.

It would appear, from the preponderance of source material examined, that the incidence of human fatalities in Death Valley during the 1850s was essentially negligible. No *reliable* account substantiates the existence of human skeletons in sufficient numbers to justify the belief that a major tragedy was ever enacted there.

It follows, then, that most of the members of the mythical doomed train must have escaped the perils of the desert. If this be true, then surely some one or more would have left written records to authenticate this conclusion. The total absence of any such records is perhaps our most unassailable proof of the non-existence of a lost wagon train. A diary, a journal, a newspaper, even a letter to a relative or friend, would assist in confirming its reality. We have already considered the extraordinarily large number of source documents written by members of the *original* train. There were numerous letters addressed to relatives back home and to one-another; there were newspaper and magazine interviews and articles; there were diaries, books, delivered lectures. The survivors, and even the descendants of these survivors, perpetuated the memory of the great adventure by organizing themselves into an active society. Correlatively, contemporary articles have been written *about* them. Yet, concerning this illusory lost wagon party, *not one source document has come down to us.*

Those who insist that a lost wagon train entered Death Valley, generally disclaim all knowledge of survivors. Rinehart, it will be recalled, assures us the entire party—man and beast—perished. "The lost wagon train and the victims," he asserts, "have never been identified. Who were the members of this wretched party? Whence did they come? What friends and relatives had they abandoned in the East? . . . These are unanswered questions." And, I may add, these are *good* questions. Intelligent answers to them are urgently required before we dare extend credibility to the very tenuous claim of a Ghost Wagon Train in Death Valley.

Hobbs tells us, in *his* lost party version, that only one survived. Dix, Colton and Burdick would have us believe there were two survivors; but they do not attempt to identify nor describe them.

Spears, who frankly admits that "the history of Death Valley is found only in tradition" and, in referring to the lost wagon train, "the facts we don't know about that party would make an interesting book, no doubt," tells us that "perhaps a dozen" of this party "of thirty souls" managed to get "beyond the Panamints."

Moreover, Spears courageously attempts to name a few of his escapees; and, in so doing, points up the irresponsibility that is characteristic of so many of the lost wagon train writers. A fellow called Towne, he says, succeeded in getting through. Also, Mrs. Towne, Sidney F. Waite and "a man named Bennett." They got through to safety, all right; but not with any *lost* wagon train group. With the exception of Mrs. Towne—of whom we have no other mention—these people all belonged to the *original* wagon train. Waite, a member of the 1849 "Sand Walking Company," the parent train from which the Death Valley contingent defected, continued into San Bernardino with the train's Captain-Jefferson Hunt. And the "man named Bennett" presumably refers to Asabel Bennett of the Bennett-Arcane group who made the long camp in Death Valley while Manly and Rogers were out scouting an escape route to Los Angeles. Even Rinehart, who lauds Spears as an impeccable source, refuses to go along with him in his unsupported statement that Bennett was a member of the doomed train. With few exceptions, the accounts assessed are found to contain garbled versions of the authentic 1849 wagon train story.

Finally, our findings do not encourage the belief that a lost wagon train *ever* penetrated Death Valley, either before or after the first printed appearance of the name in 1861. Conceivably, an occasional wagon may have entered and become trapped here during the 1860s when prospectors poured through this desert on the way to the Coso diggings. But this does not suggest the entrance of any sizeable wagon train nor any wholesale loss of human life. Had such a debacle occurred—subsequently to 1861—the entire country would have been informed of it within a matter of days.

From the year 1861 forward, this remote desert no longer housed either the isolation or the fear that once it knew. Prospectors swarmed over it and across it. Miners probed both the valley and its adjacent canyons in their never-ending quest for the elusive Gunsight and other beckoning bonanzas. An occasional death or wagon abandonment would have excited little or no comment; but any substantial loss of wagons and lives would have precipitated immediate communication to the outside world.

Elsewhere I have commented upon the almost inevitable reaction of an early-day traveler wandering through this desolate valley and coming suddenly upon a number of abandoned wagons and vast quantities of bleaching cattle bones. Such an abrupt and totally unexpected contact with anything so unusual, and in so lonely and isolated an area, would almost certainly stimulate the imagination of one not familiar with the true reason for it. The very obvious conclusion would be that a wagon party had here met with some terrible and catastrophic disaster. The scattered cattle bones would soon take on the fancied appearance of parts of human skeletons. What more logical conclusion than to assume the awful suffering and death of every man, woman and child in that doomed train?

This, I believe, is the one sensible solution to the mystery of how Death Valley received its name. Occasional visitors, mainly prospectors with no knowledge of what really occurred in the winter of 1849-50, stumbled onto the abandoned wagons of the original emigrants at McLean's Spring and the Bennett's Well areas. With understandable excitement they informed others of what they had seen. The tale became exaggerated and more gruesome with each successive telling. And thus was the sensational lost wagon train legend born.

Once formulated and set in motion, the bizarre yarn gained impetus by the recurring discoveries of abandoned wagons and human skeletons along the eastern approaches to Death Valley. The original emigrant party itself contributed to this. First at Mt. Misery in southwestern Utah, later as they crossed the barren Nevada deserts, and finally as they attempted to ascend the Funerals, these original groups were forced to abandon wagons. It is not at all improbable that some of the occupants of these and later wagons may have perished.

One lone abandoned wagon, and perhaps an occasional skeleton, could soon—in the process of telling—proliferate into a sizeable Ghost Train with its ghastly complement of bleaching skeletons. And, in keeping with desert tradition and the relation of tall tales, it would require but minimal imaginative effort to escalate the entire aggregation over the Funerals and into Death Valley.

Throughout the long years since white men first entered into it, Death Valley has claimed its share—and perhaps more than its share—of human lives. But the possibility of any appreciable number of human deaths or abandoned wagons (other than those of the first party), *at any one time*, is not only remote; in view of the evidence examined it appears absurd.

BIBLIOGRAPHY

BELDEN, L. BURR. *Death Valley Heroine.* San Bernardino. Inland Printing and Engraving Co. 1954.
——*Goodbye, Death Valley!* Palm Desert, *Desert* Magazine Press. 1956.
——*Wade Story, The.* San Bernardino. Inland Printing and Engraving Co. 1957.

BIGLER, HENRY W. Extracts from *Journal.* Utah Historical *Quarterly.* 1932. (Also in Hafen's *Journals Of Forty-Niners*; Gudde's *Bigler's Chronicle Of The West; The Overland Monthly.*) September 1887.

BRIER, REV. JOHN WELLS. *Death Valley Party Of 1849, The.* March and April issues of *Out West* Magazine. 1903.

BROWNE, J. ROSS. *Adventures In The Apache Country.* New York. Harper & Brothers, 1869.

BURDICK, ARTHUR J. *Mystic Mid Region, The.* New York. G. P. Putnam's Sons. 1904.

CANNON, GEORGE Q. *Trip To California, A.* Reprint of Cannon's original *Journal,* from the *Juvenile Instructor.* 1869.

CAUGHEY, JOHN WALTON. *Southwest From Salt Lake In 1849 And The Jacob Y. Stover Narrative.* Pacific Historical *Review.* June, 1937.

CHALFANT, W. A. *Death Valley: The Facts.* Stanford University Press. 1930.
——*Story of Inyo, The.* 1922.

COLTON, JOHN B. *Interview.* (In Dr. Margaret Long's *Shadow Of The Arrow, The.*)

COOLIDGE, DAVE. *Death Valley Prospectors.* New York. E. P. Dutton & Co. 1937.

COY, OWEN C. *Great Trek, The.* Los Angeles. Powell Publishing Co. 1931.

CRONISE, TITUS FEY. *Natural Wealth Of California.* San Francisco. H. H. Bancroft Co. 1868.

DAVIS, ALFRED. *Death Valley.* July issue of *Overland.* 1907.

DEATH VALLEY EXPEDITION. *North American Fauna No. 7.* Washington Gov't. Prtg. Office, 1893.

DIX, R. S. *Death Valley.* August issue of the *Chautauquan.* 1891.

EDWARDS, E. I. *Desert Treasure.* Los Angeles. 1948.
——*Desert Voices.* Los Angeles. Westernlore Press. 1958.
——*Into An Alkali Valley.* Los Angeles. Ward Ritchie Press. 1948.
——*Lost Oases Along the Carrizo.* Los Angeles. Westernlore Press. 1961.
——*Mystery Of Death Valley, The: How It Was Named. The Branding Iron* of the Los Angeles Corral of *Westerners.* June, 1962.
——*Valley Whose Name Is Death, The.* Pasadena. San Pasqual Press. 1940.

EGAN, HOWARD. *Pioneering The West.* Richmond, Utah. Egan Estate. 1917.

ELLENBECKER, JOHN G. *Jayhawkers Of Death Valley, The.* Marysville, Kansas. 1938.

Erkson, Alexander C. *Account.* (In Manly's *Death Valley In '49.* Also in Hafen's *Journals Of Forty-Niners.*)

Evans, John Henry. *Charles Coulson Rich—Pioneer Builder Of The West.* New York. Macmillan Co. 1936.

Evans, W. B. *Mexican Gold Trail.* (Ed. by Glenn S. Dumke.) Los Angeles. Huntington Library. Printed by the Ward Ritchie Press. 1945.

Fairbanks, Ralph J. *My 73 Years On Southwestern Deserts.* (As told to John Edwin Hogg.) June issue of *Touring Topics.* 1930.

Federal Writers Project of the W.P.A. *Death Valley: A Guide.* Boston. Houghton Mifflin Co. 1939.

Glasscock, C. B. *Here's Death Valley.* New York. The Bobbs-Merrill Co. 1940

Goodman, Jessie H. (Editor.) *Overland In 1849.* (G. C. Pearson.) Los Angeles. Privately printed. 1961.

Goodman, John B. III. *Over The Salt Lake Trail In The Fall Of '49.* (Wm. B. Lorton.) Privately printed. 1957.

Granger, Lewis. *Letters Of.* Los Angeles. Glen Dawson. 1959.

Grey, Zane. *Death Valley.* May issue of *Harpers.* 1920.

Gruwell, J. D. *Account.* (In Hafen's *Journal Of Forty-Niners.*) 1887.

Gudde, Erwin C. *Bigler's Chronicle Of The West.* Los Angeles. University of California Press. 1962.

Hafen, Le Roy and Ann. *Journals Of Forty-Niners, Salt Lake To Los Angeles.* Glendale. The Arthur H. Clark Company. 1954.

——*Supplement To The Journals Of Forty-Niners.* Glendale. The Arthur H. Clark Company. 1961.

Hanks, Henry G. *Death Valley And Its Tragical History.* San Francisco. From San Francisco *Bulletin* of Feb. 10, 1869. (In Dr. Margaret Long's *Shadow Of The Arrow, The.*)

——*Third Annual Report Of The State Mineralogist.* Sacramento. 1883.

Harrington, Mark W. *Notes On The Climate And Meteorology Of Death Valley, California.* Washington. U.S. Dept. of Agriculture. Bull. No. 1. 1892.

Haynes, Asa. *Diary.* (In Ellenbecker's *Jayhawkers Of Death Valley.*)

Hobbs, Capt. James. *Wild Life In The Far West.* Hartford. Wiley, Waterman & Eaton. 1872.

Hunt, Rockwell D. *Personal Sketches Of California Pioneers I Have Known.* Stockton. Univ. of the Pacific. 1962.

James, George Wharton. *Heroes Of California.* Boston. Little, Brown and Co. 1910.

James, T. E. and Stretch, R. H. *U.S. Government Bulletin.* Senate Report of 43 Congress. March 19, 1874.

JAYHAWKERS' FILE. Letters and papers of survivors of the Death Valley trek of 1849. Huntington Library.

KELLY, CHARLES. *On Manly's Trail To Death Valley*. February issue of *Desert* magazine. 1939. (Also in *Desert* for September 1962.)

KOCH, FRED W. *Through Death Valley*. June issue of *Sierra Club Bulletin*. Vol. 1 No. 2. 1893.

LEE, BOURKE. *Death Valley*. New York. Macmillan Co. 1930.

LONG, DR. MARGARET. *Shadow of the Arrow, The*. Caldwell, Idaho. Caxton Printers. 1941. Revised Ed. 1950.

LORTON, WILLIAM B. *Over The Salt Lake Trail In the Fall of '49*. John B. Goodman III. 1957.

LOVELACE, LELAND. (Mrs. J. Lee Loveless) *Lost Mines and Hidden Treasure*. San Antonio. The Naylor Company. 1956.

LUMMIS, CHARLES F. *Mesa, Cañon and Pueblo*. New York. The Century Co. 1925.

---*Some Strange Corners Of Our Country*. New York. The Century Co. 1892.

MAJORS, ALEXANDER. *Seventy Years On The Frontier*. Chicago. Rand, McNally & Co. 1893.

MANLY, WILLIAM LEWIS, *Death Valley In '49*. San Jose. Pacific Tree & Vine Co. 1894.

MARTINEAU, JAMES H. *Tragedy Of The Desert, A*. Salt Lake.

---*Improvement Era*. Vol. 31. No. 9. July, 1928.

MERRILL, ORIN S. *Mysterious Scott, The Monte Cristo Of Death Valley, and Tracks Of A Tenderfoot*. Chicago. 1906.

MILLER, GEORGE. *Trip to Death Valley*. Historical Society of Southern California *Ann. Publ.* Vol. XI, Part 2. 1919.

NUSBAUMER, LOUIS. *Diary*. (In J. Goldsborough Bruff's *Gold Rush* and also Dr. Margaret Long's *Shadow Of the Arrow, The*.)

PALMER, T. S. *Chronology Of The Death Valley Region In California*. Washington. Byron S. Adams, Printer. 1952.

---*Place Names Of The Death Valley Region And Nevada*. 1948.

PEARSON, G. C. *Overland In 1849*. Los Angeles. Privately printed by John B. Goodman III. Edited by Jessie H. Goodman. 1961.

PERKINS, EDNA BRUSH. *White Heart Of Mojave, The*. New York. Boni and Liveright. 1922.

PERKINS, GEORGE E. *Pioneers Of The Western Desert*. Los Angeles. Wetzel Publ. Co. 1947.

PRATT, ADDISON. *Diary*. (From Hafen's *Journals Of Forty-Niners;* also, Dr. Margaret Long's *Shadow Of The Arrow, The*.)

PUTNAM, GEORGE PALMER. *Death Valley And Its Country*. Duell, Sloan and Pearce. 1946.

RICH, CHARLES C. *Diary.* (From Hafen's *Journals Of Forty-Niners.*)

RINEHART, ROBERT E. *Naming of Death Valley.* August 16 issue of the *Illustrated Weekly* Magazine, appearing in the Los Angeles *Times.* 1908.

ROBERTS, OLIVER. (Compiled by Wm. W. Walter.) *Great Understander, The.* Aurora, Ill. William W. Walter. 1931.

ROGERS, JOHN. *Account.* Merced *Star* of April 26, 1894. (In L. Burr Belden's *Death Valley Heroine.*)

ROLLINS, JAMES H. *Recollections.* 1898. (In Hafen's *Journals of Forty-Niners.*)

SHANNON, THOMAS. *Account.* From San Jose *Daily Mercury* of November 16, 1903. (In L. Burr Belden's *Death Valley Heroine.*)

SPEARS, JOHN RANDOLPH. *Illustrated Sketches Of Death Valley And Other Borax Deserts Of The Pacific Coast.* New York. Rand, McNally & Co. 1892.

——*Miners' Homes In The Mojave Desert.* March issue of the *Chautauquan.* 1894.

——*Through Death Valley.* February issue of *California Illustrated Magazine.* 1893.

STEPHENS, L. DOW. *Life Sketches Of A Jayhawker Of '49.* 1916.

STOVER, JACOB Y. *Narrative.* (In John Walton Caughey's *Southwest From Salt Lake In 1849 and the Jacob Y. Stover Narrative;* also in Hafen's *Journals Of Forty-Niners.*)

Territorial Enterprize. Letters written by "Viator" of the Blasdel party, and published in 1866.

WALKER, ARDIS MANLY. *Death Valley & Manly: Symbols Of Destiny.* Palm Desert. *Desert* magazine. 1962. Publication No. 8 of the Death Valley '49ers, Inc.

——*Manly Map and the Manly Story, The.* Palm Desert, *Desert* Magazine Press. 1954. Publication No. 2 of the Death Valley '49ers, Inc.

WEIGHT, HAROLD O. *Lost Mines Of Death Valley.* Twentynine Palms. The Calico Press. 1953.

——*Twenty Mule Team Days in Death Valley.* Twentynine Palms. The Calico Press. 1955.

WHEAT, CARL I. *Forty-Niners In Death Valley.* Historical Society of Southern California *Quarterly.* Vol. XXI. No. 4. 1939.

——*Pioneer Visitors To Death Valley After The Forty-Niners.* California Historical Society *Quarterly,* September 1939.

——*Trailing The Forty-Niners Through Death Valley. Sierra Club Bulletin.* June, 1939.

WHEELER, LT. GEORGE M. *Annual Report Upon The Geographical Surveys West Of The One Hundredth Meridian—etc. Appendix J. J.* Washington. Govt. Prtg. Office. 1876.

——*Preliminary Report Concerning Explorations and Surveys Principally In Nevada and Arizona.* Washington. War Dept. 1872.

WOLFE, DR. JOHN E. *Route Of The Manly Party of 1849-50—Leaving Death Valley For The Coast.* 1931 (?)

WOODWARD, ARTHUR. *Camels and Surveyors In Death Valley.* Palm Desert. Desert Printers, Inc. 1961. Publication No. 7 of the Death Valley '49ers, Inc.

——(Editor.) *Jayhawkers' Oath and Other Sketches, The.* Los Angeles. Warren F. Lewis. 1949.

YOUNG, SHELDON. *Log.* (In Dr. Margaret Long's *Shadow Of The Arrow, The*; also Hafen's *Journals Of Forty-Niners.*)

INDEX

This index was prepared by Arthur H. Clark, Jr.